New Approaches to Latin American History

edited by
RICHARD GRAHAM *and* PETER H. SMITH

UNIVERSITY OF TEXAS PRESS, AUSTIN AND LONDON

Library of Congress Cataloging in Publication Data

Graham, Richard, 1934–
  New approaches to Latin American history.

  Includes bibliographical references.
    1. Latin America—Historiography—Addresses, essays,
  lectures. 2. Latin America—History—Addresses,
  essays, lectures. I. Smith, Peter H., joint author.
  II. Title.
  F1409.7.G72   980'.007'2   74-2017
  ISBN 0-292-75506-6

Composition by G&S Typesetters, Austin
Printing by The University of Texas Printing Division, Austin
Binding by Universal Bookbindery, Inc., San Antonio

TO
LEWIS HANKE

CONTENTS

INTRODUCTION

The study of Latin American history, particularly as practiced in the United States, has undergone profound alteration in the past decade or so. The most immediate sign of change is simply in quantity. Attracted by a series of exciting political events and further encouraged by the ready (and possibly excessive) availability of government and foundation funds throughout the 1960s, students moved eagerly into the field: according to a standard survey, the number of Latin American historians in this country jumped from 389 in 1965 to 566 in 1970.[1] Both new recruits and senior scholars have conducted prodigious amounts of research. New books come out by the score; anthologies flourish; even new journals appear. Keeping up with the literature—even in a narrowly specialized field—has itself become a major task.

More important than the quantitative growth in output, however, have been changes in conceptual orientation. In recent years scholars have begun to alter their thinking about Latin America—to take on new kinds of topics, to ask new sorts of questions, to experiment with novel methodologies. Students of Latin American history are now devoting, for instance, relatively little attention to formal policies and legal codes and concentrating instead on the informal patterns of actual behavior. It is to such intellectual ferment that we address this book.

It has been designed to reflect and to promote the conceptual and methodological changes that have already started to affect the study of Latin American history. To this end we invited a number of schol-

[1] Hispanic Foundation, Library of Congress, *National Directory of Latin Americanists*, 2d ed. (Washington, D.C.: Library of Congress, 1971), pp. 1, 3.

ars to contribute papers on subjects of their choice, enlarging upon their own research experience. Specifically, we had in mind a series of essays on broad historiographical problems encountered in the study of regionalism, religion, bureaucracy, entrepreneurship, ideology, urbanization, mortality control, militarism, race, etc. In each paper contributors were encouraged to do some of the following: (*a*) explain the thematic and substantive importance of a problem, (*b*) describe and evaluate standard approaches to it, (*c*) propose original hypotheses, (*d*) suggest methods for testing the hypotheses, and (*e*) indicate major difficulties—either methodological or conceptual—that have so far hampered such work.

As editors we have not imposed a strictly uniform format. Each problem has required its own treatment, and each contributor has enjoyed the right to follow individual creative bents. As a result, the essays stand as original, personal statements on the part of the authors. They are not historiographical or bibliographical surveys in the conventional sense of the term. Each paper is a speculative think-piece based on reflections derived from first-hand research.

Four out of the first five papers examine the socioeconomic bases of politics. Stuart Schwartz, pointing out the link between bureaucracy and empire, suggests that research into the social and economic ties of imperial bureaucrats can greatly advance our understanding of the decisions made or implemented in colonial Spanish America. He looks at the results and potential of collective biography and points the way for future research into the functional relationship of state and society. Frank Safford is similarly concerned with the connections between politics and society. In his essay he critically examines the extant explanations for party alignments during the first half of the nineteenth century and finds them wanting. Occupational categories, the rural-urban dichotomy, class position, capitalistic mentality, regional loyalty, dependent status, cultural variables, and racial differences are all inadequate explanatory devices. He suggests, as an alternative, that the access of an individual or a region to structures of power may have had a great deal to do with the making of political choices. Richard Graham takes up many of the same points in his examination of the conceptual difficulties inherent in any search for a link between the exercise of political power and the socioeconomic position of landowners in the nineteenth century. Of the schemes examined he finds an interest-group model most satisfactory and explores its relevance for a comparative typological study of landholders' power. Whereas Safford finds regionalism inadequate for his purposes, Joseph Love considers this phenomenon from a different perspective and considers it a fruitful way to approach the comparative study of the relationship between social development and political integration. He carefully distinguishes the various approaches and purposes of regional studies and describes research now in progress that exploits these insights.

As in Love's paper, the tools of political science are provocatively applied in Margaret Crahan's study of the administration of colonial Spanish America. She argues that historians can profitably apply such concepts as state-building, nation-building, center-and-periphery, legitimacy, elite participation, integration, and dispersion to construct more meaningful interpretations of the instruments of colonial government. In doing so they must keep in mind the parallel development or decay of political institutions in Spain, since without the imperial perspective colonial studies lose a critical dimension.

Subsequent essays focus on the social dimensions of the search for economic manpower. John Lombardi and Michael Hall, respectively, examine slavery and immigration and consider conceptual and methodological aspects involved in their study. Lombardi argues that the debate over comparative slave systems has become sterile as a result of a confusion of aims, goals, and functions within the historical profession. He suggests that a proper balance between broad synthesis and original research can be restored only if the categories are reformulated. Scholars must free themselves from a conceptual framework derived from the North American South and try to understand slavery not as a "peculiar institution" but as an integral part of socioeconomic wholes. Hall takes questions that sociologists have applied to mass migration and poses them for the historian. He suggests, not only that there is much data to be gathered, but also that the historian has a great deal to gain by applying a more rigorous methodology. Furthermore, such a study can lead to a much more systematic examination of the nature of the societies into which the immigrants moved than has heretofore been done.

Psychology is another social science that has much to offer the historian. Margaret Todaro Williams laments the failure of Latin Americanists to follow the recent example of historians of other areas in utilizing the insights of psychoanalysis. She suggests that the primary task is to uncover the symbols, the values, and the modes of psychological behavior in past times. The purpose of such investigation is not to replace standard historical approaches but to enrich them. Taking a complementary cultural approach, Peter Smith's concluding essay focuses upon the concepts and values that underlie political authority. He maintains that many North American historians and some Latin American ones have created a false dichotomy: democratic or illegitimate. In the political culture of Latin America he finds recurrent themes, regarding the legitimacy of leaders, that substantially elucidate the meaning of past political behavior.

In view of the freedom given to each author, we have been impressed by underlying unities among the papers. In one way or another, they all point to the need for placing institutions or actions in a broad societal context. The contributors present an implicit, cumulative argument against the excessive isolation of historical phenomena. Slavery and dictatorship, to take only two examples, must be understood as parts of a societal whole.

Second, the essays demonstrate the utility of interdisciplinary research. Virtually all the authors have reached out into other fields, mainly in the social sciences, for conceptual or methodological inspiration. The footnotes abound with references to sociology, psychology, and political science. For this group of historians, walls between the disciplines no longer exist.

Finally, the papers issue a latent call for rigorous comparative analysis. By focusing on broad substantive themes, the authors formulate general propositions that can best be tested and modified in a comparative fashion. Although many contributors draw heavily upon their research experiences in one country or another, they are all sensitive to the importance of a comparative approach, which, as Hall points out, "is the nearest historians can come to laboratory tests for their hypotheses."

Despite these common characteristics, however, these essays do not begin to constitute a manifesto. Nor are they meant to lay down, in imperious fashion, an exhaustive agenda for research. The essays are intended to probe, to stimulate, and to suggest—rather than to assert.

We fully expect that historical scholarship will move in a number of directions not covered here. For example, we suspect that some scholars will soon begin to investigate ecological aspects of Latin American society, exploring such problems as the connection between climatic change and social institutions. Others, we hope, will turn to the study of mortality control and epidemiology. Still others may take up the history of science. In connection with recent insights on "dependency" and "underdevelopment,"[2] there is already a resurgence—in altogether new form—of work on inter-American affairs. In all Latin American historiography we expect to find the increased use of quantitative techniques.[3]

Ultimately, our concern is not so much with substantive declaration as with the exposition of a research style: a style based on systematic doubt, an awareness of the need for conceptual rigor, and a willingness to try new methodologies.[4] Somewhat paradoxically, we believe that Latin American historians must reach out beyond Latin American history in order to understand Latin American history.

For this reason we hope that this volume will be of interest to historians in every field, as well as to students of Latin America. Though

---

[2] For an introduction to the "dependency" approach, see James D. Cockcroft, André Gunder Frank, and Dale L. Johnson, *Dependence and Underdevelopment: Latin America's Political Economy* (Garden City, N.Y.: Anchor Books, 1972).

[3] See Peter H. Smith's essay, "History," in *Quantitative Social Science Research on Latin America*, ed. Robert S. Byars and Joseph L. Love (Urbana: University of Illinois Press, 1973), pp. 14–61.

[4] For elaboration on this point see David S. Landes and Charles Tilly, eds., *History as Social Science* (Englewood Cliffs, N.J.: Prentice-Hall, 1971). We might also mention, with great pleasure, the growing tendency for social scientists to make use of historical materials.

the essays focus on Latin American phenomena, the themes they discuss—slavery, immigration, bureaucracy, regionalism, personality, and culture—are relevant to many other areas. Even more profoundly so are questions of conceptualization and methodology. This is a book about historical analysis, not about the story of a region.

It is no accident that the authors of these essays have all studied under Lewis Hanke. Because of his encouragement, guidance, and indefatigable enthusiasm, scores of graduate students, and probably thousands of undergraduates, have turned to the study of Latin American history. The great diversity among these essays provides only a glimpse of the range of his intellectual interests—and his tolerance as well! As a scholar and teacher he has exerted a deep impact upon all of us, upon the profession, and, as shown by his election to the presidency of the American Historical Association for 1974, upon the field as a whole. In view of his intense concern for problems of historiography, we hope this volume constitutes a fitting tribute to him. On behalf of all the contributors—with gratitude, affection, admiration, and pride—we dedicate this book to Lewis Hanke.

The Editors

New Approaches to Latin American History

State and Society in Colonial Spanish America: An Opportunity for Prosopography

STUART B. SCHWARTZ

Around the year 1673, Francisco Núñez de Pineda y Bascuñán, a fighter in the Araucanian wars in Chile, completed an account of his experiences in those campaigns. At various points in his manuscript, the old soldier struck out against the lawyers and government officials who lived off "the sweat and blood of His Majesty's poor subjects" and who seemed to pour into the colony, taking for themselves the spoils that men like Bascuñán had won with courage and steel.[1] The complaint was common enough. Many a nobleman in Spain or *encomendero* in the New World had voiced similar opinions, and more than one early settlment in America sought to exclude all lawyers and judges from its territory. Without realizing it, Bascuñán had simply borne witness to two major developments in the history of the modern world. In one, the overseas expansion of Europe, he acted as a willing participant; in the other, the rise of the centralized bureau-

NOTE. Prosopography is a term used increasingly by historians to describe various types of collective biography in which group characteristics rather than individuals per se are the main concern.

[1] Francisco Núñez de Pineda y Bascuñán, *Cautiverio Feliz y razón individual de las guerras dilatadas del reino de Chile* (Santiago de Chile: Imprenta del Ferrocarril, 1863); Sergio Correa Bello, *El "Cautiverio Feliz" en la vida política chilena del siglo xvii* (Santiago de Chile: Editorial Andrés Bello, 1965), pp. 100 ff.

cratic state, he stood as an interested but unhappy observer. However much Bascuñán and his comrades might wish to separate these two processes, they could not. Conquest and state, empire and bureaucracy were, at least in the Iberian world, inseparable.

The roughly contemporaneous development of overseas expansion and the centralized state stamped the Iberian nations and their empires with a distinctive legalistic and bureaucratic nature that had a profound impact, not only on their political systems, but on their societies as well. Whatever the economic, political, or spiritual motives that impelled Spaniards and Portuguese on the course of conquest in the fifteenth century, their empires were eventually molded around a legal core and a bureaucratic framework.[2] Structurally, the Iberian empires became great administrative systems designed to govern distant lands and peoples and to mobilize human and economic resources for the goals of the state. At the same time, a distinct society evolved from the process of conquest and colonization. By creating new social categories and by legislating in the area of social development, the bureaucratic state exercised considerable influence on the contours of colonial society.

While historians of the Spanish empire have long recognized the central role of the state and the importance of legal structures and administrative institutions, they have traditionally been far less interested in or able to deal with the nature of society or its relationship to the state. It is, of course, a commonplace of historiography that succeeding generations of scholars find the work of their predecessors wanting in one or another respect. Such feelings surely derive from the shifting spectrum of present interests, the availability of new sources, and the development or popularity of certain methods or approaches. At present a growing interest in social history and the refinement of a variety of research techniques have begun to direct

---

[2] Richard M. Morse, "Toward a Theory of Spanish American Government," *Journal of the History of Ideas* 15 (January 1954): 71–93; James E. McKeown, "The Legal Mentalities of the Spanish Conquistador and the English Colonizer," in *Actas del XXXIII Congreso Internacional de Americanistas* (San José, Costa Rica, 1959), II, 749–757; José Valero Silva, *El legalismo de Hernán Cortés como instrumento de su conquista* (Mexico City, 1965).

historical inquiry in new directions or toward a re-examination of old problems. The relationship of state to society is a topic in which important strides have recently been made and which appears to be drawing considerable interest. This essay is an attempt to point out the historiographical changes that have made this development possible, to underscore the major achievements to date, and to suggest those sources and lines of inquiry that seem most promising.

The generational dialectic of research and interest, the questioning of our historiographical predecessors, is no doubt healthy, but it should not blind us to their achievements. The legal or institutional approach favored by many historians of the last century did, after all, recognize the state's role in colonial history. This approach, deeply rooted in its own Hispanic tradition (it is still in vogue in Spain) and reinforced by a general European historical movement in the same direction, produced significant accomplishments in Latin American historiography.[3] Historians outlined with precision the formal organization of the colonial empire, explained the operations of its various offices, traced the development of the legal philosophy that supported it, and published valuable collections of administrative documents that invited others to follow their path. The ebb and flow of administration from creation under the Catholic kings to Hapsburg expansion and decline to Bourbon reform was delineated and explained. Great colonial administrators received detailed biographical treatment. In the present century such distinguished scholars as Roberto Levillier, Mario Góngora, José María Ots Capdequi, and Clarence Haring carried this approach to its high point in studies that demonstrated the impact and pervasiveness of the state.[4] In the hands of such sensitive

[3] Alfonso García Gallo, "El desarrollo de la historiografía jurídica indiana," *Revista de Estudios Políticos* 48, no. 70 (July–August 1953): 163–185. Evidence of the legal and institutional approach in Spanish historiography of America can be seen in the pages of *Revista de Estudios Políticos*, *Anuario del Derecho Español*, *Revista de Indias*, and *Anuario de Estudios Americanos*.

[4] Roberto Levillier, *Don Francisco de Toledo, supremo organizador del Perú, 1515–1582*, 2 vols. (Madrid: Espasa-Calpe, 1935–1940); José María Ots Capdequi, *Instituciones: Historia de América y de los pueblos americanos* (Barcelona: Salvati Editores, 1959); idem, *Historia del derecho español en América y del derecho indiano* (Madrid: Aguilar, 1969); Clarence Haring, *The Spanish Empire in America* (New York: Oxford University Press, 1947); Mario Góngora, *El estado en el*

and subtle historians as John Lynch and J. H. Parry, administrative history could at times extend beyond the operation of the state to broader questions of social and economic relationships.[5] But traditional institutional history could not do everything equally well.

As the administrative-institutional histories accumulated, it became increasingly apparent that, at least in two broad areas, they were insufficient. First, many aspects of society and economy could not be explored within the perimeters of these studies, whose emphasis, after all, lay in other directions. Society was commonly discussed simply as a context or backdrop against which an institution was placed or a viceroy ruled. Definition of class, race, and social structure were often too simple to be of much interest or too gross to be of much use. Such obvious social phenomena as patron-client relations or the role of the family were rarely treated, and the social categories employed remained curiously fixed in a Western European mold. The relationship of society and economy, the subtle impact of race on class structure, and the dynamic nature of human relations all seemed strangely absent from most studies, and many historians began to feel that the "action" in colonial history had somehow escaped them.

A second problem lay in the sources and in the very nature of the traditional approach. Based on laws, royal instructions, and administrative documents, traditional institutional history was often written from the viewpoint of Madrid or Seville rather than that of the colonies and was more the history of the administrators than of the administered. Given the nature of its sources, this approach naturally emphasized bureaucratic ideals, the way the system should have worked, and it was thus often disembodied from a reality that it tended to view as somehow pathological. The wide gap between legal

---

derecho indiano: Epoca de la fundación 1492–1570 (Santiago: Universidad de Chile, 1951).

[5] John Lynch, *Spanish Colonial Administration, 1782–1810: The Intendant System in the Viceroyalty of the Río de la Plata* (London: Athlone Press, 1958); J. H. Parry, *The Sale of Public Office in the Spanish Indies under the Hapsburgs* (Berkeley: University of California Press, 1953); idem, *The Audiencia of New Galicia in the Sixteenth Century: A Study in Spanish Colonial Government* (Cambridge: Cambridge University Press, 1948).

formulae and the actual workings of government and society became increasingly apparent, and in response historians moved toward those techniques or disciplines that seemed to offer an alternative to the traditional approach or some more effective way of dealing with the realities of colonial life. Many scholars, for example, turned to economic history, especially the quantitative *histoire série* variety popularized and to some extent pioneered in France.[6] More central to the theme of this essay, however, was the development of that field of inquiry directly concerned with society.

Social history, of course, had its own long tradition.[7] Generally considered a secondary topic, a historiographical stepchild, to most serious scholars it seemed far less important or interesting than the exploits of conquest, the lives of heroic figures, or the structure of colonial institutions. While these latter topics often contained material of direct interest to the social historian, social history as such remained a type of *costumbrismo*, the genre of "streets and costumes of Tucumán," often written by native-son amateurs and usually disregarded by professional historians. In the post–World War II era this situation began to change as students of Latin America, moved to some extent by contemporary interests and problems, increasingly turned to an examination of colonial society, not as something quaint and colorful, but as the basic theme of human experience.[8] Accompanying this shift in interest and acting as a stimulus to it were important methodological advances in the social sciences and the development of historical techniques that incorporated them. We need not recount here the achievements of sociology, ethnohistory, or historical demography to prove the point, but these disciplines expanded the horizons of social history and presented historians with new approaches

[6] On the rise of quantitative economic history and the state of the art, see Enrique Florescano, "La historia económica de la época colonial en América Latina: Desarrollo y perspectivas" (Paper read to the American Historical Association, New York, 1971).

[7] For a perceptive and stimulating essay see James Lockhart, "The Social History of Colonial Latin America: Evolution and Potential," *Latin American Research Review* 7, no. 1 (Spring 1972): 5–45.

[8] E. J. Hobsbawm, "From Social History to the History of Society," *Daedalus* 100 (Winter 1971): 20–45.

as well as the opportunity to raise wholly new historical questions.[9] Social history had become both sociological history and the history of society.

What can either type of social history offer to the study of the Spanish bureaucratic state and its relationship to society? In one case the answer is obvious. Since large-scale organizations and bureaucracy had been subjects of great concern in both sociology and political science, it was natural that scholars in these disciplines would turn to the history of the Spanish empire in search of data for their general theories or a historical arena where particular models of explanation might be tested.[10] Similarly, historians increasingly borrowed from these disciplines concepts that they hoped would provide new insights into the workings of colonial government.[11] The results of the interchange were mixed. At its best, the applications of Max Weber's or S. N. Eisenstadt's theories of bureaucratic development have provoked interesting lines of inquiry and an increased understanding of the past. But too often these theories have been mechanically applied with little concern for the particular nature of the Spanish empire, and the scholars who employ them have seldom made any attempt to push beyond the present frontiers of research. The result has been a series of conceptual models with little explanatory power that often suffer from

[9] On ethnohistory see Howard Cline, "Ethnohistory," in *Latin America: A Guide to the Historical Literature*, ed. Charles C. Griffin (Austin: University of Texas Press, 1971), pp. 124–148, and the excellent discussion in John N. Murra's "Current Research and Prospects in Andean Ethnohistory," *Latin American Research Review* 5, no. 1 (Spring 1970): 3–36. T. H. Hollingsworth's *Historical Demography* (Ithaca: Cornell University Press, 1969) discusses the field, while Nicolas Sánchez-Albornoz and José Luís Moreno, in *La población en América Latina* (Buenos Aires: Paidós, 1968), summarize work to date in Latin America.

[10] The best summary of the developments in the study of bureaucracy is presented in Nico P. Mouzelis's *Organisation and Bureaucracy* (Chicago: Aldine Publishing Co., 1968). S. N. Eisenstadt, in *The Political Systems of Empires* (New York: The Free Press, 1963), uses the Spanish empire as one of his examples. Application of political theory to an explanation of the Spanish empire can be seen in Frank Jay Moreno's "The Spanish Colonial System: A Functional Approach," *Western Political Quarterly* 20, no. 2, pt. 1 (June 1967): 308–321.

[11] John L. Phelan, "Authority and Flexibility in the Spanish Imperial Bureaucracy," *Administrative Science Quarterly* 5, no. 1 (June 1960): 47–65.

the very deficiencies of institutional formalism characteristic of the studies upon which they are based.[12]

The relationship between administrative-institutional history and the history of society is perhaps less immediately obvious, for bureaucratic institutions hardly seem fruitful orchards for the social historian. But bureaucracies are not composed only of institutions; they are created and operated by human beings. By concentrating on the individual and aggregate lives of bureaucrats, much can be done to close the gap between the legal and institutional ideals and abstractions and the reality of colonial life. Despite the innovative nature of many social-history techniques, the approach that seems to offer the richest opportunities for the study of large numbers of people and their relationship to social or political institutions is based as much on the most hallowed of historical techniques, biography and genealogy, as it is on historical demography or sociology. Called variously collective biography, multiple career analysis, or prosopography, this technique is neither new nor faultless, but it has already proven to be among the most effective historical methods for dealing with class formation, social mobility, and the ways in which social and economic factors impinge on political behavior.[13]

The basic method of prosopography is simple. A group of individuals is selected and identified. The historian then traces their lives, compiling as much detail as possible on family ties, personal relations, economic interests, political activities, and occupational performance. The result of this process is a set of biographies, often filled with fascinating details, grist for the social historian's mill. In Latin American historiography, collections of such data are an old and honored tradition. One need only glance at the dictionaries of biography, the catalogues of conquistadors and early settlers, or the sequential

---

[12] See Magali Sarfatti, *Spanish Bureaucratic-Patrimonialism in America* (Berkeley: Institute of International Studies, University of California, 1966). A fine defense of Max Weber's model is provided by William Delany in "The Development and Decline of Patrimonial and Bureaucratic Administrations," *Administrative Science Quarterly* 7, no. 4 (March 1963): 458–501.

[13] The best summary of the pleasures and pitfalls of this approach is Lawrence Stone's "Prosopography," *Daedalus* 100, no. 1 (Winter 1971): 46–79.

biographies of viceroys and bishops to see the results of such efforts.[14] The more recent studies differ, not in the nature of the data collected, but in the way it is used or analyzed. The group, not the individual, has become the unit of study. While the size of the group may vary widely from a few score people to thousands, and this—plus the historian's proclivities—will determine the extent to which quantitative techniques are employed, the recent studies share a common interest in aggregate data and the correlations between such variables as kinship, social origins, wealth, and political activity. By using the group as the unit of analysis, historians are able to deal with such elusive matters as class formation and social mobility on a somewhat firmer basis than had been possible with the impressionistic use of lapidary contemporary statements or individual examples, which, while often accurate, were always suspect as unrepresentative.

Prosopography in various forms can already boast of significant contributions to colonial history. Important and in some ways revolutionary studies have been done by James Lockhart on Peruvian society in the sixteenth century, by Armando de Ramón on the seventeenth-century Chilean elite, and by David Brading on the role of merchants in eighteenth-century New Spain.[15] A host of other topics, some as

[14] For example, Francisco A. de Icaza, *Conquistadores y pobladores de Nueva España*, 2 vols. (Madrid: Imprenta "El Adelentado de Segovia," 1923); Ricardo de Lafuente Machain, *Conquistadores del Río de la Plata* (Buenos Aires: S. Amorrotu e Hijos, 1937); Roberto Levillier, *Biografías de conquistadores de la Argentina en el siglo xvi: Tucumán* (Madrid: J. Pueyo, 1933); Enrique Udaondo, *Diccionario biográfico colonial argentino* (Buenos Aires: Editorial Huarpes, 1945); José Toribio Medina, *Diccionario biográfico colonial de Chile* (Santiago de Chile: Imprenta Elzeviriana, 1906); Manuel de Mendiburu, *Diccionario histórico-biográfico del Perú*, 11 vols., 2d ed. (Lima: Imprenta Enrique Palacios, 1931–1935). Much information on colonial elites is found in such works as Guillermo Lohmann Villena's *Los americanos en las órdenes nobiliarias (1529–1900)*, 2 vols. (Madrid: Consejo Superior de Investigaciones Científicas, 1947), and Leopoldo Martínez Cosío's *Los caballeros de las órdenes militares en México* (Mexico City: Editorial Santiago, 1946). The tradition in Latin America is more exactly called sequential biography than collective biography. See for example José Restrepo Posada, *Arquidiócesis de Bogotá: Datos biográficos de sus prelados*, 3 vols. (Bogotá: Editorial Lumen Christi, 1961–1966); Ulises Rojas, *Corregidores y justicias mayores de Tunja* (Tunja: Imprenta Departamental de Boyacá, 1963); Santiago Martínez, *Gobernadores de Arequipa colonial (1539–1821)* (Arequipa: Tipografía Cuadros, 1930).

[15] James Lockhart, *Spanish Peru 1532–1560: A Colonial Society* (Madison: Uni-

basic and crucial as the application of Marxian concepts of class to colonial society, seem particularly suited to investigation through collective biography. Moreover, this approach may be especially helpful in dealing with periods like the seventeenth century, in which the heroic figures and dramatic events favored by biography and political history are few.[16]

Obviously, the first task of collective biography is the selection of a group. Despite the wide range of possibilities, the choice of a group and the identification of its members is not an easy task. First, there is a methodological problem. Since each individual has many social roles, his inclusion by the historian in one or another group imposes a fixed category or definition on what is in effect an indivisible reality of roles and associations. Men and women may simultaneously belong to many groups or alignments, and thus their categorization by the historian is necessarily defined by his or her interests or presuppositions. This is perhaps inevitable, but the historian should at least be aware that the very act of defining the group will have an effect on the data and on the ultimate findings of the study.

A second problem is more practical in nature. There is a law of documentary elitism: that generally the more power, wealth, or prestige an individual possessed, the easier it is to find those sources needed for detailed biographical reconstruction.[17] Thus, prosopography has usually been the study of elites, since its biographical approach and the availability of sources are skewed toward viceroys and bishops rather than muleteers or field hands. While it is not im-

versity of Wisconsin Press, 1968); idem, *The Men of Cajamarca: A Social and Biographical Study of the First Conquerors of Peru* (Austin: University of Texas Press, 1972); Armando de Ramón, "La sociedad española de Santiago de Chile entre 1581 y 1596," *Revista Historia* 4 (1965); idem, "Grupos elitarios chilenos y su vinculación con la metrópoli peruana a fines del siglo xviii" (Paper read to the Congreso Internacional de Americanistas, Lima, 1970); David A. Brading, *Miners and Merchants in Bourbon Mexico 1763–1810* (Cambridge: Cambridge University Press, 1971).

16 Ursula Lamb, "Units of One and the Visible Event," *Journal of Inter-American Studies and World Affairs* 12, no. 1 (January 1971): 131–135. Cf. Donald Chipman, "The Status of Biography in the Historiography of New Spain," *The Americas* 27, no. 3 (January 1971): 327–339.

17 Lockhart, "Social History," p. 8, suggests this phrase.

possible to deal with the "common man," it is nevertheless true that, as the historian descends the social ladder in search of a group, the sources become ever thinner and the difficulties ever greater. It is in the study of these lower social strata that prosopography has shaded into the realm of historical demography, for here the demographer's skill in dealing with large numbers of people may be more useful than the biographer's concern with personal detail.[18]

Data dispersion is a corollary to the law of documentary elitism. While the historian may occasionally find a single source or set of documents that brings together biographical information, collective biography commonly demands a painstaking and time-consuming search in a wide variety of sources. Basic life data is usually accumulated in bits and pieces. It is often found in rich but difficult-to-use local sources, such as notary registers, wills, and court records, which are widely dispersed, often in poor physical condition, and usually uncatalogued. Naturally, certain sources, when available, should yield certain kinds of information. Thus a parish register can be expected to reveal a subject's date of baptism or death, and a will should indicate something about his or her property. Too often, however, the normal source for a particular kind of information is unavailable, and the historian must constantly keep watch on every available scrap in hopes of filling the gaps. The prosopographer's slow accretion of widely dispersed data might be called *histoire pastiche*; it is the methodological antithesis of the economic historian's dependence on long series of consecutive data.[19]

---

[18] E.g., Peter Boyd-Bowman, *Indice geobiográfico de cuarenta mil pobladores españoles de América en el siglo xvi* (Bogotá: Instituto Caro y Cuervo, 1964). Stone, in "Prosopography," pp. 47–48, suggests a division between the elite and mass schools of collective biography in method and social-class studies. The division does not always hold true, since under special circumstances it is possible to use "elite" techniques for analysis of nonelite groups. See for example Lockhart, *Spanish Peru*, or Mario Góngora, *Los grupos de conquistadores en Tierra-Firme (1509–1530)* (Santiago: Universidad de Chile, 1962).

[19] An example of the patience sometimes needed is provided by the work of one of the precursors of collective biography in Hispanic studies. The indefatigable Alice B. Gould patiently traced the shipmates of Columbus for twenty years in the archives of Spain. The results were published in the *Boletín de la Real Academia de Historia* between 1924 and 1944.

Since much of colonial life was structured by a system of occupational, state, and religious institutions, these organizations offer excellent vantage points from which society and its changes over time can be seen. Moreover, such bodies were usually excellent record-keepers, and thus their membership lists and internal administrative papers often provide exactly the kind of information most useful for collective biography. The Church can serve as an example. It has been the subject of administrative, institutional, economic, and theological analysis, but the Church as a great institution that pervaded the life of the Indies can also be of interest to the social historian. The vast corpus of Church-related documents is filled with useful data that social historians have only begun to exploit. The clergy, either as a distinct social category or as representative of society as whole, has been a major topic of interest. Enrique D. Dussel's extended study of the Spanish American episcopate as a missionary institution has tied prosopography to other historical approaches by carefully reconstructing the biographies of all the bishops in the Indies between 1504 and 1620 and then using this data to explain their missionary efforts.[20] Francisco Morales Valerio's social analysis of the Franciscans in New Spain demonstrates the way in which such studies reveal trends in the society as a whole. His work confirmed not only that mestizos and Indians were generally excluded from the regular clergy in the seventeenth century, but also that the sons of the conquistadors were increasingly displaced in the order by men of mercantile or bureaucratic origins.[21] Those old and unresolved questions on the nature of the secular clergy, the changing composition of the regular clergy, and the social and political role of the Inquisition are all, at least in part, approachable from the standpoint of collective biography.[22]

[20] Enrique D. Dussel, *El episcopado hispanoamericano: Institución misionera en defensa del indio*, 7 vols. (Cuernavaca: Centro Intercultural de Documentación, 1969–1970). Cf. *Les Evêques hispano-americains: Défenseurs et évangélisateurs de l'indien, 1504–1620* (Wiesbaden: F. Steiner, 1970). See also Antonine Tibesar, "The Lima Pastors 1750–1820: Their Origins and Studies as Taken from Their Autobiographies," *The Americas* 28, no. 1 (July 1971): 39–56.

[21] Francisco Morales Valerio, "Antecedentes sociales de los Franciscanos en México: Siglo xvii" (Ph.D. dissertation, Catholic University of America, 1971).

[22] Biographical materials on the regular clergy are more accessible than those on

Because it is an underlying assumption of prosopography that social and economic factors often influence or determine ideology, professional performance, and political activity, scholars have concentrated on the institutions that reveal these relationships most directly. For this reason some of the most interesting work to date has been done on the colonial municipal councils (*cabildos*), those bodies long held to be representative of colonial interests. A firm groundwork of institutional analysis has been laid so that scholars can turn their attention to patterns of membership, the influence of factions or other social groupings, and the impact of particular interests on a region's development. Who served on the town council? The question is simple, and the answer may not resolve all historical problems, but both question and answer provide a dimension that political and administrative history sorely needed. Basic studies, such as that of Aurora Flores Olea on Mexico City, have established the social composition of the councilmen at one point in time.[23] Other scholars have moved beyond this. Mario Góngora has demonstrated how the social composition of the *cabildo* of Santiago can be used as a measure of the Chilean elite in the seventeenth century. A similar study of Popayán, Colombia, by Peter Marzahl traces the rise of merchant groups to positions of power and their eventual incorporation by marriage into the original *encomendero* aristocracy of the region.[24] Such studies help to explain social and political trends and the interrelation

---

the seculars. Once again the law of documentary elitism obtains: it is easier to find information on bishops than on parish priests. Julio Caro Baroja has studied the office of inquisitor to present a different sort of collective biography in which the lives of the incumbents in an office are used to describe the operation of the office. See his *El señor inquisidor y otras vidas por oficio* (Madrid: Alianza Editorial, 1968).

[23] Aurora Flores Olea, "Los regidores de la Ciudad de México en la primera mitad del siglo xvii," *Estudios de Historia Novohispana* 3 (1970): 149–172. Two similar studies can be found in Ph.D. dissertations: William H. Hallett, "The Criollo in the Cabildo of Mexico City, 1595–1630" (Washington University, forthcoming); Dominic Azikiwe Nwasike, "Mexico City Town Government, 1590–1650: A Study in Aldermanic Background and Performance" (University of Wisconsin, 1972).

[24] Mario Góngora, *Encomenderos y estancieros* (Santiago: Universidad de Chile, 1970); Peter Marzahl, "The Cabildo of Popayán in the Seventeenth Century: The Emergence of a Creole Elite" (Ph.D. dissertation, University of Wisconsin, 1970).

between them without recourse to unnecessary abstractions. Marzahl and Góngora demonstrate that prosopography need not be highly quantitative to be useful and that the technique may yield its richest results when combined with more traditional political or economic analysis.

Government was usually a temporary concern for *cabildo* members, but for royal officials and bureaucrats it was to varying degrees a profession. The lives of these men offer particular opportunities for evaluation of the impact of social and economic factors on political life. Whereas society as a whole might view nepotism, favoritism, and graft as only morally reprehensible (if even that), in a state bureaucracy designed for the achievement of administrative and political goals such behavior was officially considered illegal, dysfunctional, and often punishable. It was, therefore, continually checked and recorded. Such activities are those that the prosopographer often finds most interesting, for they are exactly the points where social and economic considerations directly impinge on political affairs. The operation of government in the Spanish empire was a complex equation of royal interests, expressed through laws and bureaucratic norms; the bureaucrats' class, professional, and personal goals; and the desires and aspirations of various colonial groups. Beneath the rigid formulations of laws lay a variety of personal and professional options open to the bureaucrats, who, acting as mediators between crown and colony, could provide the links between government and society.

There were, of course, many echelons of bureaucracy in the Spanish empire. The personnel of almost any level or office could be profitably examined. Intendants, *alcaldes mayores*, or even clerks can all be studied within the context of collective biography, but since the imperial bureaucracy was based on a judicial core, it was perhaps epitomized by its most professional members, the university-trained *letrados*, the laywers and judges for whom government was an occupation and a way of life.

The *letrados* rose to prominence as the power of the centralized state expanded. Responding to the growing needs of royal government after the fourteenth century, the king's household evolved into a large and complex bureaucratic apparatus staffed by royal servants, functionaries, and professional bureaucrats who advised the crown, enforced the laws, collected taxes, and kept the records of government. These men, drawn from a variety of social backgrounds, became in effect a bureaucratic class.[25] The Laws of Toro (1480) marked their ascendancy in Castile. Although some observers described their rise to power in almost allegorical terms as a competition between military virtues and the values of humanism (arms versus letters), the most perceptive saw the struggle for what it was: a political conflict in which the monarchy sought to impose its authority over various individual and corporate rights and powers.[26] In this process the bureaucracy became the king's weapon and the *letrados* its cutting edge.

In the New World as in Europe, *letrados* became the most direct representatives of the Spanish monarchy. The crown charged them with the difficult mission of curbing centrifugal forces generated by private interests (Columbus, Pizarro, Cortez), aristocratic pretensions (*encomenderos*), or corporate ambitions (*cabildos*, the Church).[27] While waging these battles for the crown, the *letrados* sometimes used their authority for personal advantage. They became in effect a social class linked by profession to the state and by interests and aspirations to the society in which they lived.

While *letrados* staffed many offices, ranging from viceroy to legal

[25] Juan Beneyto, "La gestación de la magistratura moderna," *Anuario de la Historia de Derecho Español* 23 (1953): 55–82; José Antonio Maravall, "The Origins of the Modern State," *Journal of World History* 6, no. 4 (1961): 789–805; idem, "Los 'hombres de saber' o letrados y la formación de su conciencia estamental," *Estudios de historia del pensamiento español* (Madrid: Ediciones Cultura Hispánica, 1967), pp. 345–380; Jaime Vicens Vives, "Estructura administrativa estatal en los siglos xvi y xvii," in idem, *Coyuntura económica y reformismo burgués* (Barcelona: Ediciones Ariel, 1969), pp. 100–141.

[26] Ricardo del Arco y Garay, *La sociedad española en las obras de Cervantes* (Madrid: Patronato del IV Centenario del Nascimiento de Cervantes, 1951), especially Ch.15, "Académicos o letrados."

[27] Javier Malagón Barceló, "The Role of the *Letrado* in the Colonization of America," *The Americas* 18 (July 1961): 1–17. My discussion centers on the *letrado* as judge, but there is available considerable biographical material on the practicing lawyers and the legal profession. See Hector García Chuecos, *Abogados de la colonia* (Caracas: Imprenta Nacional, 1958); Archivo General de la Nación, *Los abogados de la colonia* (Caracas: Imprenta Nacional, 1965); Javier González Echenique, *Los estudios jurídicos y la abogacía en el reino de Chile* (Santiago: Universidad Católica de Chile, 1954).

scribe, the *audiencias* (royal high courts of appeal) best represented their presence in America. The creation of the *audiencia* of Santo Domingo (1511) signaled the crown's desire to establish the judicial bureaucracy in the Indies on a permanent basis. Eventually, fourteen such courts were established in Spanish America. Their wide range of administrative as well as judicial duties, their constant contact with other colonial institutions, and their persistence over long periods of time all present a wide range of historical opportunities. Perhaps two thousand *letrados* (*oidores*) eventually served in the American *audiencias* during the colonial period—a number large enough to offer a wide variety of historical examples, yet still small enough to be managed statistically without great difficulty.[28] Importance, political activities, size, and persistence over time make the *audiencias* excellent institutions from which the collective biography of bureaucracy can be written.

Despite the central role of the *audiencias* and the importance of the *letrados*, few studies have been devoted to either.[29] The great chancellery courts of Spain—Valladolid and Granada—remain unstudied.[30] In Spanish America few *audiencias* have received book-

[28] I have used *oidor* to mean any *letrado* in an *audiencia*, including *alcaldes del crimen* and *fiscales*. Ernesto Schäfer, in *El Consejo Real y Supremo de las Indias: Su historia, organización y labor administrativa hasta la terminación de la Casa de Austria*, 2 vols. (Seville: Escuela de Estudios Hispano-Americanos de Seville, 1935–1947), II, 439–525, lists over 1,400 *audiencia* appointments between 1511 and 1700. More complete listings that include the eighteenth century do exist for some tribunals. See Vicente de Paula Andrade, "Los oidores de Nueva España," *Boletín Bibliográfico Mexicano* 196–197 (May–June 1956): 16–25.

[29] Haring's *Spanish Empire*, Ots Capdequi's *Instituciones*, and especially Schäfer's *El Consejo Real* are excellent introductions to the subject. General studies are provided by Francisco de Pelsmaeker e Ibáñez, *La audiencia en las colonias españolas de América* (Madrid: Tipografía de la "Revista de Archivos," 1925); Pío Ballesteros, "La función política de los reales chancillerías coloniales," *Revista de Estudios Políticos* 15, nos. 27–28 (1946): 47–109; Jesús Abadía Lalinde, "El régimen virreino-senatorial en Indias," *Anuario de Historia del Derecho Español* 37 (1967): 5–244.

[30] See F. Mendizával, "Investigaciones acerca del origen, historia y organización de la real cancillería de Valladolid," *Revista de Archivos, Bibliotecas, y Museos* 31 (1914). Curiously, the *audiencia* of the Canary Islands has been better studied than the peninsular tribunals. See José María de Zuaznávar, *Noticias histórico-legales de la real audiencia de Canarias*, 2d ed. (Santa Cruz de Tenerife, 1864); Benjamín Artiles, *Sobre las ordenanzas de la real audiencia de Canarias* (Las Palmas, 1949); Leo-

length treatment, and the great tribunal of Mexico still awaits its historian.[31] High-court judges were powerful men, but their activities were not the sort that attracted biographers. The few biographers of *oidores* are devoted to exceptional figures like Juan de Solórzano Pereira, Antonio de León Pinelo, Juan de Matienzo, or Alonso de Zorita, men who are remembered primarily as great legal thinkers, political theorists, or social critics. Only a handful of biographies deal with everyday life of the ordinary judge or bureaucrat.[32] For most purposes, the *letrados* remain an unstudied social and professional

---

poldo de la Rosa Oliveira, "La real audiencia de Canarias: Notas para su historia," *Anuario de Estudios Atlánticos* 3 (1957): 91–164.

[31] C. H. Cunningham, *The Audiencia in the Spanish Colonies as Illustrated by the Audiencia of Manila, 1583–1800* (Berkeley: University of California Press, 1919); Parry, *The Audiencia of New Galicia*; John L. Phelan, *The Kingdom of Quito in the Seventeenth Century: Bureaucratic Politics in the Spanish Empire* (Madison: University of Wisconsin Press, 1967); Javier Malagón Barceló, *El distrito de la Audiencia de Sto. Domingo en los siglos XVI a XIX* (Ciudad Trujillo: Universidad de Santo Domingo, 1942). I have not been able to consult Vera L. Brown, "A Study of the Audiencia in Peru" (Ph.D. dissertation, Bryn Mawr College, 1913).

[32] Guillermo Lohmann Villena has produced three *oidor* biographies in his introductions to Antonio de León Pinelo's *El gran canciller de las Indias* (Seville: Escuela de Estudios Hispanoamericanos, 1953) and *oidor* Juan de Matienzo's *Gobierno del Perú (1567)* (Paris-Lima: Institut Français d'Etudes Andines, 1967) and in his study, *Les Espinosa: Une Famille d'hommes d'affaires en Espagne et aux Indes à l'époque de la colonisation* (Paris: S.E.V.P.E.N., 1968), which deals with the activities of Lic. Gaspar de Espinosa. Francisco Javier de Ayala, in *Ideas políticas de Juan de Solórzano* (Seville: Escuela de Estudios Hispanoamericanos, 1946), sketches the life of that *letrado*. Ralph H. Vigil's "Alonzo de Zorita, Oidor in the Indies" (Ph.D. dissertation, University of New Mexico, 1969) is a portrait of that judge as a loyal official. A good study of him is also provided in Benjamin Keen's introduction to Zorita's *The Lords of New Spain* (New Brunswick, N.J.: Rutgers University Press, 1963). Paul Lietz's "Vasco de Quiroga: Oidor Made Bishop," *Mid-America* 32 (1950): 13–32, and Fintan B. Warren's *Vasco de Quiroga and His Pueblo-Hospitals of Santa Fe* (Washington, D.C.: Academy of American Franciscan History, 1963) are both studies of a *letrado* remembered for his social, not his judicial, activities. More pertinent to the matter of a judge's career is Emilio Robeledo's *Bosquejo biográfico del señor oidor Juan Antonio Mon y Velarde, visitador de Antioquia, 1785–1788,* 2 vols. (Bogotá: Banco de la República, 1954). The most detailed *oidor* biography to date is Ricardo Donoso's *Un letrado del siglo xviii: El doctor José Perfecto de Salas,* 2 vols. (Buenos Aires: Universidad de Buenos Aires, 1963).

category, whose importance many proclaim, but whose position in colonial history few have pursued.

There are three basic and not necessarily mutually exclusive approaches that might be used for a social analysis of the *audiencia* bureaucracy. The first, a "total" quantitative analysis of all *oidores* from 1511 to the end of the colonial era, has not yet been attempted and is probably best left to last. There is much biographical information about *oidores* now in print, but the size and complexity of such a project present a considerable challenge.[33] More important, serious deficiencies in the present state of knowledge place severe restrictions on possible results. Historians of a colonial situation work slightly off center, since decisions, policies, and actions affecting their subject are often the result of the metropolitan situation. The state of peninsular historiography thus places certain limits on the study of government in Spanish America. Little has been done on the *letrado* bureaucracy in Spain, aside from Richard Kagan's excellent study of the Hapsburg period.[34] Thus, it is difficult to place the American or "Indies" bureaucracy in a proper historical context. If, for example, we find that a certain percentage of *oidores* in America had artisan backgrounds and we do not know how this compared to the *letrado* bureaucracy as a whole, then the possible significance of the data has been lost. The blame is not all in Spain. The relative lack of studies on the American *audiencias* also places limits on a general approach. While it is not necessary to have a detailed monograph on every *audiencia* before attempting a general study, until more is known about the hierarchy of promotion within and between *audiencias*, the system of professional rewards, and the possible goals of the judges, nuances and subtleties of the quantitative data will be lost.

[33] Biographical material on *oidores* is widely scattered in biographical dictionaries. It has occasionally been brought together in such works as José María Restrepo Sáenz's *Biografías de los mandatarios y ministros de la Real Audiencia, 1671–1819*, Biblioteca Historia Nacional, no. 84 (Bogotá: Editorial Cromos, 1952), and Manuel Moreyra y Paz-Soldán's *Biografías de oidores del siglo xvii y otros estudios* (Lima, 1957).

[34] Richard Kagan, "Education and the State in Hapsburg Spain" (Ph.D. dissertation, Cambridge University, 1968).

Both other approaches concentrate on a single tribunal, but differ in the nature of their temporal dimension. One attempts the study of an *audiencia* over an extended period of time, analyzing its formal institutional structure and its informal operations as seen through the lives of its judges.[35] The other attempts to isolate the tribunal and its magistrates at a specific point in time, when, in a period of crisis or tension, certain general characteristics and tendencies become manifest. The Bourbon reforms of the mid-eighteenth century provide just such a situation. Royal investigators sent from Spain to discover and eliminate abuses overturned many stones and revealed the dark underside of government practices. The findings of these investigators have already served historians as the basis for a re-evaluation of the *audiencia* bureaucracy in that era.[36] Such sweeping empire-wide reforms were rare, however, and historians must turn to other sources for other periods.

Among the most promising documents are the judicial reviews and examinations (*visitas* and *residencias*), which periodically checked bureaucratic behavior and which created strains that revealed the inner workings of the court. John Phelan's excellent study of the *audiencia* of Quito is basically an examination of that body through the *visita general* of Lic. Juan de Mañozca in the 1620's. Phelan clearly demonstrates the utility of such sources.[37] The fact that these judicial inquiries treat infractions of legal norms makes them especially valuable,

[35] Parry's *Audiencia of New Galicia*, although primarily administrative in approach, is the best example to date. Cf. Stuart B. Schwartz, *Sovereignty and Society in Colonial Brazil: The High Court of Bahia and Its Judges, 1609–1751* (Berkeley: University of California Press, 1973), which attempts this approach for an analogous Brazilian tribunal.

[36] Brading, *Miners and Merchants*, pp. 37–44; Leon G. Campbell, "A Colonial Establishment: Creole Domination of the Audiencia of Lima during the Late Eighteenth Century," *Hispanic American Historical Review* 52, no. 1 (February 1972): 1–25; Mark Burkholder, "From Creole to *Peninsular*: The Transformation of the Audiencia of Lima," ibid. 52, no. 3 (August 1972): 395–415. See also Jacques Barbier, "Elite and Cadres in Bourbon Chile," ibid. 52, no. 3 (August 1972): 416–435.

[37] Phelan, *Kingdom of Quito*. A similar approach is used in Constance Crowder Carter's "Law and Society in Colonial Mexico: Audiencia Judges in Mexican Society from the Tello de Sandoval Visita General, 1543–1547" (Ph.D. dissertation, Columbia University, 1972). William L. Sherman's "Indian Slavery and the Cerrato

for they reveal the actual operation of government in contrast to the ideal situation as set forth in the laws and regulations. Since many of the infractions involve the personal behavior of the judges and violation of their theoretical isolation from society, these investigations provide excellent sources for the social historian. There are problems here too. The documentation of most of these judicial reviews is fragmentary. Often the charges or accusations remain, but not the refutation or sentence. Given the prosopographer's natural inclination to believe the worst (the operation of selfish interest), such sources may be unfairly used to corroborate the historian's thesis. The risk, however, is not limited to this particular type of source, and the problems or deficiencies of such materials should not obscure their rich potential.[38]

Whatever the unit of study, social analysis of the *letrado* bureaucracy has concentrated on four major life areas: (*a*) education, (*b*) career patterns, (*c*) social relations, (*d*) economic interests. Each of these life areas is assumed to be a factor of potential influence on personal, political, and professional behavior. While research on these topics has already produced significant results, it has also raised a large number of questions and underlined certain problems of sources and methodology that demand attention.

Education

All *letrado* bureaucrats shared one common attribute, university training with a degree in canon or civil law. University archives and

Reforms," *Hispanic American Historical Review* 51, no. 1 (February 1971): 25–50, is basically an analysis of the *audiencia* of Guatemala, based on *visita* materials.

[38] Guillermo Céspedes del Castillo, "La 'visita' como institución indiana," *Anuario de Estudios Americanos* 3 (1946): 984–1025; José María Mariluz Urquijo, *Ensayo sobre los juicios de residencia indianos* (Seville: Escuela de Estudios Hispanoamericanos, 1952). A glance at José María de la Peña Cámara, *A List of Spanish Residencias in the Archive of the Indies, 1515–1775* (Washington, D.C.: Library of Congress, 1955) reveals the richness of these sources. Not all the extant *residencia* papers are housed in Seville. See the listing in Luis Sánchez Belda's *Guía del Archivo Histórico Nacional* (Madrid: Dirección General de Archivos y Bibliotecas, 1958), pp. 140–144. There are sixty or seventy *visitas*, of which only six are complete. This and other deficiencies are discussed in Schäfer's *El Consejo Real*, II, 128–157.

matriculation records often contain information on the social and geographical origins of the student body and are thus valuable to the collective biographer, but there is more of interest in the universities than their role as keepers of records. In these schools the would-be bureaucrats learned the skills of their profession and the political principles of the state. As the demands and needs of government changed, so too did the nature and function of the universities. It is now clear that six *colegios mayores* in major Spanish universities served as seedbeds for the upper echelons of the state bureaucracy in the Hapsburg era. Richard Kagan has demonstrated that the *colegios mayores* also affected the operations of government in less formal ways. He shows clearly that old school ties and common educational affiliations significantly influenced promotion and career opportunities within the hierarchy of office.[39] His work should stimulate colonial historians to pose similar questions, but university studies have been far more concerned with internal intellectual developments than with the relationship of the colonial schools to the workings of the state. While much remains to be done on the university's role in the socialization and professionalization of the *letrado* bureaucracy, historians might turn to these studies of the intellectual and philosophical milieu of the law faculties for some help in rectifying collective biography's usual inability to integrate ideology into the explanation of human behavior.

Many questions about the impact of the university and university life remain unanswered. It would be interesting to know the relative weight or advantage of a peninsular degree as compared with a diploma from Lima or Mexico. It is possible that preferential treatment and advancement depended not on social origins or place of birth but on place of education. Certainly, the existence of numerous American universities where creoles, born, raised, and educated in the New World, could be prepared to serve a metropolis they had never seen raises interesting questions of identity and loyalty. The effects of this situation have never been fully explored and call for comparison with the situation in Brazil, whose *letrados* were all schooled and prepared for royal service at Coimbra, Portugal. Did Brazilians and Spanish

[39] Kagan, "Education and the State," pp. 163–207.

Americans develop different attitudes toward state and nationality partially in response to the difference in their bureaucratic opportunities and training?

Professional Life

Magistracy was a full-time occupation, usually a lifetime career, and certainly a major point of personal orientation for those *letrados* who entered the judicial bureaucracy.[40] Career patterns, both individual and aggregate, become a major concern, since professional achievements, goals, and the very nature of the bureaucratic structure may have been important factors influencing personal or group behavior. The social historian seeks not only to reconstruct individual careers but also to discover general patterns of recruitment, promotion, reward, and censure. The extent to which *letrado* bureaucrats sought only those goals and rewards prescribed by the crown as compatible with the operation of government is what is at question here. Obviously, the crown hoped to direct *letrado* aspirations in this direction, but it is also clear that professionalization never fully overcame a competing set of personal goals that led the judges to act in their own interest and not that of the state.

The professional life of the *letrados* complicates the task of the social historian, who must deal with them not only as part of the larger social structure but also as participants in a distinct subsystem, the bureaucracy, with its own set of norms and values. The bureaucratic dimension also has its bright side, however, since administrative records are abundant and relatively well preserved in Spanish archives. Discussions (*consultas*) of various administrative bodies, letters of appointment and promotion, correspondence to and from the

---

[40] A general but basically administrative study of the imperial judiciary is Enrique Ruiz Guiñazú's *La magistratura indiana* (Buenos Aires: Universidad de Buenos Aires, 1916). See also Louis G. Kahle, "The Spanish Colonial Judiciary," *Southwestern Social Science Quarterly* 32 (June 1951): 26–37. Ricardo Zorraquín Becú in *La organización política argentina en el período hispánico* (Buenos Aires: Emecé Editores, 1959), presents a perceptive discussion of the judiciary's function in the structure of the state. Also based on regional sources but with wide application is Nestor Meza Villalobos's *La conciencia política chilena durante la monarquía* (Santiago: Universidad de Chile, 1958).

judges, and reports about their activities by others make up a significant part of the materials available in Simancas, Seville, and Madrid.[41] Thus, while the professional dimension raises difficult questions of interpretation, bureaucratic records make it relatively easy to reconstruct careers and often cast considerable light on many other aspects of a judge's life.

The availability of data on the operation of bureaucracy has not, however, eliminated historical disagreements. Most scholars admit that patronage played some role in appointment and promotion within the *letrado* ranks, but there is little agreement on its extent or impact. J. H. Parry suggested in 1963 that *audiencia* judgeships were rarely, if ever, sold, but recent evidence indicates that by the close of the seventeenth century many *oidores* had bought their positions.[42] John Phelan believes that few *letrados* who served in the American *audiencias* later returned to positions in Spain and that the American promotional structure was virtually a separate system within the Spanish bureaucracy. Richard Kagan is far less convinced of this.[43] Collective biography or, a better term in this case, multiple career analysis can provide a definite answer.

Primary Social Relations

Kinship, patron-client links, and other primary social relations have traditionally played a dominant role in Latin American society, and

[41] Ricardo Magdaleno's *Títulos de Indias: Catálogo XX del Archivo General de Simancas* (Valladolid: Dirección General de Archivos y Bibliotecas, 1954) is a guide to the letters of appointment. The *consultas* of the Council of the Indies are usually found in the Archivo General de Indias in Seville. Also important is the *Consejos suprimidos* section of the Archivo Histórico Nacional (Madrid), which contains information on *letrado* appointments made by the Cámara de Castilla.

[42] Parry, *The Sale of Public Office*. Cf. Antonio Domínguez Ortiz, "Ventas y extensiones de lugares durante el reinado de Felipe IV," *Anuario de Historia del Derecho Español* 34 (1964): 163–208; Burkholder, "From Creole to *Peninsular*," p. 397; Campbell, "A Colonial Establishment," pp. 5–15. See also M. A. Burkholder and D. S. Chandler, "Creole Appointments and the Sale of Audiencia Positions in the Spanish Empire under the Early Bourbons, 1701–1750," *Journal of Latin American Studies* 4, no. 2 (November 1972): 187–206.

[43] John L. Phelan, "The Spanish Colonial Bureaucracy under the Hapsburgs" (Paper read to the American Historical Association, New York, 1969); Kagan, "Education and the State," p. 54.

there is little reason to believe that they did not exercise considerable influence on government as well. The history of colonial government is, in fact, filled with references to family protection, nepotism, favoritism, and the use of office for personal advantage. The *letrado* bureaucracy, as the most professional branch of government, should have been the least influenced by these phenomena, but scratching the surface of almost any historical event or epoch reveals a web of personal relations in which *oidores* are often involved. Bishop Bartolomé de las Casas probably exaggerated in 1545 when he claimed that confiding in the *oidores* of Guatemala was like "entrusting very tame sheep to hungry wolves," but hardly an *audiencia* escaped similar charges.[44]

It is clear that the crown sought to isolate judges from society and make them impartial guardians of the law fully pledged only to the king's interests. The *Recopilación* of 1680 and subsequent legislation severely restricted a magistrate's access to friendship, kinship, and other social or economic ties within the area of his jurisdiction.[45] *Letrados* constantly ignored this legislation or found loopholes in it.

[44] Las Casas, Gracias a Dios, to Prince Philip, November 9, 1545, in *Etudes sur Bartolomé de las Casas,* by Marcel Bataillon (Paris: Centre de Recherches de l'Institut d'Etudes Hispaniques, 1966), p. 240. For examples of similar criticism and of the kind of sources available on these matters see Manuel Moreyra y Paz-Soldán, "Introducción a documentos y cartas de la Audiencia y del Virrey Marqués de Montesclaros," *Revista Histórica* 19 (1952): 239–243; Carlos Deustua Pimentel, "Un informe secreto del Virrey Gil de Taboada sobre la Audiencia de Lima," *Revista Histórica* 21 (1954): 274–287; *Cartas del licenciado Jerónimo de Valderrama y otros documentos sobre su visita al gobierno de Nueva España, 1563–1565* (Mexico City: Editorial Porrúa, 1961), pp. 205–252; Roberto Levillier, ed., *La Audiencia de Charcas: Correspondencia de presidentes y oidores; documentos del Archivo de Indias,* 3 vols. (Madrid: J. Pueyo, 1918–1922); idem, *Gobernantes del Perú: Cartas y papeles, siglo xvi; documentos del Archivo de Indias,* 14 vols. (Madrid: Sucesores de Rivadeneyra, 1921–1926); Ricardo Beltrán y Rózpide, ed., *Colección de las memorias o relaciones que escribieron los virreyes del Perú,* 2 vols. (Madrid: Imprenta de Asilo de Huérfanos del S. C. de Jesús, 1921–1930).

[45] *Recopilación de las leyes de los reynos de las Indias,* 4 vols. (Madrid, 1681), II, título xvi, 53, 54, 57–60, 65–70; cf. Richard Konetzke, ed., *Colección de documentos para la historia de la formación social de Hispanoamérica, 1493–1810,* 3 vols. (Madrid: Consejo Superior de Investigaciones Científicas, 1953–1962), passim; Antonio Muro Orejón, ed., *Cedulario americano del siglo XVIII,* 2 vols. (Seville: Escuela de Estudios Hispano-Americanos 1956–1959), I, 356–357, II, 474–475. For a *letrado*'s opinion, see Matienzo, *Gobierno del Perú,* p. 200.

By doing so, they established relations with local society that subverted their supposed disinterest and professionalism.

Marriage between *oidores* or their dependents and members of the local population constituted one of the commonest links between *audiencia* and society and one of the easiest for the historian to reconstruct. Despite repeated prohibitions against these unions, *oidores* continually found spouses for themselves and their dependents among the colonial elite.[46] In theory, all judges who wished to marry within their area of jurisdiction had to obtain a royal dispensation from the standing ordinances against such unions. Those who failed to do so could be removed from office. Ernesto Schäfer has pointed out, however, that the Council of the Indies had a "varied and sometimes very strange" history in dealing with this problem. The scandal at times was so great that the crown had to act. In 1568, for example, a Lic. Peralta, *oidor* in Santo Domingo, was removed from office after he had kidnapped and married an eight-year-old Cuban heiress![47] Punishment of such infractions was apparently outweighed by numerous incidents in which prohibited unions either were unnoticed or were allowed after some "service" to the crown, usually in the form of cold cash. The crown's vacillating policy on prohibited marriages cannot be fully explained in financial terms. Since many judges spent most of their life in the Indies, it was impractical to deny them the opportunity to marry colonials. Instead, the crown tried half-heartedly to regulate these marriages and to prevent judges from marrying socially unacceptable women or those whose personal ties were sure to lead to future difficulties.

Despite these inconsistencies, the Spanish crown believed and the social historian assumes that marriage between judges and members

---

[46] Richard Konetzke, "La prohibición de casarse los oidores o sus hijos e hijas con naturales del distrito de la Audiencia," in *Homenaje a Don José María de la Peña y Cámara* (Madrid, 1969), pp. 105–120. For some specific examples of the disruptive nature of these social relations, see Richard E. Greenleaf, "The Little War of Guadalajara—1587–1590," *New Mexico Historical Review* 43 (1968): 119–135; Juan B. Iguíniz, "Acusación contra el doctor Santiago de Vera presidente de la Real Audiencia de Guadalajara," *Estudios de Historia Novohispana* 4 (1971): 187–216.

[47] Schäfer, *El Consejo Real*, p. 123.

of the colonial elite created consanguineal and affinal ties that influenced the enforcement of law and the operation of government. One famous case can serve as an example. In 1660, Doña Catalina de los Ríos y Lisperguer, "La Quintrala," was brought to trial before the *audiencia* of Santiago, charged with numerous homicides. Her eventual acquittal in the face of massive evidence of guilt can only be explained by her familial connections. La Quintrala was related to two *oidores* of the *audiencia* of Santiago, to an *oidor* in Lima, and even to the state's chief investigator in the case. Proof that these ties resulted in her acquittal cannot be given, but the probability seems high. It was exactly such situations that the crown hoped to avoid by limiting contacts between bureaucrats and society.[48]

Marriages between *letrado* judges and members of the colonial elite had results beyond their direct influence on the operation of law and administration. Not only did *oidores* themselves enter into competition for the social and economic resources of the colonies, but their children joined the sons and daughters of *encomenderos* and hacendados in the ranks of the colonial elite. An advantaged "bureaucratic" element that had at least theoretical access to political power continually intruded into the colonial social structure. Its role in the formation of the colonial elite has never been fully explored. These vertical or cross-generational ties between *oidores* and society add considerable complexity to any evaluation of the political impact of primary relations.

Tracing such relations is the traditional task of the old and often maligned science of genealogy, upon which so much of prosopography ultimately rests. In Latin America, genealogical studies have flourished for centuries, and, while they have often been motivated by aristocratic antiquarianism and filiopiety, to dismiss or ignore them because of these biases would be a serious loss. Latin Americans have long considered lineage and kinship important social phenomena, and genealogists have compiled a great variety of data on the growth of regional and national elites that the social historian can now appropri-

---

[48] Benjamín Vicuña Mackenna's *Los Lisperguer y La Quintrala*, 3d ed. (Santiago de Chile: F. Becerra M., 1908), is the best source. I wish to thank Mr. Malcolm Bochner for a lead to this information.

ate. Manuel Moreyra Paz-Soldán and Pedro Rodríguez Crespo, in their studies of the *audiencia* of Lima, have both demonstrated how genealogical sources can be used to reveal the primary relations affecting bureaucratic behavior.[49] Much more can be done along these lines, but genealogy must also be set into a broader social context. The history of the family itself remains unwritten. Until more is known about the demographic features of the colonial family, the role of clientage within an extended kindred, and the mechanisms by which certain families have maintained control of social and economic resources over long periods of time, genealogical evidence remains highly suggestive and possibly deceptive.[50]

The kinship ties normally the concern of genealogy are at least relatively easy to trace. The same cannot be said of the variety of other social relations that also may have influenced the operation of government. Fictive kinship (*compadrazgo*), for example, is often posited as an important system of social linkage that, in addition to its religious functions and *Gemeinschaft* qualities, also served as a mechanism that established or reinforced patterns of dominance and dependency.[51] While parish records contain the information needed to study this phenomenon, at present virtually nothing is known about the patterns or functions of *compadrazgo* in colonial Latin America. It has been suggested that the patron-client aspects of the institution

[49] Paz-Soldán, *Biografías*; idem, "Dos oidores del primer tercio del siglo xvii," *Mercurio Peruano* 27 (1946): 537–551; Pedro Rodríguez Crespo, "Parentescos de los oidores de Lima con los grupos superiores de la sociedad colonial," *Tercer Congreso de la Historia del Perú* (Lima, 1965), pp. 232–237.

[50] Three possible approaches are found in Elda R. González and Rolando Mellafe, "La función de la familia en la historia social hispanoamericana colonial," *Anuario del Instituto de Investigaciones Históricas* 8 (1965): 57–71; Woodrow Borah and Sherburne F. Cook, "Marriage and Legitimacy in Mexican Culture: Mexico and California," *California Law Review* 54 (1966): 946–1008; and Mary Felstiner, "The Larraín Family in the Independence of Chile" (Ph.D. dissertation, Stanford University, 1970). A computer-aided study of kinship is Stephanie Blank's "Social Integration and Social Stability in a Colonial Spanish American City, Caracas (1595–1627)," mimeographed (Bloomington: Latin American Studies Program, Indiana University, 1972).

[51] S. N. Eisenstadt, in "Ritualized Personal Relations," *Man* 96 (July 1956): 90–95, summarizes the literature and major questions. The remark on "*Gemeinschaft* [community] qualities" is owed to Richard Morse.

were waning in fifteenth-century Spain but were resuscitated by the
realities of the New World.[52] No one has followed this lead. While
there are a large number of modern anthropological studies of *compadrazgo*, they, unlike genealogy, concentrate almost invariably on
Indian communities or on the urban proletariat and thus provide little
guidance for the understanding of the institution's operation among
the colonial bureaucratic elite.[53]

Finally, historical analysis of primary social relations, especially
those of kinship, as factors influencing political or professional behavior has its limitations. As descendants of Adam all men are at
least allegorically related. Thus, discovering remote or even immediate
kinship does not necessarily prove access to influence (*enchufe*). Some
people, in fact, hate their relatives. Establishing kinship or associa-
tional ties suggests only a range of possible influences. Each individual selectively calculates those bonds that he considers operative,
and there is no reason to believe that this calculation remains constant
through time. Using genealogical and other sources, the historian is
able to point out the existence of kinship or association. In colonial
Latin America the presence of such primary relations may suggest a
high probability of mutual influence between the people who shared
them, but they do not constitute, in and of themselves, an explanation
of political and economic behavior.

Economic Interests

Calculating the effect of private economic interest on political behavior has been a popular approach of collective biography since
Charles Beard's classic study on the American Constitution. Royal of-

---

[52] George Foster, "Cofradía and Compadrazgo in Spain and Spanish America,"
Southwestern Journal of Anthropology 9, no. 1 (1953): 1–28; see also Sidney W.
Mintz and Eric R. Wolf, "An Analysis of Ritual Coparenthood (Compadrazgo),"
Southwestern Journal of Anthropology 6, no. 4 (1950): 341–364.

[53] The literature is extensive. Howard Cline, in "Mexican Community Studies,"
Hispanic American Historical Review, 32 (1952): 212–242, summarizes the major
issues. For non-Indian studies, see Eva Hunt, "The Meaning of Kinship in San
Juan: Genealogical and Social Models," *Ethnology* 8, no. 1 (January 1969): 37–
53; Arnold Strickon, "Class and Kinship in Argentina," *Ethnology* 1 (1962)·
500–515.

ficials in colonial Spanish America engaged in a wide variety of economic activities, despite prohibitory laws designed to eliminate conflict of interests and guarantee judicial probity. *Letrado* economic activities are difficult to disassociate from the matrix of social relations in which they were often embedded. Distinction should be made, however, between those activities that, while varying in their legality, were primarily the result of a judge's participation in the economy of an area and those actions of economic benefit to him resulting from the corruption of office.

As men living in a society, the *audiencia* magistrates were naturally drawn into the economy. Through inheritance, dowry, or other legal means, *oidores* acquired houses, land, capital, and even encomiendas. While the crown sought to discourage the accumulation of these interests, little could be done to prevent them. As open and legal property, these interests were duly recorded and admitted by the judges and, therefore, are relatively easy for the historian to reconstruct from such sources as notarial records. Of course *oidores* sometimes engaged in economically gainful and thoroughly criminal activities, such as smuggling, extortion, and theft, which are more difficult to document, but which also gave them independent sources of income and thus weakened the force of professional motivations.

Particularly interesting are those activities not illegal for society as a whole but prohibited to *oidores* and other royal officials. Trade, investment, or partnership within the area of a magistrate's authority were specifically disallowed, but as John Phelan and Guillermo Lohmann Villena have shown, statutes alone did not eliminate these activities.[54] The constant involvement of *oidores* in such activities raises interesting questions about the depth to which bureaucratic norms were internalized. Perhaps on this issue *oidores* followed and colonial society recognized a standard of behavior that differed from the crown's requirements. Violations of the laws in this sphere might be wrong, but not very wrong, especially when the judge had placed family responsibility or friendship above the demands of the pro-

[54] Phelan, *Kingdom of Quito*, pp. 243–264; Lohmann Villena, *Les Espinosa*, pp. 181–245. For similar activities of peninsular *letrados*, see Bartolomé Bennesar, *Valladolid au siècle d'or* (Paris: Mouton and Co., 1967), pp. 121–137.

fession. Determining this standard of accepted behavior that lay
somewhere between law and practice is an important historical task
that will tell us a great deal about the interplay between colonial
government and society.[55] Naturally, *oidores* did not make these deal-
ings public, and, as with the wholly criminal activities, the historian
depends on evidence revealed in administrative reports and judicial
investigations. Care must be used with this material, since backbiting
and false accusations were common features within the bureaucracy,
and not every charge could be substantiated.

The economic benefits resulting from the corruption or abuse of
office always drew the most ardent complaints from both crown and
colonists. Graft, venality, malfeasance, and the use of power or influence for personal and familial ends were common features of
colonial government even among the professional magistracy.[56]
Whether the reason for this lay in a relatively low salary scale, as
Phelan suggests,[57] or in a simple acquisitive desire facilitated by power
à la Lord Acton remains open to question. Perhaps both are true. Certainly the image of the *audiencia* that emerged from the *Recopilación*
as an isolated, frugal, loyal, impartial, and wholly upright body is
constantly contradicted by contemporary reports like that of Antonio
de Grambela y Arriaga, which revealed the *oidores* of Mexico in 1624
profiting from their position and living in lavish circumstances far
beyond their supposed means.[58] Power or influence and the ability to

[55] Robert Berkhofer, *A Behavioral Approach to Historical Analysis* (New York:
The Free Press, 1969), pp. 104–107.

[56] Since a corrupt judge or his colleagues controlled access to the courts, colonists
were often frustrated in their attempts to bring charges. In 1553, Juan Becos of
Mexico City complained against Oidor Lorenzo de Tejada and advised the crown
that " . . . se le quitara la vara hombres obiera que osaran decir verdad, y teniendo
el cargo, no suspenderselo callaba todo el mundo" (Francisco del Paso y Troncoso,
ed., *Epistolario de Nueva España, 1505–1818*, 16 vols. [Mexico City: J. Porrúa e
Hijos, 1939–1942], III, 364: "if the rod of justice had been taken from him, men
would have dared to tell the truth; but since he continued to hold the position,
everyone kept silent").

[57] Phelan, *Kingdom of Quito*, pp. 147–176.

[58] Antonio de Grambela y Arriaga, "Relación en favor del marqués de Galves,
virrey que fue de esta Nueva España, cerca del tumulto que hubo en esta ciudad de
México el 15 de enero de 1624," in *Documentos para la historia de Méjico*, 2d
ser. (Mexico City: J. R. Navarro, 1853–1857), vol. 3.

use them for personal goals characterized the bureaucratic element in Spanish American society. How this ability contributed to its social and economic position, facilitated mobility, and led to social change are all matters of concern to the social or even the economic historian. It would be interesting to know, for example, the extent to which capital generated by the corruption of office was invested in economically productive activities, and if this differed from region to region.

Even more central to the relationship of state and society are those forms of corruption that involved an exchange between a judge and an individual, usually a trade of judicial or political influence for economic or social benefit. Abuses of this sort naturally linked the judges to society and by doing so influenced the operation of the state. Royal officials in general and *oidores* in particular became "brokers" between the demands of the state and the realities of colonial society. Such a position obviously jeopardized their professional performance but was not wholly disruptive to government. It did allow certain colonial interests to influence the application of policy in an imperial system that gave them little opportunity to participate in its formulation. Obviously, such a situation favored the wealthy and prestigious and simply increased their advantage by giving them access to limited political power as well. Prosopography, through a careful accumulation of evidence, can trace the patterns of exchange between bureaucrats and the colonial elite. Interpretation is another matter. A whole literature now exists in the fields of sociology, political science, and public administration on the issue of bureaucratic corruption, especially in developing nations.[59] Many of these studies eschew moral judg-

[59] Matienzo recognized the problem when he wrote, " . . . no hay justicia contra el rico y poderoso, que es la cosa mas perniciosa que hay en el mundo, y la que destruye todo gobierno y justicia" (*Gobierno del Perú*, p. 200: "there is no justice against the rich and powerful, which is the most pernicious thing that there is in the world, and which destroys all government and justice"). Functional models can be seen in O. P. Dwivedi, "The Case for Bureaucratic Corruption," in *Bureaucracy in Historical Perspective*, ed. Michael T. Dalby and Michael S. Werthman (Glenview, Ill.: Scott Foresman and Co., 1971), pp. 88–95; Robert O. Tillman, "Emergence of Black-Market Bureaucracy: Administration, Development and Corruption in New States," *Public Administration Review* 28, no. 5 (September–October 1968): 437–444; James C. Scott, "The Analysis of Corruption in Developing Nations," *Com-*

ments and point to the functional benefits of corruption. The historian may wish to do the same, but, in any case, he cannot avoid the implications of bureaucratic corruption for the nature of colonial society and the operation of the state.

Underlying the concern with economic activities and kinship is a basic assumption that self-interest is a factor, and probably the most important one, determining human action. When, for example, we find that Lic. Alonso de Maldonado, president of the *audiencia* de Los Confines (Guatemala), refused to enforce legislation protecting the Indians by curtailing the *encomenderos*, it comes as no surprise to learn that he held Indians in encomienda through his marriage to a daughter of the conquistador Francisco de Montejo.[60] The question of the extent to which similar interests influenced the government's response to political crises or the use of the "obey but do not comply" formula remains to be answered. There is a high probability that personal interests of the *oidores* had an even greater effect on purely judicial matters than on those issues that involved imperial policy and were, therefore, closely scrutinized by the crown. The testing ground for this statement lies in the enormous and relatively untapped body of trial records, which, analyzed in the light of private interests and legal philosophy, will provide insights into both law and society.[61]

Studies of *audiencia* personnel and the use of prosopography for a study of colonial government in general are just beginning to bring

---

parative *Studies in Society and History* 2, no. 3 (1969): 315–341; David H. Bayley, "The Effects of Corruption in a Developing Nation," *Western Political Quarterly* 19, no. 4 (December 1966): 719–732.

[60] Sherman, "Indian Slavery," p. 27.

[61] Much remains to be done on the judicial process and the actual operation of the courts. Jesús Abadía Lalinde, in "Los gastos del proceso en el derecho histórico español," *Anuario de Historia del Derecho Español* 34 (1964): 249–416, points out just one area about which little is known. Part of the problem lies in the state of judicial archives. The Archivo Nacional of Lima has a vast body of papers in its Real Audiencia sections. They are organized by type (*civiles, criminales*, etc.) and year, but there is no guide or catalogue except for the section Gobierno Supremo. Other papers of the colonial *audiencia* of Lima are housed in the archive of the Supreme Court. These too are uncatalogued. The situation is still worse in Quito, where the Archivo de la Corte Suprema de Justicia is in unfortunate condition. Cf. Lino Gómez Cañedo, *Los archivos de la historia de América*, 2 vols. (Mexico City: Instituto Panamericano de Geografía y Historia, 1961).

results, but our image of the past has already been modified by them. Research in the four principal life areas of *letrado* bureaucrats in the *audiencia* of Lima has revealed the web of social and economic ties underlying the operation of government. Moreover, the often cited exclusion of Americans from high office and of creoles from serving in their native province has now been disproven. Four of the six *oidores* of Lima in 1705 were *limeños*. Between 1740 and 1751 all fourteen judges appointed to that tribunal were creoles, and eleven were *limeños*. When in 1777 royal investigator Antonio de Areche tried to reform the Lima High Court, he found that seven of the eight judges were creoles and five were natives of the city. These findings, results of work by Jorge Tovar de Velarde, Leon G. Campbell, and Mark Burkholder, lay to rest the old shibboleths about creole exclusion.[62] Along with a similar study by Brading on Mexico, they indicate that the Bourbon reforms marked the increasing exclusion of creoles from office. Colonial complaints really dated from the 1780s, not from time immemorial, and they were probably directed as much against the disruption of existing patterns of influence as against the principles involved. Here collective biography has reopened a question of central importance to our understanding of both the colonial regime and the origins of independence.

Not all the advances will be as startling or revolutionary. Prosopography is but one approach among many. It has serious methodological problems both in its assumptions about human nature and in its techniques of research. It may sometimes call for statistical analysis beyond the competence of many historians, and its concern with the small details of life will challenge the patience and *sitzfleisch* of archival seekers. But, in resolving such problems as the relation-

[62] Jorge Tovar de Velarde, "La audiencia de Lima (1705–1707): 3 años de gobierno criollo en el Perú," *Revista Histórica* 23 (1957–1958): 338–348; Campbell, "A Colonial Establishment"; Mark Burkholder, "José Baquijano and the Audiencia of Lima" (Ph.D. dissertation, Duke University, 1970); and especially idem, "From Creole to *Peninsular*." For an overview see John J. TePaske, "El crisis del siglo xviii en el Virreinato del Perú," in *Historia y sociedad en el mundo de habla española*, ed. Bernardo García Martínez, et al. (Mexico City: El Colegio de México, 1970), pp. 263–280.

ship of state to society, prosopography has a real contribution to make. Its detailed description of men and women as members of social groupings once again makes mankind the central concern of the historian. By doing so, prosopography places historical flesh on the bones of sociological abstraction and at once makes the past both interesting and understandable.

Spanish and American Counterpoint: Problems and Possibilities in Spanish Colonial Administrative History

by MARGARET E. CRAHAN

Spanish colonial administration has long been studied in an effort to understand the nature and consequences of the enterprise that Spain undertook in the late fifteenth century. The discovery and conquest of America and the creation of a far-flung empire gave Spain a unique opportunity to disseminate its political forms and culture. An investigation of the nature of these political forms at the outset of the colonial period, their permutations over time, and their trans- ference to America will provide insights into such phenomena of current interest as imperialism, colonialism, and economic de- pendency.

The purpose of this essay is to examine some aspects of the Spanish state in order to suggest productive directions for future research. While some links between metropolitan and colonial developments have long been noted, a good portion of the available data has not been capitalized upon. The topics dealt with in this survey of the effects of certain internal Spanish developments on colonial policy were se- lected on the basis of utility and interest to the scholar and were also limited by the research available. To some degree it emphasizes, as an

NOTE. I wish to thank David A. Brading, Elizabeth Wilkes Dore, Franklin W. Knight, Harry Magdoff, Patrick V. Peppe, Stuart B. Schwartz, Brooke Larson, and Stanley J. Stein for giving of their time to read and criticize this essay in manu- script form.

example, the Viceroyalty of Peru. Not every hypothesis suggested will be applicable to all of Spanish America, but, insofar as there was a replication of patterns and phenomena, it will illuminate Spanish colonial administration as a whole. This paper is not intended to imply that colonies can only be studied from the perspective of the metropolis, nor is it a recommendation to ignore special circumstances in the Indies that resulted in deviation from peninsular norms. Rather, its purpose is to urge a re-examination of comparable and related processes in Spain and America.

NATURE OF THE SPANISH STATE IN THE IMPERIAL PERIOD

Colonial administration can profitably be seen from the point of view of Spanish advances in state- and nation-building and against a background of increasing absolutism. A Spanish state, that is, a political entity that was successful over time in imposing its will throughout most of the Iberian Peninsula, emerged concurrently with the acquisition of the American empire. Spain was not, however, in 1492 a new nation-state, as has sometimes been assumed. Instead, the country was, as Juan Linz has noted, "a case of partial early state-building in Castile and delayed state-building of Spain." Linz goes on to differentiate a state from a nation by holding the former to be "an organization based on certain chances of compliance with authority," whereas it is "the solidarities based on certain attitudes and sentiments reflected in certain behaviors, that transform a social group into a 'nation.' " Linz argues that it is only "when both processes coincide—the creation of an organization for the exercise of authority and that of a specific sense of solidarity in the face of other groups" that the result is a nation-state. It is this that Spain failed to achieve.[1]

[1] Juan J. Linz, "Early State Building and Late Peripheral Nationalisms against the State: The Case of Spain," in *Building States and Nations: Models, Analysis and Data across Three Worlds*, ed. S. N. Eisentadt and Stein Rokkan (Beverly Hills: Sage Publications, forthcoming). For further discussion see José Cepeda Adán, *En torno al concepto del estado en los Reyes Católicos* (Madrid: Consejo Superior de Investigaciones Científicas, Escuela de Historia Moderna, 1956); José Antonio Maravall, "The Origins of the Modern State," *Journal of World History* 6 (1961): 789–808; Jaime Vicens Vives, "Estructura administrativa estatal en los

The chronological conjunction of state-building, nation-building, and empire-building under an increasingly absolutist monarchy resulted in an interweaving of these weapons. Spain under Isabel and Ferdinand was a personal union of kingdoms, each being administered separately and retaining its own laws, institutions, and customs. The Catholic Monarchs accepted a high degree of regional autonomy and concentrated on making Castile the base for an increasingly absolutist monarchy. They left to their successors the tasks of state- and nation-building. Under Charles I (1516–1556) and Philip II (1556–1598) and with the wealth and prestige accruing from the Indies, some advance was made. Charles's grand chancellor, Mercurino Gattinara, tried to create a broader-based central administration, but his efforts and those of the Council of State were relatively unsuccessful. In America, however, the crown established an administration based on Castilian structures, which allowed royal authority greater scope than did the regional privileges, laws, and institutions of other peninsular kingdoms. The chief unifying principle in both America and Spain continued to be the person of the king. Philip II attempted to reduce the autonomy of the peripheral regions of Spain and the power of the aristocracy, in addition to tapping their resources for royal purposes. Resistance to this policy caused social, political, and economic tensions, and, while royal authority was strengthened, the monarchy had to recognize the necessity of some regional devolution. Under the less able seventeenth-century Hapsburgs, Philip III (1598–1621), Philip IV (1621–1665), and Charles II (1665–1700), attempts at state-building and national integration helped precipitate revolts of the Catalonians and Portuguese, and administrative decentralization and aristocratic influence were reinforced.

Decline of monarchial authority was reversed with the advent of the Bourbons to the throne of Spain. The defeat of Catalonia, which had supported the Hapsburg candidate, provided the monarchy with an opportunity to limit the autonomy of that region and subordinate it more fully to Castile. Aragon was accorded similar treatment. The

---

siglos XVI y XVII," in *Rapports: Onzième Congrès International des Sciences Historiques* (Göteborg: Almqvist and Wiksell, 1960), IV, 1–24.

result was the Castilianization of Spain, not the building of a national state. More than the Hapsburgs, the Bourbons realized that, to expand their base of power, it was necessary to redistribute the benefits of empire. Progress in this respect under Philip V (1700-1746), Ferdinand VI (1746–1759), and Charles III (1759–1788) was diminished during the reign of Charles IV (1788–1808) and curtailed by the Napoleonic invasions. To quote Linz once again:

The delay in building the Spanish state in the period of maximum glory, prestige of its kings and influx of wealth from America, made the task more difficult in a period of decadence. That delay in turn was the result of the early success in Castile, of the need to go slowly considering the problems of the extra-Spanish territories of the Crown in Italy and central Europe, that would have been threatened by such institutional changes. The advantage offered in the administration of overseas Spain of the incorporation into Castile rather than the transfer of the complex institutions of the Crown of Aragon was another factor.[2]

The implications of this interpretation are rich with meaning for the history of Latin America.

IMPACT OF THE CASTILIANIZATION OF SPAIN AND THE INDIES

The incorporation of the Indies into the crown of Castile sprang from the personal nature of the union of the Spains.[3] The Alexandrine bulls recognized this in specifying that the American discoveries were the possessions of Isabel and Ferdinand and of their heirs who succeeded to the thrones of Castile and León.[4] The exclusion of Aragon was in line with the monarchs' objective of promoting absolutism. Among the more obvious consequences was the transplantation

---

[2] Linz, "Early State Building."

[3] The classic study of the reasons for and implications of this step is Juan Manzano Manzano's *La incorporación de las Indias a la corona de Castilla* (Madrid: Ediciones Cultura Hispánica, 1948).

[4] For the texts of these documents see Francisco Javier Hernáez, ed., *Colección de bulas, breves y otros documentos relativos a la iglesia de América y Filipinas,* 2 vols. (Brussels: Impr. de A. Vromant, 1879). See also Manuel Giménez Fernández, *Nuevas consideraciones sobre la historia, sentido y valor de las bulas alejandrinas de 1493 referentes a las Indias* (Seville: Escuela de Estudios Hispano-Americanos de la Universidad de Sevilla, 1944).

of Castilian political structures and laws to the Indies. This did not, however, prevent Spanish colonists from seeking to introduce into the New World municipal, regional, or parliamentary traditions that allowed greater self-determination.[5] Such efforts have been little studied, though such studies would be useful to gauge colonial interest or lack of interest in self-rule and royal response.

The dominance of Castile in colonial matters encouraged the growth of an alliance of Castilian and Andalusian interests whose composition, activities, and impact need to be more closely analyzed.[6] Their influence was exercised not only through such bodies as the Council of the Indies and the Casa de Contratación, but also by means of Castilian governmental organs.[7] The cortes of Castile, though it suffered a decline as a result of the growth of monarchical authority, was initially involved in colonial administration, particularly in forming commercial, military, tax, emigration, and Indian policies.[8] Analy-

[5] See, for example, Guillermo Lohmann Villena, "Las cortes en Indias," *Anuario de Historia del Derecho Español* 18 (1947): 655–662.

[6] Information concerning the Sevillian component of the Castilian-Andalusian axis has been provided by Ruth Pike's works: *Aristocrats and Traders: Sevillian Society in the Sixteenth Century* (Ithaca: Cornell University Press, 1972) and *Enterprise and Adventure: The Genoese in Seville and the Opening of the New World* (Ithaca: Cornell University Press, 1966). See also Huguette Chaunu and Pierre Chaunu, *Séville et l'Atlantique, 1504–1650*, 8 vols. (Paris: A. Colin, 1955–1960); Jaime Vicens Vives, ed., *Historia social y económica de España y América* (Barcelona: Editorial Teide, 1957), III.

[7] Since Ernesto Schäfer's study of the Council of the Indies, *El Consejo Real y Supremo de las Indias: Su historia, organización y labor administrativa hasta la terminación de la Casa de Austria*, 2 vols. (Seville: Escuela de Estudios Hispano-Americanos de Sevilla, 1935–1947), little has been written on the topic, except for Demetrio Ramos's *El Consejo de Indias en el siglo XVI* (Valladolid, 1970). Knowledge of the workings of the Casa de Contratación is also limited. Information concerning it is contained in the Chaunus' work previously cited, Clarence Haring's *Trade and Navigation between Spain and the Indies in the Time of the Hapsburgs* (Cambridge: Harvard University Press, 1918), and José Pulido Rubio's *El piloto mayor de la Casa de la Contratación de Sevilla: Pilotos mayores, catedráticos de cosmografía y cosmógrafos* (Seville: Escuela de Estudios Hispano-Americanos de Sevilla, 1950).

[8] José Martínez Cardós, "Las Indias y las cortes de Castilla durante los siglos XVI y XVII," *Revista de Indias* 16, no. 64 (April–June 1956): 207–265; no. 65 (July–September 1956): 357–411. In the eighteenth century this body became, in effect, the cortes of Spain, with little influence in colonial affairs.

sis of the geographical origins of colonial officials could help clarify the relative importance of Castile and other areas of Spain in colonial administration.[9]

Many of the Castilian and Andalusian interests that benefited from the acquisition of the empire promoted the Castilianization of the peninsula. Participation in colonial profits predisposed them to accept the expansion of royal authority. In return, Castile was expected to bear a heavy tax burden.[10] The drain of European warfare and other imperial enterprises on a contracting economy in the late sixteenth and seventeenth centuries encouraged migration to the more lightly taxed regions of the peninsula. Emigrants also sought opportunities in the overseas possessions. It would be useful to compare the resultant growth patterns of the colonial and peripheral populations and economies and possible links that were forged between them in this period.[11] Economic and demographic shifts in the peninsula and the growth of the bourgeoisie encouraged the periphery to intervene more frequently in Castile and America and to expect more from the state. The latter's capacity to respond was determined to an extent by the

[9]Data useful for such studies can be found in Peter Boyd-Bowman's works, especially his *Indice geobiográfico de cuarenta mil pobladores españoles de América en el siglo XVI*, 2 vols. (Bogotá and Mexico City: Instituto Caro y Cuervo, 1964–1968); Richard Konetzke, ed., *Colección de documentos para la historia de la formación social de Hispano-América, 1493–1810*, 3 vols. (Madrid: Consejo Superior de Investigaciones Científicas, 1953–1962); idem, *La emigración española al Río de la Plata durante el siglo XVI* (Madrid: Instituto "Gonzalo Fernández de Oviedo," Consejo Superior de Investigaciones Científicas, 1952).

[10] Antonio Domínguez Ortiz, "La desigualdad contributiva en Castilla durante el siglo XVII," *Anuario de Historia del Derecho Español* 21–22 (1951–1952): 1222–1272. For some of the implications for peripheral regions of Spain and on the colonies see J. H. Elliott, *The Revolt of the Catalans: A Study in the Decline of Spain, 1598–1640* (Cambridge: Cambridge University Press, 1963); María Encarnación Rodríguez Vivente, *El tribunal del consulado de Lima en la primera mitad del siglo XVII* (Madrid: Ediciones Cultura Hispánica, 1960); idem, "Los caudales remitidos desde el Perú a España por cuenta de la Real Hacienda: Serie estadística (1651–1739)," *Anuario de Estudios Americanos* 21, (1964): 1–24.

[11] David A. Brading's study of Guanajuato in the eighteenth century, *Miners and Merchants in Bourbon Mexico, 1763–1810* (Cambridge: Cambridge University Press, 1971), has illustrated the considerable impact of immigration on a regional economy, as has Brian R. Hamnett's *Politics and Trade in Southern Mexico, 1750–1821* (New York: Cambridge University Press, 1971).

vagaries of royal access to colonial resources. In this manner the American possessions served as a safety valve for peninsular pressures and helped stabilize the monarchy, thereby promoting absolutism.

Castilianization impeded peninsular political and economic integration, while geographic, ethnographic, racial, and cultural heterogeneity in Spain and America reinforced regional identity. Metropolitan and colonial distinctions were emphasized by Spain's concentration on the exploitative aspects of empire. While the creoles regarded themselves as Spaniards, there was no Spanish nation with which they could identify. The object and symbol of their loyalty was the monarch. As long as the creoles perceived sufficient benefits from the colonial connection, they maintained their allegiance to the metropolis. When these benefits appeared to diminish, the desire for independence increased. Spain's retention of the colonies for more than three hundred years under these circumstances may be somewhat elucidated by an examination of the role of the monarch as an object of loyalty and the effectiveness of the imperial structure in inculcating this loyalty and in mediating between metropolitan and colonial interest groups.

ROLE OF THE MONARCH AND EFFECTIVENESS OF IMPERIAL ADMINISTRATION IN MAINTAINING THE EMPIRE

In order for the Spanish monarchs to expand their power in Spain and America it was necessary for them to assert and legitimize their control, identitfy themselves as the interpreters and implementers of common objectives, gain the support and participation of the elites and their institutions, and obtain and maintain a sufficient flow of revenue to cover expenditures. Isabel's and Ferdinand's efforts in this direction gave form to administrative structures in Spain and America and contributed to peninsular state-building. The monarchs' objective, after the Castilian-based monarchy had expanded its control in the peninsula and the Indies, was to consolidate and stabilize that hold. Throughout this period the crown utilized the personal nature of its jurisdiction in the New World, especially its authority over land and Indian labor, to reward its supporters. This technique reinforced the personalism of monarchical rule, which was reflected in administrative structures.

As a consequence, political participation by individuals or institutions required not only a power base but also the favor of the head of government. This situation reinforced the role of the monarch as ultimate arbiter and source of all authority—executive, legislative, and judicial. While officials were theoretically responsible to both their constituencies and the monarchy, the latter attempted to exact greater allegiance. A bureaucracy arose to carry out the will of the monarch and see to the distribution of benefits to royal supporters. Such a bureaucracy lacked rationality in the Weberian sense, in that its goals "were focused around 'ad hoc,' particularistic regulative and distributive activities, rather than on the more continuous, specialized, and universalistic criteria," and dealt with the demands of "kinship, territorial, religious, personal or family" groups in both the center and the periphery.[12]

This quality was in accord with the patrimonial nature of the Spanish empire[13] and was further reflected in the lack of definition of functions and responsibilities of officials and government agencies, the overlapping jurisdictions, and the unification of legislative, judicial, and executive authority in single individuals or bodies. While these characteristics flowed from a desire to concentrate authority, the realities of governing an area geographically removed from the core

[12] S. N. Eisenstadt, "Traditional Patrimonialism and Modern Neo-Patrimonialism," in *Social Change*, ed. J. A. Jackson (Cambridge: Cambridge University Press, forthcoming). Of value would be the undertaking of studies of Spain similar to Ernest Barker's *The Development of Public Services in Western Europe, 1660–1930* (Hamden, Conn.: Archon Books, 1966), which details the shift from estate patrimonialism to the patrimonialism of the absolute monarchs in France, Prussia, and England.

[13] On patrimonialism see William Delany, "The Development and Decline of Patrimonialism and Bureaucratic Administrations," *Administrative Science Quarterly* 7, no. 4 (March 1963): 458–601; S. N. Eisenstadt, "Patrimonial Systems: Introduction," in *Political Sociology: A Reader*, ed. idem (New York: Basic Books, 1971), pp. 138–145; Max Weber, *The Theory of Social and Economic Organization*, ed. Talcott Parsons (New York: Free Press, 1966); Guenther Roth, "Personal Rulership, Patrimonialism and Empire-Building in the New State," *World Politics* 20, no. 2 (January 1968): 194–206.

resulted in decentralization and devolution. Attempts to counteract this tendency through a hierarchical government that placed a priority on access to the court, whether viceregal or royal, impeded effective administration. The objectives of those interest groups capable of influencing decision-making were often attained or not according to the needs of the monarchy at the time. The demands of the interest groups inclined the Spanish monarchy toward expansion rather than toward more intensive exploitation of peninsular resources, to which the crown had limited access. To deal with such groups complex administrative machinery was evolved to allocate national and imperial resources.

The expansion of conciliar and ministerial government in the imperial period multiplied the means and number of individuals who affected peninsular and colonial policy and administration. Under Isabel and Ferdinand, councils were reorganized, bureaucratized, and made more active. Charles I consulted the specialized or regional councils to a greater degree than his Council of State, thereby according more weight to individuals with specific knowledge or training than to the high nobility. Philip II's inclination to control all aspects of administration circumscribed the roles of his councils, though they operated efficiently and effectively during his reign. The relative abdication of executive responsibility by his successors meant that the councils could carve out for themselves larger roles, though they were limited by the authority of crown favorites. Under Philip III the Council of State was able to take advantage of this situation, aided by the apparent indifference of the king's *valido*, the Duque de Lerma.[14] Widespread patronage resulted in such offices becoming by

[14] Philip III's dependence on the Duque de Lerma and Philip IV's on the Conde Duque de Olivares transmuted personal rule by the monarch into rule by royal favorites and their coteries. Literature on the *validos* does not include very much information on their impact on colonial policy. For a general study see Francisco Tomás Valiente, *Los validos en la monarquía española del siglo XVII: Estudio institucional* (Madrid: Instituto de Estudios Políticos, 1963); E. Rott, "Philippe III et le duc de Lerme," *Revue d'Histoire Diplomatique* 1 (1887): 201–216, 363–384; Julian Juderías, "Los favoritos de Felipe III," *Revista de Archivos, Bibliotecas y Museos* 19 (1908): 309–327; 20 (1909): 16–27, 223–240; Gregorio Marañón, *El conde-duque de Olivares (la pasión de mandar)* (Madrid: Espasa-Calpe, 1959). Olivares is the subject of a study in progress by J. H. Elliott.

the late seventeenth century sinecures for individuals not necessarily qualified by age, abilities, or interest. By 1700 the councils were to a considerable extent serving the hereditary and robed aristocracy rather than the monarchy, and attempted reforms were unavailing.[15]

Under the Bourbons, councils and juntas were used in conjunction with ministers to produce more coherent policies and more efficient administration. The creation of secretariats and ministries rationalized administration, and, with the appointment of competent individuals, the administrative centralization of Spain progressed. With the establishment of a Council of Ministers in 1787 the supremacy of ministerial over conciliar government appears confirmed.

The advantages and disadvantages of both forms of government affected colonial administration. Insofar as councilors and ministers were competent, knowledgeable, and permitted to do so by the crown, they could serve to give direction to colonial officials and institutions. Otherwise, tendencies toward delay and corruption were compounded. Only limited work has been done on the involvement in American affairs of the councils, including the body most concerned—the Council of the Indies. This agency was initially closely linked to the Council of Castile, sharing as it did the same councilors, and this fact reinforced the predominance of Castilian interests in the New World. As the council resided at the court, unlike those in other peninsular kingdoms, such as Aragon, it was heavily influenced by the political maneuvering that surrounded the king. Members were drawn primarily from the elite, many possessing legal backgrounds and a few having overseas experience. The council grew considerably during the

---

[15] Nepotism appears to have been a more serious problem among upper-echelon officials than the sale of public office, which was extensive in the Indies. The Hapsburg period witnessed the evolution of a bureaucratic aristocracy that became intermingled with the titled nobility. By the end of the seventeenth century this group was fairly concentrated, with power being wielded by a relatively few families. For the evolution of the *letrado* aristocracy and its relationship with the titled nobility see Richard L. Kagan, "Bureaucracy in Habsburg Spain: A Study in Family History" (Paper delivered at the American Historical Association Meeting, New Orleans, 1972). It would be useful to have a study comparable to J. H. Parry's *The Sale of Public Office in the Spanish Indies under the Hapsburgs* (Berkeley: University of California Press, 1953) to examine the impact of such a practice on peninsular office-holding.

reign of Philip II, and councilors continued to be drawn from the nobility.

In the seventeenth century the proliferation of special juntas made the bureaucratic network that had developed in the sixteenth century more complex and precipitated occasional disputes over jurisdiction. The juntas served as means by which such individuals as the Duque de Lerma could control multiple aspects of government either by serving on these bodies themselves or by filling them with allies.

While the general outline of the history of the Council of the Indies is known, there is a great deal that remains to be studied. In particular, the actual extent of its influence throughout the colonial period remains somewhat obscured. The manner by which Spanish, and particularly Castilian, interests used it for their own benefit must still be ascertained. Also relatively unexplored is the degree to which the council served interests in the colonies. Of additional import in determining the influences molding Spanish colonial policy and administration are the roles of such individuals as secretaries and other upper-echelon royal bureaucrats.[16] The former exercised considerable influence, for it was they who decided what materials the king and councils would see. They also served as the king's liaison to the councils and were able, as a consequence, to influence their deliberations. This power and their access to the monarch led them to use their positions to distribute *mercedes* in order to build power bases for themselves. Competition for the favor of such individuals, particularly by rival aristocratic factions, came increasingly to dominate Spanish administrative concerns. This tendency became exaggerated under Philip III, Philip IV, and Charles II.

In 1714, at the outset of the Bourbon period, Philip V created five secretaries of state who served in conjunction with the traditional councils. During the reign of Charles III these offices developed into ministries. The effectiveness of the ministers was a product of their

---

[16] Philip II's secretary, Antonio Pérez, has been the object of considerable attention, e.g., José García Mercadel, *Antonio Pérez, secretario de Felipe II, una vida borrascosa* (Madrid: Ediciones Morata, 1943); Gregorio Marañón, *Antonio Pérez (el hombre, el drama, la época)*, 2 vols. (Madrid: Espasa-Calpe, 1958). Others, whose careers were not as flamboyant, have received less attention.

own abilities and the responsibility Charles placed on them. Their expanded role, and in particular that of the secretary or minister of the Indies, has not yet been fully studied. The efficiency and administrative creativity of the Caroline period did not persist under Charles III's successors. Closer examination of the effect of these developments on colonial administration is warranted. Perhaps most important is the investigation of the emergence of the bureaucracy as an interest group and of the degree to which their growing sense of self-identification affected administration.

Further research also needs to be done on the impact of Spain's European policy and involvements on America.[17] Although Charles I was also Emperor Charles V, he possessed neither an integrated imperial policy nor a unified administrative system. The efforts of his grand chancellor, Mercurino Gattinara, to provide them were unsuccessful, and decisions continued under Philip II to be made largely in response to special circumstances.[18] Philip's consolidation of monarchical authority on a Castilian base, his acquisition of Portugal, and his struggle to maintain Hapsburg political and spiritual hegemony in Europe, while interrelated, were not coordinated. Hence decisions in one area were sometimes counterproductive in others. This is not to deny that there was some validity in individual responses to different situations. However, the decline of strong direction from Spain in the seventeenth century and the increasing pressure of domestic problems, together with the effects of excessive patronage, resulted in less coherence in colonial policy. The autonomy this incoherence encouraged in the Indies allowed for considerable development of colonial interests.

The eighteenth-century changes reflected fundamental differences in Hapsburg and Bourbon policies. Under the former, colonial administration was aimed more at assuaging fiscal needs than at imposing an economic system of control on the colonies. The Bourbons,

[17] An exemplar of a broadly conceived study of the type needed is Fernand Braudel's *El mediterráneo y el mundo mediterráneo en la época de Felipe II*, 2 vols. (Mexico City: Fondo de Cultura Económica, 1953).

[18] While this was essentially the case in France and England in the same period, both of these countries developed more coherent imperial policies during the seventeenth century.

particularly Charles III, sought to augment colonial revenues by increasing the productive capacity of the colonies and improving tax collection. This policy constituted a stricter imposition of mercantilism than the Hapsburgs had ever attempted.

Some Effects of Peninsular State- and Nation-Building on Colonial Structures

If, having said this, we turn to a consideration of specifically colonial structures, we can see the reflections upon them of the same pressures, the same contradictions, the same frustrated aspirations. State-building outdistanced nation-building, with dire consequences, in the end, for the imperial system. Colonial structures originally conceived by the metropolis to permit penetration and exploitation of the colonies necessarily benefited some American interests. At times, these benefits were extended consciously; at others, they were the result of the creoles' determined expansion of their influence and participation in the governance of the Indies. While the crown recognized from the outset the need to reward colonists for their efforts in Hispanicizing and Christianizing the New World, it was intent on keeping their power within certain limits. Hence one of the chief concerns of the crown was the maintenance of the independence of colonial officialdom and the dependence of colonial interest groups upon it. The monarchy attempted to accomplish this by granting authority while circumscribing jurisdiction, emphasizing prestige rather than power, impeding alliances between officials and local elites, and maintaining a complex system of vertical and horizontal checks. No matter where we look—colonial law, bureaucratic recruitment and restriction, the office of viceroy, the institutions of *audiencia*, *corregimiento*, and *cabildo*, the intendancy, or the Church— we will find a reflection of the peninsular tensions that accompanied state-building but slowed nation-building efforts.

In the period of conquest and expansion the monarchy was a legitimizing principle and source of authority for the Spaniards in America. The special circumstances of those years caused the crown to delegate authority. These two factors increased and reinforced the mutual dependency of crown and subjects. By the 1570s, however, the formal organization of the empire was well underway, and Philip II attempted to reconcentrate and expand royal power. During the seventeeth century, as Stanley and Barbara Stein have pointed out, colonial structures were modified by "the interaction of legally sanctioned monopoly and of private interest [which] inevitably produced an atmosphere in which corruption was tolerated and aggressive individualism was concealed or disguised by the apparent functional corporative nature of society based upon scholastic natural law, [and] liberty was exercised within the corporative body. Those involved in the administration of the colonies found its principles and practice anything but oppressive. And where colonial legislation conflicted with local interest, it could always be suspended or ignored as suggested by the often utilized formula 'to be obeyed but not executed.' "[19] In the viceroyalties this was an era of privilege and considerable self-rule, with a decline in the degree to which royal interests were pursued. Able royal officials were often frustrated by lack of support from Madrid.[20] There were some who promoted reform partly out of a desire for a more effective government that they would control. This attitude in Spain led some to support a Bourbon successor to Charles II, and Spain's administrative and economic revival in the eighteenth century appeared to confirm the wisdom of this position.

The utility of Spanish law as a source for understanding such developments has been debated for some time. Lewis Hanke has asserted

[19] Stanley J. Stein and Barbara H. Stein, *The Colonial Heritage of Latin America: Essays on Economic Dependence in Perspective* (New York: Oxford University Press, 1970), pp. 74–75.

[20] Among Peruvian officials in the latter part of the Hapsburg period, the viceroys —Conde de Castellar and Duque de la Palata—brought considerable energy to their posts and were able to make some progress in increasing administrative effectiveness. Castellar, however, was forced out by commercial interests in Lima, and Palata received little or no royal support for the reforms he attempted. See Elena Sanguineti E., "Memorias del Virrey de Castellar," *Letras* 30 (1945): 128–137; Margaret E. Crahan, "The Administration of the Duque de la Palata, Viceroy of Peru, 1681–1689," *The Americas* 27, no. 4 (April 1971): 389–412; Ronald D. Hilton, "The Career of Melchor de Navarra y Rocafull, Duque de la Palata, with Special Reference to His Viceregency in Peru, 1681–1689" (M.A. thesis, University of Bristol, 1967).

that "Spaniards were a legalistic and moralistic people whose laws and polemics tell us what they thought life ideally should be. One of the best ways to find out what evils the Spanish crown was attempting to abolish is by studying the laws themselves. . . . Historians will have much less material to work with if they ignore the traditions and attitudes imbedded in sixteenth-century Spanish law. They also will be ignoring one of the fundamental aspects of the intellectual history of Spain."[21] The corollary of this statement is the necessity of examining the actual implementation of laws and the operation of legal structures.[22] As Constance Carter found in her study of the *audiencia* in sixteenth-century New Spain, "law seems to have derived in great measure from what happened during the early years of Spanish tenure in the new world. Law originating in the metropolis was greatly modified in its practical application by overseas officials."[23]

The study of law in the Spanish colonial system is complicated by the fact that legislative, executive, and judicial powers were not clearly distinguished and were exercised concurrently by the same individuals and agencies. This mix began with the monarch who was not only a law-giver but also an executor and adjudicator.[24] This triple role was the source of the moderating capacity of the crown, by which the monarch not only upheld justice but also mediated

[21] Lewis Hanke, "A Modest Proposal for a Moratorium on Grand Generalizations: Some Thoughts on the Black Legend," *Hispanic American Historical Review* 51, no. 1 (February 1971): 117.

[22] There has been little study of actual court cases dealing with even such hotly debated topics as the relationship between colonial legislation and the treatment of slaves. An exception is Norman A. Meiklejohn's "The Observance of Negro Slave Legislation in Colonial Nueva Granada" (Ph.D. dissertation, Columbia University, 1968). Meiklejohn finds some basis for the thesis that the existence of protective laws served to reduce abuse. Until more studies like this are done, our knowledge of the impact of colonial legislation will continue to be for the most part speculative.

[23] Constance Ann Crowder Carter, "Law and Society in Colonial Mexico: Audiencia Judges in Mexican Society from the Tello de Sandoval Visita General, 1543–1547," (Ph.D. dissertation, Columbia University, 1971), pp. 143–144.

[24] For some of the implications of this, see Frank Jay Moreno, "The Spanish Colonial System: A Functional Approach," *Western Political Quarterly* 20, no. 2 (June 1967): 312.

among conflicting interests.[25] It decreased the possibilities for developing avenues of political struggle and served to concentrate authority more fully in the monarch. It also served as the rationale for the direct access of Spanish subjects to the king. Some scholars have concluded that the monarch served as a sort of impartial arbitrator of conflicts.[26] While this impartiality is suggested by the legal structure, it appears that when the crown was able to pursue its own interests it did so without too many scruples. Hence an image of the monarch as the promoter of royal interests and mediator of others would seem to have more validity than an image of the monarch as an impartial arbitrator, though it was useful to the crown to encourage this latter impression. This role allowed for some apparent flexibility in an authoritarian structure that contributed to the stability of the regime.

Direct appeal to the crown, however, encouraged disregard for local administrators and was useful in delaying enforcement of directives. When combined with the somewhat unrealistic nature of Spanish legislation, this practice impeded implementation and increased administrative inefficiency. Frank Jay Moreno views this situation as stemming from the Roman heritage of Spanish law, which transmitted a conception of law that stated ideals rather than attempting to regulate actual situations.[27] Constance Carter disagrees, having

[25] A species of moderating power appeared in some of the early constitutions adopted by the Latin American republics in the ninetieth century. Simón Bolívar incorporated such a concept in the 1821 Constitution of Gran Colombia, and it infused the principle of *amparo* in Mexico. See Manuel Aguilar Arriaga, *El Amparo de México y sus antecedentes nacionales y extranjeros* (Mexico City: Universidad Nacional Autónoma de México, 1942); Antonio Beltrán Martínez, *Comentarios a los antecedentes extranjeros y nacionales del juicio de amparo* (Mexico City: Universidad Nacional Autónoma de México, 1934).

[26] For example, in her study of civil-ecclesiastical relations in eighteenth-century New Spain, Nancy Farriss posits that the Hapsburgs, when dealing with disputes between religious and secular authorities, were "generally impartial arbitrators" (*Crown and Clergy in Colonial Mexico, 1759–1821* [London: Athlone Press, 1968], p. 89). A closer examination of the Hapsburg period reveals that this was more theoretical than actual. See Margaret E. Crahan, "Civil-Ecclesiastical Conflict in Hapsburg Peru" (Paper delivered before the American Historical Association, Boston, December 1970).

[27] Moreno, "Spanish Colonial System," p. 310, passim. In commenting on the

found that in pre-1550 New Spain citizens did not ignore the ethical content of laws and hierarchical colonial structures, but used them, selectively and astutely, to further the colonists' purposes.[28] Such a situation allowed for disregard of the law without implying disloyalty to the crown. From his comparative study of imperial bureaucracies, S. N. Eisenstadt has concluded that in such patrimonial societies,

the trend was toward differentiating the basic legitimation of the rulers (kings, etc.) from their concrete policies and the policies of the various government organs. This trend's manifestations were the distinctions made between the norms regulating basic loyalty to the ruler and the norms pertaining to attitudes about different concrete policies, and the shifting interrelations among various social groups and between them and the rulers.

Although the first type of norms and values was usually very traditional and ascriptive the other was far more flexible and given to change. Much of the political struggle was focused on the concrete definitions and derivations of the latter types.[29]

This statement is in accord with John Phelan's conclusion that noncompliance with the law among Spanish bureaucrats often sprang from goal ambiguity and conflicting standards.[30]

There was, however, variance in the degree to which noncompliance with the law was allowed. During the Hapsburg period there appears to have been less preoccupation on the part of the crown over inobservance and less inclination to regard it as a challenge to royal authority. In the eighteenth century persistent violations of royal regulations were met with increasing royal displeasure and attempted stricter enforcement. External threats to the security of

Spanish colonial economic system, John Lynch appears to agree by holding that mercantilistic legislation "was so perfect that it could not be administered" (*Spanish Colonial Administration, 1782–1810: The Intendant System in the Viceroyalty of the Río de la Plata* [London: Athlone Press, 1958], pp. 8–9).

[28] Carter, "Law and Society," p. 143.

[29] S. N. Eisenstadt, *The Political Systems of Empire: The Rise and Fall of the Historical Bureaucratic Societies* (New York: The Free Press, 1969), p. 305.

[30] John Leddy Phelan, "Authority and Flexibility in the Spanish Imperial Bureaucracy," *Administrative Science Quarterly* 5 (June 1960): 63–64.

the empire and the Bourbons' growing fear that creoles, mestizos, and Indians would unite against Spain spurred them on. There was also concern about the subversive potential of those who enjoyed immunity from the civil judicial system, particularly clerics. Such fears did not result in substantial policy changes until the second half of the eighteenth century.[31]

In John Phelan's opinion, the conflicting standards inherent in the Spanish colonial system allowed officials a discretionary role in decision making. He further holds that, in Weberian terms, the Spanish colonial bureaucracy partook more of substantive rationality than formal rationality; that is, the prime criterion was the performance of tasks rather than the following of specified procedures. Constance Carter demurs, having found that in the early colonial period the absence of clear-cut lines of authority was not as intentional as Phelan implies. She argues that lack of clarity concerning jurisdiction resulted in part from the desire of royal officials not to publicize the limits of their powers, thereby allowing themselves more flexibility.[32] It appears, consequently, that the definition of royal power was an ongoing process that flowed not only from the monarchy but also from colonial officialdom. Clearly the monarchy in this period was not particularly successful in utilizing its officials as a counterweight to special interests. The conflict between official standards and private interest was lost by the crown to a large extent because of the inability of the central government to enforce standards. In the colonies the increasing number of creole officials reflected this failure.

In the late Bourbon period attempts were made to reverse this trend, and the monarchy began to re-emphasize peninsular domination of colonial offices. There was also some attempt to improve the quality of officeholders. Concern for defense inclined the crown toward military appointees for civil posts. Major factors in securing office, however, continued to be favor at court and service to the

[31] For an examination of the Caroline campaign against ecclesiastical immunity see Farriss, *Crown and Clergy*; for a contrasting situation with respect to the military see Lyle N. McAlister, *The "Fuero Militar" in New Spain* (Gainesville: University of Florida Press, 1957).
[32] Carter, "Law and Society," p. 137.

monarchy. This was the case with many who were appointed intendants.[33] Common defects of colonial officeholders did not disappear, as inadequate salaries encouraged corruption, competition among officials and unclear jurisdiction inhibited effective action, and local power relationships discouraged fulfillment of royal objectives.

While the Spanish colonial system was relatively successful in encouraging loyalty of its officials to the person of the monarch, it was less successful in encouraging loyalty to the metropolis. A prime reason for this was a deficient incentive system. This placed a greater burden on coercive elements, such as *residencias* and *visitas*. With the numerical expansion of the bureaucracy, the task of supervision became more difficult. It became impossible with the decay of the monarchy.

The role of the Spanish American bureaucracy in the imperial structure has not been studied in depth. For example, variations in salaries have not been examined sufficiently to evaluate their impact on loyalty and service to the crown. The role of the bureaucrats as personal servants of the king, rather than corporate agents, has not been fully analyzed, nor has the influence of their socioeconomic backgrounds on their official actions.[34] In addition, the royal court in Spain has been the object of far greater attention than have the

[33] Lynch, *Spanish Colonial Administration*, p. 73.

[34] Recent contributions in this area include, in addition to David Brading's and Constance Carter's works previously cited: Jacques Barbier, "Elites and Cadres in Bourbon Chile," *Hispanic American Historical Review* 52, no. 3 (August 1972): 416–435; Mark A. Burkholder, "From Creole to *Peninsular*: The Transformation of the Audiencia of Lima," ibid., pp. 395–415; Leon G. Campbell, "A Colonial Establishment: Creole Domination of the Audiencia of Lima during the Late Eighteenth Century," ibid., no. 1 (February 1972): 1–25. These expand and modify the conclusions of Jaime Eyzaguirre, *Ideario y ruta de la emancipación chilena* (Santiago de Chile: Editorial Universitaria, 1957), and Guillermo Céspedes del Castillo, "La sociedad colonial americana en los siglos XVI y XVII," in *Historia social y económica*, ed. Vicens Vives, III, 388–494. Scholars interested in the evolution of society in seventeenth- and eighteenth-century Latin America would do well to compare their findings with those of Antonio Domínguez Ortiz, in *La sociedad española en el siglo XVII* (Madrid: Consejo Superior de Investigaciones Científicas, 1963) and *La sociedad española en el siglo XVIII* (Madrid: Consejo Superior de Investigaciones Científicas, 1955).

viceregal courts. While studies have been done of individual viceroys, even these are for the most part limited in their conception.[35]

As the viceroy was the direct representative of the king, investigations of the evolution of this office could reveal a good deal about the exercise of royal authority in the colonial context. There were obvious variations in the freedom and discretion exercised in eras of weak metropolitan control, as opposed to those when peninsular influence was reasserted. There were also variations in the ability and initiative of officials. Although we have some information on the degree to which upper-echelon officials controlled and manipulated the colonial bureaucracy, our knowledge is still limited. The complex of working relationships that grew up in the colonies is not well understood. There are also indications that colonial appointments were occasionally made to remove real or potential competitors for power and influence from Spain.[36]

While the viceroy was the chief royal official in the colonies, the *audiencia* had perhaps more influence, for in the Spanish system it was the judicial role of a governing body that accorded it pre-eminence.[37] Isolation and distance eventually resulted in these courts' enjoying certain powers not exercised by the *audiencias* in Spain.[38]

[35] Our understanding of viceregal history will be advanced tremendously upon completion of Lewis Hanke's projected publication of the *Memorias* of the viceroys in the Hapsburg period. This series will contain biographical sketches and additional information that will markedly increase our knowledge in this area. For a description of the project and an extensive bibliography see Lewis Hanke, *Spanish Viceroys in America: The Smith History Lecture* (Houston, 1972). Useful general studies are Jesús Lalinde Abadía's "El régimen virreinosenatorial en Indias," *Anuario de Historia del Derecho Español* 27 (1967): 5–244, and Sigfrido Radaelli's *La institución virreinal en las Indias: Antecedentes históricos* (Buenos Aires: Editorial Perrot, 1957).

[36] The chief minister, the Duque de Medinaceli, apparently urged Charles II to name the Duque de la Palata to the Viceroyalty of Peru in 1680 in order to lessen the latter's influence in Spain. In order to convince him to go to the New World, Palata was given permission, contrary to law, to fill twelve colonial posts with members of his retinue (Crahan, "Palata," p. 390).

[37] John Leddy Phelan, *The Kingdom of Quito in the Seventeeth Century: Bureaucratic Politics in the Spanish Empire* (Madison: University of Wisconsin Press, 1967), p. 38.

[38] For the authority of the *audiencia* as defined by royal legislation see Lillian

The *audiencias* served as a means of mediating differences between colonial and metropolitan or intracolonial interests. The functioning of the *audiencias* and their judges has recently been coming under closer scrutiny, but by and large the field is still unworked.[39] Most notably, light has been shed on the degree to which judges were linked politically and economically to local interests. They reveal that the expansion of *audiencia* authority was not substantially impeded by overlapping jurisdiction and that the system of checks was to a large extent ineffective. *Audiencias* in peripheral areas, such as Chile and Panama, acted with considerable autonomy, and even in the colonial capitals, *audiencias* expanded their power at the expense of both viceregal and royal authority. This was possible because the relatively stable tenure of judges gave their deliberations more continuity than those of other more transitory royal appointees. While historians have noted that *oidores* and viceroys engaged, at times, in disputes, what has not been looked at closely is their cooperation in the advance of their own and local interests. This failure results, in part, from the fact that much of the research has been based on official correspondence with Spain that is unlikely to include much information concerning such matters. The portrait that is beginning to emerge is that of a court subservient to the wishes of the local elites in spite of royal restrictions. The implication is that the crown's attempt to reassert itself in colonial affairs through imperial reforms

---

Estelle Fisher, *Viceregal Administration in the Spanish-American Colonies* (New York: Russell and Russell, 1967), pp. 133–141.

[39] Considerable advance has been made by the studies of Mark A. Burkholder, Leon G. Campbell, Constance Carter, and John Leddy Phelan already cited. Of value for comparison is Stuart B. Schwartz's *Sovereignty and Society in Colonial Brazil: The High Court of Bahia and Its Judges, 1609–1751* (Berkeley: University of California Press, 1973). These studies have revised some of the conclusions of Charles Henry Cunningham, *The Audiencia in the Spanish Colonies as Illustrated by the Audiencia of Manila: 1583–1800* (Berkeley: University of California Press, 1919); Javier Malagón Barceló, *El distrito de la audiencia de Sto. Domingo en los siglos XVI a XIX* (Ciudad Trujillo: Universidad de Santo Domingo, 1942); J. H. Parry, *The Audiencia of New Galicia in the Sixteenth Century: A Study in Spanish Colonial Government* (Cambridge: Cambridge University Press, 1948); Francisco de Pelsmaeker e Iváñez, "La audiencia en las colonias españolas de América," *Revista de ciencias jurídicas y sociales* 8 (1925): 291–304, 383–423, 465–506; 9 (1926): 5–20.

in the latter part of the eighteenth century caused considerable tension.

While viceroys and *oidores* were the chief royal officials in the colonies, it was the treasury officials, governors, and *corregidores*, among others, who attended to local administration. As the chief concern of Spain was insuring a steady flow of income from the New World, the institutions and individuals involved in the collection of royal revenues were of utmost importance. Surveys of royal correspondence with the colonies reveal the depth of the metropolis's preoccupation with the mobilization of colonial resources and collection of taxes. Yet colonial financial administration has been, to a surprising degree, ignored, and hence the extent to which the colonists were able to avoid the full financial burden of their colonial status is yet to be established.[40]

The *corregidores* were also of supreme importance to Spanish colonial administration, for they were the local officials who represented the authority of the mother country to the vast majority of Spain's subjects.[41] We can only speculate about the degree to which they enforced the royal will. Moreover, the crown's intention that the *corregidores* serve to counterbalance the power of the *encomenderos* faded as it became clear that the impulse towards cooperation for their mutual benefit was often stronger than their commitment

[40] Of interest are José Miranda, *El tributo indígena en la Nueva España durante el siglo XVI* (Mexico City: Colegio de México, 1952); Robert S. Smith, "Sales Taxes in New Spain, 1575–1770," *Hispanic American Historical Review* 28, no. 1 (February 1948): 2–37; Mario Briceño Perozo, *El contador Limonta* (Caracas: Impr. Nacional, 1961); Guillermo Céspedes del Castillo, "Reorganización de la hacienda virreinal peruana en el siglo xviii," *Anuario de Historia del Derecho Español* 23 (1953): 329–369; Carmen Bancora Cañero, "Las remesas de metales preciosas desde el Callao a España en la primera mitad del siglo XVII," *Revista de Indias* 19, no. 75 (1959): 35–88; Edberto O. Acevedo, "Los impuestos al comercio cuyano en el siglo XVIII, 1700–1750," *Revista Chilena de Historia y Geografía* 126 (1958): 34–76.

[41] See Carlos Molina Arguello, "Gobernaciones, alcaldías mayores, y corregimientos en el reino de Guatemala," *Anuario de Estudios Americanos* 17 (1960): 105–132; Guillermo Lohmann Villena, *El corregidor de los indios en el Perú bajo los Austrias* (Madrid: Ediciones Cultura Hispánica, 1957). Of particular value would be additional studies similar to Lohmann Villena's.

to royal objectives. This was similar to the alliance between the rural land-holding aristocracy and local officials in the peninsula.

A colonial institution that was intended to serve the Spanish Americans' needs directly was the *cabildo*.[42] This municipal council, sometimes described as the only element of representative government in the Spanish colonial system, served as a mediator between royal and town interests.[43] In the sixteenth century, while these councils possessed some vitality, there was competition within the creole elite for membership. In the following century, as more important offices became available, interest in membership decreased. *Cabildos* became hamstrung by lack of financial resources, although this problem was remedied somewhat during the intendancy period.[44] This development also had some untoward results, for as the *cabildos* revived they became more demanding. The restoration of Ferdinand in

[42] While the *cabildos* have been accorded more attention than some other colonial institutions, many of these studies have lacked analysis. Useful data are included in studies by Ellen Douglas Howell, "Continuity and Change: A Comparative Study of the Composition of the Cabildos in Seville, Tenerife, and Lima," *The Americas* 24, no. 1 (July 1967): 33–45; John Preston Moore, *The Cabildo in Peru under the Hapsburgs, 1530–1700* (Durham: Duke University Press, 1954); idem, *The Cabildo in Peru under the Bourbons: A Study in the Decline and Resurgence of Local Government in the Audiencia of Lima, 1700–1824* (Durham: Duke University Press, 1966); Fredrick B. Pike, "The Cabildo in Spanish American Colonial Administration" (Ph.D. dissertation, University of Texas at Austin, 1956); Francisco Xavier Tapia, *El cabildo abierto colonial: Un estudio de la naturaleza y desarrollo del cabildo abierto durante los tres siglos de la administración colonial española en América* (Madrid: Ediciones Cultura Hispánica, 1966); Julio Alemparte-Robles, *El cabildo en Chile colonial: Orígenes municipales de las repúblicas hispanoamericanas* (Santiago: Ediciones de la Universidad de Chile, 1940); Charles R. Boxer, *Portuguese Society in the Tropics: The Municipal Councils of Goa, Macao, Bahia, and Luanda, 1510–1800* (Madison: University of Wisconsin Press, 1965).

[43] Towns themselves functioned, as Richard M. Morse has observed, "as the [crown's] principal agency for colonizing and nucleating the population, distributing land, and converting overseas Spaniards from predatory to sedentary pursuits. Creation of orderly urban nuclei, though they were potentially ungovernable and separatist, seemed the only alternative to a human landscape of adventurism and vagabondage" ("Trends and Issues in Latin American Urban Research, 1965–1970 [Part 1]," *Latin American Research Review* 6, no. 1 [Spring 1971]: 12).

[44] Lynch, *Spanish Colonial Administration*, pp. 201–202, 212–220; J. R. Fisher, *Government and Society in Colonial Peru: The Intendant System, 1784–1814* (London: Athlone Press, 1970), p. 200.

1814 and the rejection of desired reforms fueled creole discontent. There was some variety, however, in the attitudes of the colonial *cabildos* toward the central government in the immediate preindependence period that is correlated to the benefits they received from ties with Spain. Lima and Mexico City, for instance, had less critical attitudes than cities like Buenos Aires and Caracas, where the commercial elite was more closely tied to a world market. Yet even the *cabildo* of Lima was increasingly discontent with a peninsular government that was incapable of guaranteeing local interests the advantages they were accustomed to.

It is notable that the areas where the intendancies were first tablished were peripheral ones—Cuba, Venezuela, and Buenos Aires. This reflected the growing concern of Madrid for the defense of her American possessions and the autonomy of those areas. Recent studies have indicated that, while there was some progress toward achieving these objectives, the imposition of the intendancies was in some respects counterproductive in achieving greater imperial unity.[45] The weakening of direction from the core of the empire combined with the defense of local autonomy to impede the crown's objective of more effective administration. The practice of checking the power of one official or institution with that of another did not make the acceptance of the new offices of intendants and subdelegates and their occupants any easier. As a consequence, much energy was channeled into jurisdictional disputes. The success of the system was predicated on cooperation between those occupying the traditional offices and new officials. Efforts to deal with sources of tension, such as the New Ordinance of Intendants (1803), were generally unsuccessful due to lack of implementation. By the beginning of the nineteenth century, it was evident that the system that had been instituted to integrate the empire was malfunctioning.

The Caroline reforms contributed to increased divisions within the colonies, for they alienated some of those who had previously benefited from lax administration and disappointed others who had hoped for increased participation in government and promotion of their

---

[45] Notably Fisher, *Government and Society*, and Lynch, *Spanish Colonial Administration*.

interests. Regional divisions were also reinforced: economic reforms that encouraged imports through such ports as Buenos Aires worked against producers in the interior of the Platine region; the creation of an *audiencia* in Cuzco and greater autonomy in Upper Peru added to increased economic independence in that area, which was resented by the Limean merchants.

The role of the creole elite in the Indies was analogous to that of the aristocracy in Spain. After the initial period of exploration and colonization the creoles concentrated on the consolidation and distribution of power among themselves. Royal manipulation blocked somewhat the emergence of class cohesion but not of class interest. Distance, difficulties of communication, the heterogeneous population, and other factors contributed to the development in the New World of strong competitors to royal power. Furthermore, members of the elite in the capitals enjoyed an advantage over peripheral elites as a result of their proximity to the locus of power. Such central elites attempted to limit the exercise of authority by peripheral elites and monopolize the profits from colonial resources. This effort caused resentment in other areas, not only against the central elites, but also against the monarchy for sanctioning such disparity.

The situation was made more complex by the privileged status of the Church. The crown depended on it for moral and material support, including a supply of disinterested officials. However, a recent survey of the Peruvian episcopacy shows that approximately 70 percent of these prelates were engaged in economic pursuits that tied them to the secular elite in the colonies or peninsula or both.[46] As a consequence, individual clerics and religious groups actively participated, at times, in the struggle between the crown and various secular interest groups, as well as in the competitive efforts of the latter. Co-

---

[46] Elizabeth Wilkes Dore, "The Training of an Elite: The Bishops of Peru and Chile in the Colonial Era" (M.A. Thesis, Columbia University, 1973). For three revealing examinations of religious institutions that served the socioeconomic needs of the colonal elite see Asunción Lavrin, "The Feminine Orders in Colonial Mexico," James Riley, "Jesuit Hacendados: Estate Management by the Colegio Máximo de San Pedro y San Pablo of Mexico," and Susan Soeiro, "Flagellants and Financiers: The Nunnery in Bahia" (Papers delivered before the American Historical Association, New Orleans, December 1972).

operation among the elites was necessary for stability, and, in particular, Iberian control in the colonies depended on that of the creole aristocracy, clergy, and bureaucracy. While some attention has been paid by scholars to the alienation of these groups from the monarchy, considerably less has been paid to changing relationships among them. Bourbon ecclesiastical policy, for example, might have been much more difficult to implement if there had not been a growing distance between colonial ecclesiastical and secular elites.

Throughout the colonial period the Catholic Church remained substantially loyal to the monarchy, and crown concern over its subversive potential was exaggerated. This preoccupation also reflected the special nature of the colonists' identification with Spain, intertwined as it was with devotion to Catholicism. The intermingling of religious and political orthodoxy was revealed in the reinvigoration of the Inquisition as a political instrument in the late eighteenth century.[47] Increasing colonial self-interest and nonpeninsular identification made any decrease of the Church's contribution to imperial stability seem particularly threatening. Such a perception would help explain royal overreaction to the relative independence of the Jesuits and to claims to ecclesiastical immunity. In addition, it would appear that there was a decrease in the congruence of civil and ecclesiastical goals. Hence, the monarchy's traditional dependence on the Church for legitimation, for moral and material support, and as a source of officials for royal service, began to lessen. The Bourbons felt less need for Church sanction of their actions than had the Hapsburgs, and royal access to colonial resources increasingly seemed to be impeded by ecclesiastical holdings and influence.

The role of the Church in the Spanish American empire needs to

[47] The findings of Henry Charles Lea in *The Inquisition in the Spanish Dependencies* (New York: The Macmillan Company, 1908) and José Toribio Medina, for example in *Historia del Tribunal de la Inquisición de Lima 1569–1820*, 2 vols. (Santiago de Chile: Fondo Histórico y Bibliográfico J. T. Medina, 1956), are somewhat lacking in analysis and balance. This is not the case with the many works of Richard Greenleaf relating to the Inquisition, e.g., *The Mexican Inquisition of the Sixteenth Century* (Albuquerque: University of New Mexico Press, 1969) and *Zumárraga and the Mexican Inquisition, 1536–1593* (Washington, D.C.: Academy of American Franciscan History, 1962).

be re-evaluated with a greater attention not only to the institutional loyalty of its officers, but also to the socioeconomic entanglements of individual clerics and ecclesiastical institutions. Evidence of these raises the question of whether the role of the Spanish cleric was significantly different than that of the lay Spaniard. Re-examination of the Church's impact has already resulted in a de-emphasizing of the role of the Church as a Hispanicizing instrument, for, according to James Lockhart, "the great mechanism of Europeanization was not formal instruction but ordinary contact between Europeans and Indians, measured in man-hours, and . . . the primary Europeanizing agent was the local Iberian and already Iberianized population going about its daily business—not the church, except insofar as it was a part of that population."[48] It would appear that not only the influence but also the motives and attitudes of the Spaniards in the New World varied little according to lay or clerical status. This lack of differentiation led to confused expressions of class interest by ecclesiastics, many of whom were surprisingly quiescent in the face of regalist moves. Like the secular elite, churchmen were bound to the empire as a result of a unity of interest, particularly with respect to the control of the Indians. Such a situation was accepted not only as furthering the purposes of the Church, but also as being in the best interest of the Indians, for it helped them fit into the secular and ecclesiastical order.

IMPERIAL DEPENDENCY: RECIPROCITY AND EXTENT

The enslavement of the Indian and African in Spanish America flowed from Spain's exploitation of two prime American resources: land and precious metals. The Spanish elite, whether in Spain or in the colonies, were united in their efforts to control Indian and African labor in the New World. The Spaniards in the Indies relied on the metropolis for legal, spiritual, moral, and sometimes coercive authority to maintain their dominance. The numerical disparity between the elite and the subject population helped reinforce this dependence on the metropolis.

[48] James Lockhart, "The Social History of Colonial Spanish America: Evolution and Potential," *Latin American Research Review* 7, no. 1 (Spring 1972): 10.

In turn, Spain became largely dependent on the Indies for the maintenance of the existing order in the peninsula. The implications of this connection have been relatively unexplored by scholars. Ultimately, the possession of the colonies made it unnecessary to restructure

the Spanish semi-feudal, land-based, aristocratic economy and society. . . . The process was more than atrophy, however, for if essential productive sectors shrivelled, certain consuming sectors—aristocracy, bureaucracy, the service occupations, the church—burgeoned. The resulting symptoms of pathology were apparent in government as in society and economy in the new as in the old world. After 1600 when the modernizing states of Europe were questioning concepts and practices of privilege, of the 'absolute state,' of the church militant, of private usufruct of public power, of bullion rather than production of wealth, these institutions and attitudes took new root in Spain and Spanish America.[49]

Thus the discovery and colonization of the New World served to undercut pressures for change in Spain, reinforced a mercantilist colonial structure, and discouraged peninsular industrialization.

Economic and political developments in northern Europe and particularly in England relegated Spain and her colonies to a subordinate position. Furthermore, Castilian and Andalusian pre-eminence in the colonial venture contributed to multiple levels of dependency.[50] The emergence of competing interests in peripheral areas of the peninsula and empire and their interrelations are fertile fields for research. Such studies would help test the conclusion that there was a major shift in the economic core of the empire from Spain to America in the seventeenth century.[51] In addition, Stanley and Bar-

[49] Stein and Stein, *Colonial Heritage*, p. 20.

[50] Brading, in *Miners and Merchants*, describes the dependent role played by northern New Spain vis à vis the central provinces, while Brooke Larson has elucidated the dependent position of portions of Upper Peru in "Merchants and Economic Activity in Sixteenth Century Potosí" (M.A. thesis, Columbia University, 1972). More light will be shed on this topic with the publication of Peter and Judith Bakewell's current study of Potosí, which should benefit from insights gleaned in Peter Bakewell's book, *Silver Mining and Society in Colonial Mexico: Zacatecas, 1546–1700* (Cambridge: Cambridge University Press, 1971).

[51] John Lynch, *Spain under the Hapsburgs*, vol. 2: *Spain and America, 1598–*

bara Stein note the apparent shift of social and political power "from metropolis to periphery—to the colonial hacendado, mineowner, merchant." This transfer was accompanied by a process of economic regionalization, or "compartmentalization," which in turn gave rise to "incipient" national feelings on the part of creoles.[52] The stirrings of nationalism in the colonies in the face of the weakness of metropolitan national sentiments has not been accorded the attention it deserves, though it could help explain the fragmentation of the Indies once independence was gained.

The Bourbon response was to attempt to increase imperial integration in order to better protect and profit from the colonies. This goal was to be accomplished by making Spain less dependent on northern Europe through reform of both the peninsular and the colonial economies. Such a policy involved systematic plugging of the gaps in the imperial monopoly.[53] Explorations for new mineral deposits were undertaken, and the expansion of production of certain agricultural commodities was encouraged—actions that tended to reinforce some of the anarchronisms of the imperial economy. Increasing prosperity in some portions of the empire helped expand the monarchy's base of support, but it also introduced new groups with their demands into imperial political struggle. As long as the crown responded to these groups, they helped stabilize it; when it did not or could not, they often became passive or withdrew their support.[54] Throughout, the crown did not attempt to change substantially its

---

1700 (New York: Oxford University Press, 1969), p. 9; Tulio Halperín Donghi, *Historia contemporánea de América Latina* (Madrid: Alianza Editorial, 1970), p. 20.

[52] Stein and Stein, *Colonial Heritage*, p.66.

[53] For studies of intracolonial trade see Woodrow Borah, *Early Colonial Trade and Navigation between Mexico and Peru* (Berkeley: University of California Press, 1954); Guillermo Céspedes del Castillo, *Lima y Buenos Aires, repercusiones económicas y políticas de la creación del Virreinato de la Plata* (Seville: Escuela de Estudios Hispano-Americanos de Sevilla, 1947); Eduardo Arcila Farías, *Comercio entre Venezuela y México en los siglos XVI y XVII* (Mexico City: Colegio de México, 1950); Francisco Morales Padrón, *El comercio canario-americano (siglos XVI, XVII, y XVIII)* (Seville: Escuela de Estudios Hispano-Americanos, 1955).

[54] For some of the vagaries of peninsular support see Richard Herr, *The Eighteenth-Century Revolution in Spain* (Princeton: Princeton University Press, 1958).

traditional bases of support, continuing to rely on the peninsular and colonial elites. Bourbon policies, in some respects, bolstered interests with a strong commitment to maintaining the status quo. Thus, the monarchy attempted to accomplish greater consolidation of its empire through policies that reinforced some of the impediments to it. In the eighteenth century, monopoly was not abandoned; instead, the number of those with such privileges increased, as indicated by the creation of trading companies.[55] At the same time, commercial ties between the colonies and European countries other than Spain increased. Moreover, established economic interests in Spain took advantage of free trade to increase the volume of trade—and hence their profits—and increased their dependency on northern European suppliers rather than on peninsular ones. Contrary to royal expectations, the loosening of the monopoly did not stimulate peninsular manufacturing to the degree desired. All this points to the need for research on the impact of eighteenth-century reforms in order to establish more clearly the gains and losses of Bourbon economic policy and relate them not only to the independence movement but also to the subsequent development of the economies of the new republics.[56]

Misdirected and inadequate colonial reforms are only a partial explanation for the independence movement. The Industrial Revolution in Europe, which encouraged the search for large new markets and sources of raw materials, turned northern European attention to Spanish and Portuguese America. Such interest encouraged colonial

[55] See Roland D. Hussey, "Antecedents of the Spanish Monopolistic Overseas Trading Companies (1624–1728)," *Hispanic American Historical Review* 9, no. 1 (February 1929): 1–30; idem, *The Caracas Company, 1728–1787: A Study in the History of Spanish Monopolistic Trade* (Cambridge: Harvard University Press, 1934); Vicente de Amezaga Aresti, *Hombres de la Compañía Guipuzcoana* (Caracas: Banco Central de Venezuela, 1963). There is considerable opportunity for additional research in this area.

[56] Contributions in this area have been made by Eduardo Arcila Farías, *El siglo ilustrado en América: Reformas económicas del siglo XVIII en Nueva España* (Caracas: Ediciones del Ministerio de Educación, Dirección de Cultura y Bellas Artes, 1955), and J. H. Parry, *Trade and Dominion: The European Overseas Empires in the Eighteenth Century* (New York: Praeger, 1971).

merchants and manufacturers to define their interests somewhat differently than previously. With the disappointment of the erratic Bourbon reforms and the disruption caused by the French Revolution and European warfare, discontent grew among the commercial elite and increased their affinity for ideas propounded by the Enlightenment and the French and American revolutions.

STATE, NATION, AND EMPIRE BUILDING: CONCLUDING OBSERVATIONS

The initial reaction to the events of 1808 in Spain and the colonies was one of loyalty and, particularly in the peninsula, of unity against a foreign invader. This latter impetus was not so present in the Indies, although fear of potential Indian uprisings played something of a similar role. Subsequent events in Spain, however, particularly the rapid succession of various ruling bodies of different orientations, contributed to disaffection in the colonies. In Peru the weakness of metropolitan direction exacerbated tensions that contributed to rebellions in areas where little benefit was felt from the imperial connection, as exemplified by outbursts in Upper Peru and Quito in 1809. The creole elite in the viceregal capital cooperated in putting down these disturbances, but continued chaos in the peninsula and the specter of liberalism alienated more creoles. The restoration and reassertion of metropolitan control convinced the colonial elite of the need to replace royal authority with self-rule.

With a limited geographical and class base in Spain the monarchy in the nineteenth century entered into a period when its very existence was challenged. In the colonies the search for stability and legitimacy in the early years of independence led to a search for a unifying factor, either in an individual or in a constitution, or both. Neither was sufficient, and political struggle among those with some access to power continued. The liberal/conservative and federalist/centralist conflicts of the nineteenth century had their counterparts in metropolitan Spain. Rather than comparing the Latin American wars of independence to that of the United States or to the French Revolution, it would be more illuminating to compare them to the Basque and Catalonian separatist movements of the nineteenth century.

Spain did not become a nation-state during the imperial period. This was, in part, the result of the acquisition of an American empire, which encouraged Iberian stagnation and dependency and decreased pressures for change. Shorn of its colonies, Spain erupted into civil war, dynastic struggles, and ineffectual political experimentation. The colonies turned in upon themselves, inherent splits within the ruling elites surfaced, and regionalism and centrifugalism marked the political lives of the new countries. The failure of Spain to create an integrated state during the imperial period worked against the identification of the colonists with the Spanish state. In addition, the anti-state and illiberal attitudes of the peninsula influenced Spanish America, contributing to the difficulties the new republics had in establishing and maintaining their new governments.

The special nature of the Spanish sense of history also contributed to peninsular and American problems. Rather than capitalizing on Spain's experience in the imperial period, there was a tendency to reject the political developments of that epoch and to harken back to the medieval era, as a glorious period of constitutionalism and representation.[57] Thus, little of Spain's experience during the imperial period was used for nation-building efforts in the nineteenth and twentieth centuries. Similarly, the new Latin American republics turned to North American and French models.

What occurred in Spain during the imperial period was the building of an absolutistic monarchy on a narrow base, which restricted the resources available to the central government. The limitations, particularly financial, of this system were alleviated by access to colonial wealth. With a weak, economically dependent bourgeoisie tied to the northern European economy, an oppressed peasantry, and an uncommercialized nobility, possibilities for economic development and political integration were circumscribed. Stagnation was partially obscured by the wealth and prestige accruing from the Indies. The colonies helped maintain a defective system longer than it might otherwise have survived. Spain found itself at the outset of the nineteenth century with outmoded metropolitan and colonial structures

---

[57] Herr, *Eighteenth-Century Revolution*, pp. 341, 347, 440–441.

that were not well adapted to meet the challenges presented by the Industrial and French revolutions.

Hapsburg recognition of the Spanish possessions as separate kingdoms and limited national and imperial integration had helped lighten the burden of royal absolutism and metropolitan exploitation. The inefficiency of the imperial administrative machinery that contributed to this, however, came under attack during the Bourbon period. Charles III and his ministers tightened the mainspring of centripetal authority in an attempt to increase efficiency, security, and profit. This effort produced tension, particularly in peripheral areas. With the relaxation of authority under Charles IV and during the Napoleonic period, such areas in the colonies sought greater self-determination. Although separatist sentiments in the peninsula were undercut by the presence of French troops on Spanish soil, the colonies were freer to pursue their autonomous impulses. The tendency to break away from central authorities was directed not only against Madrid, but also against Lima, Mexico City, and, within peripheral areas, against such centers as Buenos Aires. The desire for independence was clearly related to the degree of satisfaction with the allocation of power and benefits within the imperial system. Discontent spurred not only separation from Spain but also fragmentation within Latin America.

Spain was able to maintain her empire for more than three hundred years largely as a result of mutual interests among crown, peninsular elites, and creole elites. Conflicts between Spanish and American interests and within Spain and the Indies were assuaged through the institutionalization of conflict and the creation of mediatory instrumentalities. Competing forces were useful in the maintenance of the supremacy of monarchical authority. As long as the moderating functions of official structures worked well, the level of conflict was controlled; however, when the crown attempted to abandon them for more absolute control in the latter part of the eigthteenth century, separatist pressures intensified. The Bourbon reforms marked a departure from the tradition of dealing with competitors for power by allocating benefits sufficient to retain the support of one group without alienating another or causing the groups to combine for mutual advantage at the expense of central authority.

In the Indies, the crown was preoccupied by possible collaboration among the bureaucracy, the creole elites, and the religious. From the outset of the colonial period the tendency for royal officials to identify with local elites was apparent, a situation that became more of a threat to crown authority when creoles occupied high positions in colonial officialdom. Efforts to combat this presence in the second half of the eighteenth century by cutting back on the number of creole officials did not have the desired effect. Further administrative reforms, such as the introduction of intendants, caused disaffection among some colonial bureaucrats. In addition, some sectors resented economic reforms because they either altered the status quo or did not alter it enough. Bourbon ecclesiastical reforms also threatened the privileged position of the Church in both Spain and America, where difficulties were generated by the conflicts between regalism, ultramontanism, and new intellectual currents. Support for royal policies was simply not sufficient to counter colonial discontent and passivity.

The independence movement marked the breaking down and inadequacy of the traditional controls and mediatory instrumentalities that the metropolis used to maintain its authority. The task was perhaps an impossible one, given the contradictions involved in meeting royal objectives and those of the monarchy's potential supporters. Attempts to rationalize the royal bureaucracy in the eighteenth century ran into difficulty because circumstances in the previous two hundred years had already provided the modes and forms according to which it functioned. The fixing of Spanish objectives in the sixteenth century, in part under the impetus of the acquisition of empire, made adaptation in the seventeenth and eighteenth centuries difficult and contributed to nineteenth- and twentieth-century strife. Bourbon reforms might have integrated the empire more effectively if objectives had been substantially reoriented in the light of building a more viable political entity and responding to social and economic changes that had taken place during the eighteenth century. Instead, royal efforts were concentrated on modifying forms so that original imperial goals could be more effectively fulfilled. These reforms and imperial structures neither preserved the empire nor served particularly to prepare the colonists for self-government under republican forms. Schooled in a patrimonial system, Latin America in the nineteenth century moved into a period of neopatrimonialism. Attempts to graft on political theories and models developed in other contexts contributed to postindependence difficulties. The impulse toward centralized administrations was opposed by peripheral elites who regarded the creation of the republics as an opportunity to increase their influence and participation. The demands they posed emerged concurrently with the central elite's desire for more active support from those areas.[58] The removal of traditional authorities and elimination of the monarchy as an object of loyalty resulted in a competition among the creoles for legitimacy, in part through definition of national goals in the constitutions. There was a tendency for these documents and the political forms that flowed from them to change as power shifted within the elite.

Latin American phenomena have often been examined in the light of models developed outside the Hispanic world, with consequent misunderstandings and misrepresentations. If the intention is to try to fathom the Latin American reality, then more attention must be paid to the profound complexity of the Spanish colonial system and its relationship to political developments within Spain.

[58] Eisenstadt, "Traditional Patrimonialism and Modern Neo-Patrimonialism," p. 71.

Bases of Political Alignment in Early Republican Spanish America

FRANK SAFFORD

This essay deals with some of the problems arising from attempts to describe the socioeconomic bases of political alignments in Spanish America in the first half century of the republican period. As this was a time of beginnings, individuals in making their political commitments could not consult a well-established family tradition, as would be the case after the middle of nineteenth century. Thus the role that socioeconomic factors may have played in shaping political choices is of particular interest. This essay refers solely to alignments among the political elite, the more-or-less visible elements in politics. The analysis uses the history of Colombia as its principal reference point but takes sidelong glances at Mexico, Venezuela, and other variants.

Specifying the socioeconomic factors underlying political divisions in this period is fraught with complications. Most obviously there is the problem of the considerable diversity in the circumstances of the

NOTE. The thoughts presented here were developed with the encouragement of a grant from the Council on Intersocietal Studies, Northwestern University. Parts of the analysis, applied more specifically to Colombia, appeared in different form in the *Journal of Social History* 5, no. 2 (Spring 1972): 344–370. I am grateful for comments volunteered by Charles Berry, Woodrow Borah, David Brading, and Charles Hale, at an early stage in the analysis, and, latterly, by Richard N. Adams, Peter Eisenberg, William Glade, and, most particularly, Richard Sinkin.

new republics—their differing sizes, terrain, population distribution, ethnic characteristics, economics, colonial traditions, and recent experience. Mexico's deeply entrenched colonial institutions (most prominently the Church), its large sedentary peasant population, and its mining and manufacturing interests created a different set of political forces and a different set of issues than were to be found in Argentina or Venezuela, with their smaller populations, simpler economies, and shallower institutional foundations. Chile, with its concentrated population and closely linked economic interests, was much less disturbed by regional conflict than larger or less-integrated countries like Mexico or Colombia.

Differing economic relations with the European metropolis also played a part in varying the political patterns of the Spanish American republics. In countries, like Mexico or Colombia, with relatively weak commercial links to European markets before 1850, such questions as the role of Church institutions and the survival of colonial taxation systems were central issues. Finding their countries' economic growth (as measured in that era) frustrated, leaders in such places tended to blame the obstructions posed by the continuing control of resources by Church corporations as well as by the survival of colonial fiscal systems. In countries that entered the export economy easily, there was less reason to look upon the colonial inheritance as a critical obstruction.

As the issues varied according to geography, economy and historical tradition, so did the ways in which political groups defined themselves. The political debate in many places came to be between "liberals"and "conservatives." But in Argentina the centralists were liberals in economic and cultural terms; the federalists, defenders of colonial tradition. And there are other less well-known anomalies— in Venezuela, for example, liberals who were landowners and paternalists, conservatives who were defenders of economic liberalism.

Analysis of political alignments in the early republican era is further complicated by the fluid character of politics in the period. Between 1820 and 1850, the political systems of Spanish America were still in a formative stage. Political groups, like the republics in which they functioned, were going through a process of self-discovery and self-definition. Groups continually fragmented and reformed, and the political coloration of individual politicians changed. The historian interested in the definition of structures therefore confronts, perhaps in a more acute form than usual, the problem of making his subject sit still.

The many variations in the economic and political patterns of the Spanish American countries make it difficult to construct generalizations that deal usefully with all of them. One might construct a typology that would encompass the most significant variants of the first half century of the republican era. But elaboration of such a typology is not the purpose of the present essay. This essay examines a variety of approaches to the analysis of nineteenth-century politics that have been or may be used. It deals first with analyses based upon economic class or occupation, then turns to those founded upon regional economic interests and other aspects of regionalism. It concludes with an outline of an approach that I consider useful and appropriate to the subject. Obviously no single approach to analysis is sufficient. This essay aims, not to lay down some monistic doctrine, but to offer reflections that may lead to more analytical precision.

As they focus on social determinants, the following comments do not deal with the role of individual psychologies or with the role of rational thought in making political choices. Individuals presumably were affected in various degrees by both. This analysis, however, is based upon the assumption that there exists some general, more or less predictable relationship between structural characteristics in the society and political affiliations that were established in the formative era. The problem is to discover which structures are the most relevant, and the most helpful and illuminating way of defining and viewing them.

POLITICAL GROUPS IN THE FORMATIVE YEARS

The character of political alignments varied a good deal from country to country. In some places politics for most or all of the period consisted of little more than a competition among factions based upon personalist attachments. Bolivia and Peru may be considered salient examples. In these cases, the shifting political alignments may have had some broad social significance, but it is obscure and hard to ferret out. In some other countries personalist politics was quite evident, but there were also at least temporary divisions among the elite based upon issues of some broad social and economic significance. Venezuela and probably Ecuador may be said to fit this category. Finally, some of the republics—notably Mexico, Colombia, and (in different ways) Chile—were evolving in this period from a politics of personalist factions toward one of competition among groups that may be thought of, at least in nineteenth-century terms, as political parties. The present essay is concerned primarily with those cases in which politics was more or less structured and in which social issues and social forces came into play in some significant ways.

The parties that had emerged in even the most structured polities by the middle of the nineteenth century lacked many of the characteristics of parties as conceived in the twentieth century. Among other things they had no formal party organizations and mass bases. Before 1850 they generally did not have formally organized hierarchies or central directorates; nor were there party whips in the congresses. Even in the countries with relatively complex political parties, both personalism and factional flux continued to be evident, and individuals or factions of two opposing parties occasionally joined together to form a third force (as happens in modern parties). Finally, the political groups of the early nineteenth century were of course upper-class parties, in which the lower orders participated very little, except in time of civil war and then, one may assume, unwillingly in most cases.

But at least by the middle of the nineteenth century there existed political groups that had a strong sense of party identity, reflected more than the personal ambitions of a caudillo, were relatively complex in composition, and endured for long periods of time. In such places as Mexico and Colombia there had developed a sense of party identity that had considerable force. After mid-century even dissident factions in these countries usually thought of themselves as the true interpreters of the doctrines and tradition of the party from which they emerged.

The evolution of party alignments in the structured polities can be divided into three stages, corresponding very roughly to the decades between 1820 and 1850. The politics of the 1820s were characterized by extreme fragmentation, with political attachments formed on both personalist and regional bases. Alignments fluctuated rapidly, depending on the variable fortunes of certain leading figures. In many cases the alignments evident in this decade did not persist much beyond it.

During the 1830s, however, there occurred a coagulation of various conservative interests into identifiable establishment groups. The Chilean regime led by Joaquín Prieto and Diego Portales is the most famous case. But others follow the pattern—for example, the Venezuelan adherents of Gen. José Antonio Páez and the *moderados* of Colombia. Often these early republican establishments were composed of groups that had been at odds, or at any rate quite distinct, in the 1820s. Thus, Colombia's *moderados* were in many cases liberal republicans who had followed Gen. Francisco de Paula Santander in the 1820s but became disenchanted by his support for Gen. José María Obando in the 1830s; others were former Bolivarians who found in the *moderados* a means of re-entry upon the political stage. In Chile, the Prieto-Portales regime was founded upon an alliance of the *pelucones*, generally identified with large landowners, and the *estanqueros*, an insider business element.

Finally, in the 1840s there occurred a kind of political crystallization in many countries, with emergent groups rebelling against the establishments of the 1830s. In the process there formed political groups with sharp ideological differences and strong party identities. Factionalism continued to flourish within parties, but in many places the politically active part of the population now thought of itself as belonging to either of two parties. Most commonly they came to be called "liberal" and "conservative." Such terms, particularly *liberal*, had been used during the 1820s and 1830s, but before the 1840s they were not the exclusive property of one party; until the 1840s, everyone considered himself "liberal." By the end of the 1840s, however, these terms had become firmly attached to particular parties and were the banners under which they went to war. In many countries the alignments formed in the 1840s tended to be more or less enduring.

The political crystallization of the 1840s was furthered by various external events. Charles Hale points to the Mexican War as a cataclysm that created more obvious political fissures in Mexico than had been evident before.[1] But other countries that experienced nothing like the Mexican War were going through the same process of political definition during the 1840s. In several cases, the hazards of the export economy produced internal tensions that were reflected in political polarization. In Venezuela depressed international prices of coffee and other commodities in the 1840s created a sharp, albeit temporary, division between "conservatives," representing capital interests, and "liberals," representing many planters.[2] And, in both Venezuela and Colombia, movement toward free trade and the increased pressure of imported goods mobilized artisans who became, at least temporarily, supporters of liberal parties. Finally, in most countries in Latin America the emergence of hardened, more or less ideologically defined divisions was encouraged by the European Revolution of 1848. The drama of the European revolution encouraged Spanish American politicans to strike political poses in imitation of their European mentors. Suddenly class revolution, or at any rate a limited activation of lower-class groups, came into vogue. Some liberals began to style themselves "socialists,"[3] and conservatives now embraced the European term that applied to their role.

This "radicalization" of politics at the end of the 1840s and in the early 1850s in turn divided some of the newly crystallized parties. The liberal parties in Mexico, Colombia, and Venezuela divided on slightly varying grounds between radical and moderate wings. Nevertheless, the mid-century alignments remained of enduring signifi-

---

[1] Charles Hale, *Mexican Liberalism in the Age of Mora, 1821–1853* (New Haven: Yale University Press, 1968), pp. 11–38.

[2] Robert Wayne Butler, "The Origins of the Liberal Party in Venezuela: 1830–1848" (Ph.D. dissertation, The University of Texas at Austin, 1972).

[3] Robert L. Gilmore, "New Granada's Socialist Mirage," *Hispanic American Historical Review* 36, no. 2 (May 1956): 190–210.

cance. For no matter how bitter the divisions between the wings of the post-1850 parties, their members in most cases continued to think of themselves as indelibly marked as either liberal or conservative.

By mid-century, in New Granada at least, a few individuals in each party constituted a competitive but also cooperative ideological leadership. This did not prevent the various factions within a single party from presenting and persisting in supporting their own candidates for the presidency. After 1850, when a sense of party identity became more marked, parties began to develop more unity of action. By 1850, the locus of party leadership had become evident—certain individuals were generally recognized as expounders of party doctrine; others formed a stable of likely presidential candidates. The parties continued to present many factional candidates long after mid-century, but in general as the elections drew near there was a tendency to rally to a single party representative. By 1860 in New Granada there were signs that party directorates, with power to form policy and choose candidates, existed.

Though formal party hierarchies were not common before mid-century, there were other modes of party organization dating from the 1820s or 1830s. Throughout the entire century, Colombian politicians "ran" for the presidency by soliciting support from those assumed to be sympathetic. This "campaigning" was carried on *sotto voce*, but many letters survive testifying to its occurrence. Leading politicians, even those not seeking office at the time, kept up a febrile correspondence with agents in far-flung provinces, seeking information and giving marching orders. Party newspapers also kept the active members of the upper class oriented on doctrinal matters as well as on the chicaneries of the opposition. There was also electioneering of sorts, including promises made to special interest groups like the artisans of Bogotá. Finally, of course, throughout the century, patronage, spiced and graced by party ideology, helped to hold the party faithful to the cause.

Party affiliation must have been a question of great moment to members of the upper classes. Otherwise it is hard to explain the bitterly fought internecine conflicts of the nineteenth century. Much civil disruption amounted to little more than caudillistic coups d'état, in which broad interest often may not have been engaged; this was particularly true of those countries, like Peru and Bolivia, in which there was relatively little party development. But in Mexico, Colombia, and Venezuela, relatively greater party articulation meant that political conflict was more likely to occur on a broad scale.

What did party affiliation mean to the upper classes? For many it was largely a matter of government jobs. Lacking other economic opportunities in most places and lured on by the Spanish tradition of government service, those with secondary education often viewed political position as their principal economic resource. Even for those not directly involved as politicians, party affiliation meant access to or denial of favorable treatment in customs offices, in the settlement of government debts, in speculative purchases of public lands. In time of civil war, all substantial citizens knew that their party affiliations would determine whether or not forced loans would be exacted from them. For many members of the upper class, therefore, a political party was a brotherhood for their economic protection.

If nineteenth-century parties were simple mechanisms for economic protection, their composition might be of no more significance than that of two contending families of the Mafia. The present essay does argue that the kind of differentiation suggested in leading interpretations exaggerates the social and ideological differences between the parties. Nevertheless, it would be going too far to suggest that the distribution of politicians was random, with no evident pattern.

OCCUPATION AND ECONOMIC CLASS AS DISCRIMINATING FACTORS
The Role of Occupation In Current Interpretations

When general statements are framed on nineteenth-century poliitcs, they often are extensions of a particularly well-known model, in most cases that of Mexico, sometimes also that of Argentina. Generalizations based on the Mexican model view the politics of the period from 1820 to 1870 as a conflict between the remnants of the "colonial order" and the "emerging" classes. As a general proposition this conception has merit. Most of the existing statements about the sociopolitical dynamic of the period fail, however, because of the way they specify who formed part of the colonial order and who was emerging. Generally, the former are identified as landowners, clergy, and military, and the latter as merchants, lawyers, and intellectuals.

The conception of rural conservatism pitted against urban liberalism, widely accepted for Mexico, is often applied more generally to the rest of Latin America, notably by John J. Johnson and, more recently, by Stanley and Barbara Stein.[4] One particularly simplistic statement of this theme, influenced apparently by the imaginative disquisitions of Domingo Faustino Sarmiento, is the Marxist Noël Salomon's assertion that "from Argentina to Mexico" the period is one of antagonism between *campo* and *ciudad*, *barbarie* and *civilización*, feudalism and capitalism.[5]

In Johnson's brief synthesis an urban "middle sector," which provided intellectual leadership in the fight for independence, was then "everywhere forced to surrender leadership to elites composed of the landed aristocracy, the hierarchy of the Catholic Church, and the officer corps of the armed forces." In an authoritarian environment, with force rather than reason the basis of power, the "middle sectors" were overwhelmed, and then often co-opted, by caudillos representing the interests of the landed elite. Economically as well as politically, the landed elements eclipsed the urban ones, for their estates were much less affected by civil war than the urban economy, and, in any case, the cities "played a distinctly secondary role in the economic system maintained by the elites."[6]

Johnson eschews the use of the term *class*, apparently because he believes (rightly) that the intermediary group between upper and lower lacks the consistency and coherence of a class. He therefore substitutes the terms *elite* and *middle sectors*. But he does not thereby avoid engaging in a species of class analysis. For Johnson misuses

[4] John J. Johnson, *Political Change in Latin America: The Emergence of the Middle Sectors* (Stanford: Stanford University Press, 1958), pp. 15–26; Stanley J. Stein and Barbara H. Stein, *The Colonial Heritage of Latin America: Essays on Economic Dependence in Perspective* (New York: Oxford University Press, 1970), pp. 140–141, 168.

[5] Noël Salomon, "Féodalité et capitalisme au Mexique de 1856 à 1910," *La Pensée*, no. 42–43 (May–June, July–August 1952): 123–132; and in a slightly revised version with the same title in *Recherches Internationales à la Lumière du Marxisme*, no. 32 (July–August 1962): 180–196.

[6] Johnson, *Political Change*, pp. 15, 17–20, 24–25.

the term *elite*, in effect equating it with *upper class* or *aristocracy*; and *middle sectors* to him clearly means *middle class*, but simply fudged a bit.

Whatever the merits of Johnson's categories for the twentieth century, they tend to muddle matters when applied to the nineteenth. They have the virtue of suggesting that some kind of struggle for power and preference was going on among the literate inhabitants of these republics—a struggle between established factions and challengers. But the categories mislead by dividing the established and the challengers into two separate classes on the basis of their occupations or economic functions (landowners versus lawyers and merchants). This procedure is inappropriate to nineteenth-century Spanish America. For in this period it is hard to distinguish a professional or bureaucratic middle sector from a landowning elite. Whether the role was urban intellectual or rural hacendado, they all formed part of a single upper class. If there was a middle sector in the nineteenth century, it consisted not of the mercantile or intellectual-professional elements, but of artisans and small tradesmen.

Some of the more obvious problems with Johnson's treatment are obviated in Tulio Halperín Donghi's somewhat parallel interpretation of the period. Halperín avoids the spongy concept of the "middle sectors." He does not generalize quite so loosely about all of Latin America—he gives some sense of the particular characteristics of the individual countries. While sharing Johnson's view of urban elements being eclipsed by landowners and caudillos in the postindependence period, he distinguishes more clearly than Johnson between an urban sector that stemmed from the colonial period and a newer bourgeoisie that emerged toward the middle of the century. Halperín also improves on Johnson by conceiving of the military not merely as a tool of landed interests but also, at least in Ecuador, Peru, and Mexico, as an arbiter or mediator among various economic interests. Nevertheless, with all its refinements, Halperín's interpretation agrees with Johnson's in portraying a landed aristocracy separate from and dominating the urban sector.[7]

[7] Tulio Halperín Donghi, *Historia contemporánea de América Latina* (Madrid: Alianza Editorial, 1969), pp. 141–147, 173–174, 187–189.

Halperín and some others who view nineteenth-century politics in terms of contending economic groups see a dynamic that has its point of dramatic climax at mid-century. The better accounts agree that a kind of crystallization of politics occurred in such countries as Mexico, Venezuela, and New Granada in the years between 1845 and 1855. From several of the more interesting interpretations (most notably those of Germán Colmenares, for Colombia; Jan Bazant, for Mexico; and Tulio Halperín Donghi overall),[8] one can extract the following synthesis. In the political confusion and relative economic stagnation of the 1830s, the landowning-clerical-military coalition was able to dominate the urban sector rather easily. The development of export economies and commercial expansion in the 1840s in some countries, however, fostered the emergence of a new merchant class, which began seriously to challenge the dominance of the traditional power groups. At the same time, the expansion of foreign trade undermined native artisans, making them susceptible to the blandishments of the emergent bourgeois who would challenge the established power-holders. In the conflict between the old landed and the new commercial element, both sides made elaborate appeals to ideology in their efforts to curry popular support. The ruling coalition of landowners, aided by the clergy and military, responded to the middle-class challenge by making an intensified appeal to religion as a symbol that could hold the masses. The "new middle classes" (merchants, professionals), in many cases representing a new political generation, for their part held up the banners of a new secular religion—compounded of economic liberalism and the democratic republican spirit of the Revolution of 1848—attracting the loyalty of artisans, small merchants, and other lower elements in the society. These ideological conflicts of mid-century were most clearly dramatized in the Reforma in Mexico and in Colombia's upheavals of the years 1849–1854. In both cases, allegedly, the new bourgeoisie

---

[8] Germán Colmenares, *Partidos políticos y clases sociales* (Bogotá: Ediciones Universidad de los Andes, 1968); Jan Bazant, *Alienation of Church Wealth in Mexico: Social and Economic Aspects of the Liberal Revolution, 1856–1875* (Cambridge: Cambridge University Press, 1971); Halperín, *Historia contemporánea*.

emerged politically triumphant but then, through purchases of land (often former Church property), became incorporated in and assimilated to the traditional landowning aristocracy.

Many of the major points of this synthesis seem sound. The development of export economies did produce stresses that forced adjustments among the upper classes as well as mobilizing adversely affected elements of the lower class. In this period of stress, occurring in most cases between 1840 and 1860, established and emergent upper-class leaders in some places—certainly in Mexico and Colombia—did more or less consciously use religion and liberalism as symbols to manipulate and control disrupted lower-class groups. But it is doubtful that the established groups may be clearly identified with landowning and the socially emergent with the urban professions. Even the best syntheses have exaggerated the extent to which an urban elite was dominated by the combined forces of landowners and military warlords of the independence period. And the very idea of a clear split between urban and rural or "bourgeois" and "traditional" groups seems open to question.

Power Relationships Between Rural and Urban Elites

Turning first to the relationship between caudillos (presumably landowner-backed) and the urban elite, accounts of the politics of a number of countries generally suggest that the former were able to dominate the latter. This is the picture we are given of Argentina in the epoch of Juan Manuel de Rosas, Bolivia of the *caudillos bárbaros*, and even, perhaps less accurately, of Venezuela under Páez and Mexico under Antonio López de Santa Anna. Such a conception, however, surely needs modification. To identify a government with its principal figure is to substitute a metaphor for serious description of the system.

In most cases the caudillo depended upon an elite of lawyer-administrators to carry much of the burden of governance. Just as Portales provided direction for the rule of General Prieto, so did Lucas Alamán for Santa Anna (at least in the 1830s). In Venezuela, caudillos frequently were manipulated by their intellectual secretaries,[9] and a host of lawyer-bureaucrats influenced Colombia's governing generals. While these urban administrators were formally subservient to the military presidents, the two were in fact mutually dependent, for many caudillos relied heavily upon civilian administrators to determine policy in large and in detail. Civilian administrators who wished to maintain their positions may have had to observe certain modes of deference, but it is a mistake to view such deference toward the caudillo as proof of his effective exercise of power.

If the relationship of the caudillo to the urban administrator was ambiguous at least, what of the landowners' position vis-à-vis the city elite? It has been suggested that the economic strength of the urban sector was more sapped by the post-1810 warfare than was that of the landowners; that, in any case, landowners enjoyed greater prestige than the city folk, whose principal capital was their wits; and that, for both reasons, landowners were able to control, manipulate, and co-opt the urban elite.[10] Each of these propositions is in need of some clarification.

In the first place, one must distinguish, for analytical purposes, between the political-administrative and mercantile sectors of the urban elite. The administrator element did depend to some degree on the political support of the propertied, and it *was* weakened economically by chronic civil war. Often receiving much of their salary in depreciated government credit documents, the administrators constantly were in danger of sliding through the material zone in which gentility could survive. Nevertheless, economically weakened and politically dependent upon the rural lords as they might be, these urban administrators were not necessarily in a relationship of subservience to the hacendados. Rather it seems that the urban political specialists provided leadership to the rural-dwelling landowners, who were relatively passive and relied upon the urban political elite for information and political direction.

The merchant-capitalist elements in the urban elite were in a quite

---

[9] Robert L. Gilmore, *Caudillism and Militarism in Venezuela, 1810–1910* (Athens: Ohio University Press, 1964), pp. 54–55.

[10] Halperín, *Historia contemporánea*, pp. 142–147; Bazant, *Alienation*, pp. 6, 89.

different position from the administrators. For, whatever their role in politics, they generally were in a stronger economic position than the landowners. In time of war, nothing was more certain than the seizure of horses and cattle by passing armies. Merchant-capitalists also were mulcted of their ready cash, and sometimes more than that. But they had the advantage of being able to keep much of their working capital abroad and untouchable by political warriors, an option not available to landowners. Civil war also offered opportunities for speculative profits in imported merchandise as well as for loans at exorbitant rates of interest to governments suffering from postwar hangovers.

As for another important element in the urban elite, the lawyers, these stormy petrels profited from any kind of strife. Aside from the opportunities for litigation opened up by war-caused economic disruption, many lawyers found postwar employment as claims agents for provincials whose property had been seized or damaged in time of civil war.

One may say that the interests of the bourgeoisie as a class were harmed by caudillistic civil war, in that it prevented the creation of banks and other instruments of capital development. But as individuals many members of the urban elite seem not to have been affected more adversely than landowners. And, though it would be hard to establish quantitatively, capital concentrated in urban hands appears to have grown in this period in relation to that in the hands of mere landowners.

If the urban elite was not necessarily more debilitated than landowners during the disorders of the 1810–1860 period, did it nonetheless recognize the proprietor class as its master? Was land universally recognized as the sole measure of power and social prestige? And did such prestige then serve as a lever for the manipulation of urban subordinates? I am inclined to doubt this. Even in the relatively simple societies to be found in Spanish America of the 1810–1860 period, there did exist a variety of reference groups within the upper class and therefore several different ladders of prestige. Within the ranks of each group—commercial, landed, military, professional, literary—a man could obtain the security of recognition. In addition, to some degree members of each group recognized the claims of the others. A merchant was likely to respect most those merchants who equaled or surpassed him in wealth, but he was also likely to concede something to those in other groups who could wield some power, whether economic, political, military, or intellectually manipulative. The point is, however, that each group had an independent claim to power and prestige. And it would be hard to establish a general status ranking upon which everyone in the society would have agreed.

If this was the case, how then does one explain the perennial tendency of merchants to buy land? Does this not represent the purchase of status by individuals still unsure of their social position? Perhaps. But it may also be taken as an indication of the accumulation of wealth in commercial hands. One should consider also the possibility that many merchants bought land simply as one of many investments and not necessarily for status reasons. Finally, in considering the land-buying merchant one should also note the phenomenon of the landowner who takes up commerce.[11]

One final consideration regarding landowner power. It is not at all clear that most large landowners had much to do with national politics. Presumably substantial hacendados wielded considerable power locally and could exert a certain amount of electoral influence if they wished. But those hacendados who lived outside the capital and the principal provincial towns had only a remote connection with the national government. Rather few government policy decisions affected most landowners. Occasionally there might be a measure dealing with local roads or the acquisition of government or Indian community lands. But by and large the government was irrelevant to most hacendados, and many therefore may be presumed not to have exercised their potential for power. In contrast, members of the urban elite living in the capital city may have lacked the landowners' natural power base. But as they lived at the political nerve-center and, as their livelihood as lawyers and merchants often depended heavily upon political influence, they were more attuned to politics and tried

[11] Frank Safford, "Social Aspects of Political Alignments in Nineteenth-Century Spanish America: New Granada, 1825–1850," *Journal of Social History* 5, no. 2 (Spring 1972): 351.

to maximize their power potential. I would suggest, therefore, that the urban elite—whether peddling influence, shaping political ideas in the newspapers, or teaching the sons of upper-class youths in *colegios*—may have had more effective power at the national level than landowners.

Economic Categories and Party Affiliation

An economic class analysis of party divisions among the political elite has great appeal. If couched in terms of occupations or a city-rural split, it is simple. The idea of a conflict between a landed aristocracy and emerging urban groups fits the Marxian conception of the feudal-bourgeois evolution on which we all have been nurtured. And it corresponds to what has been presumed to be the familiar pattern of European history.

The generally accepted conception of a clear-cut conflict between a conservative coalition of landowners, higher clergy, and military officers and an emerging urban sector also is supported by a good deal of scholarly authority. In his recent study, *Church Wealth in Mexico*, Michael Costeloe reaffirms the long-held idea that the widespread indebtedness of landowners to church corporations tended to cement their solidarity in a conservative coalition. Similarly, Costeloe has documented the role of ecclesiastical corporations in financing and organizing at least one military attempt against a liberal government (the rebellion of the Polkos in 1847).[12] Students of Colombian history, with some reason, have viewed the conflicts of the 1840s as between established landowners particularly entrenched in the Cauca Valley (and around Bogotá) and an emerging commercial class from the northern provinces.[13]

It also appears that some nineteenth-century politicians viewed the party struggles of their era in these class terms. In Mexico, conservatives like Alamán and Mariano Paredes y Arrillaga and liberals like

---

[12] Michael P. Costeloe, *Church Wealth in Mexico: A Study of the "Juzgado de Capellanías" in the Archbishopric of Mexico 1800–1856* (Cambridge: Cambridge University Press, 1967), p. 28; idem, "The Mexican Church and the Rebellion of the Polkos," *Hispanic American Historical Review* 46, no. 2 (May 1966): 170–178.

[13] Colmenares, *Partidos políticos*.

Mariano Otero agreed in considering the conservative party that of the property-owners and the higher clergy, the liberal party that of the lower strata of society.[14] In Colombia, the conservative José Eusebio Caro, who was himself not a large property-owner, seems to have thought of his party as that of the landowners.[15] One may consider that the nineteenth-century political writers, ever attuned to Europe for their ideological orientations, may have described their parties in accord with imported conceptions. Nevertheless, their writings must carry some weight in the proceedings.

For all the authority behind it, the conception of nineteenth-century politics as a conflict between landowners and an urban bourgeoisie is not convincing. In the first place, the nature of most Latin American economies was such that there was not a clear opposition of interests between property-owners and merchants. In most places the overwhelming majority of the upper class had a stake in developing export economies—the landowners as producers for export and as consumers of imported luxury goods, the merchants as expediters of this exchange, and the lawyers as principal actors in the drama of land aggrandizement. The most common upper-class vocations were complementary. Party affiliation therefore was unlikely to express a particular occupational interest within the upper class.

Even where one can perceive, in large, an opposition between urban and rural interests, as a practical matter it is hard to make a clear distinction between individuals or families belonging to a rural landed class and those belonging to an urban sector of merchants, professionals, and intellectuals. Most of Latin American society was not sufficiently developed for there to be a clear specialization of function. A member of the upper class active in politics was likely to be at once a landowner, lawyer, merchant, educator, littérateur, government employee, and, on occasion, military officer. Even in

[14] Jesús Reyes Heroles, *El liberalismo mexicano*, 3 vols. (Mexico City: Universidad Nacional Autónomo de México, 1957–1961), II, 87–144, 331–344.

[15] José Eusebio Caro, New York, to Blasina Tobar de Caro, July 13, 1851, in José Eusebio Caro, *Epistolario*, Biblioteca de Autores Colombianos (Bogotá: Editorial ABC, 1953), p. 164.

those cases where an individual can be assigned to a "major" function, the members of his immediate family, all with the same political
affiliation, are likely to have encompassed most of the upper-class
vocations. It is therefore very difficult to distinguish among individuals or families in the elite in terms of economic function.

It is even more difficult to make these groups correlate to party affiliations. Even pushing individuals into the pigeonholes of their
predominant functions, it appears that representatives of the various
specialities, at least in Colombia, fall into both leading parties in
roughly equal parts. There may be a functional reason for this—to
survive, each party needed the various contributions that could be
made by landowners, merchant-capitalists, lawyer-ideologists, and,
certainly, military men. In this respect one might view each party as
something like the *panelinha* of twentieth-century Brazil, as described by Anthony Leeds.[16]

In conclusion, in Colombia and, I suspect, elsewhere, elites of
both contending parties were homogeneous in terms of occupation.
They were so, in fact, almost by definition. Although they might
differ strikingly in terms of social origin, by the time individuals
reached maturity and positions of political significance, they tended
both to be possessors of some wealth and education and to range in
similar ways across several types of activity. This being the case, it
would seem to be more useful to attempt to discriminate among the
groups in terms of social origins rather than social arrivals.

CAPITALISM AS A DISCRIMINATING FACTOR
The Mexican and Colombian Cases

If liberals and conservatives were similar in formal occupation,
was there nevertheless a difference between them in economic style?
A number of accounts view liberals as capitalist in spirit, conservatives as resistant to capitalist institutions and behavior. This is a
notable feature of Jan Bazant's richly paradoxical *Alienation of
Church Wealth in Mexico*. Bazant begins his sinuous analysis with

---

[16] Anthony Leeds, "Brazilian Careers and Social Structure: A Case History and
Model," in *Contemporary Cultures and Societies of Latin America*, ed. Dwight B.
Heath and Richard N. Adams (New York: Random House, 1965), pp. 379–401.

the point-blank assertion that in the political conflicts of the era "the
social classes were divided vertically." And in several of the localities he analyzes, particularly in Puebla, Mexico City, and San Luis
Potosí, he emphasizes the interpenetration of upper-class economic
interests—land, commerce, manufacturing, and the exercise of the
professions. In each of these places members of the bourgeoisie were
at once engaged in commerce, manufacturing, and landowning. Although Bazant attempts to depict these urban-based bourgeois landowners as mostly liberal, it is clear from his account that many salient
members of the Mexican bourgeoisie were either conservative or
"moderate" in political inclinations or attempted to be apolitical.[17]
Thus, Bazant seems to demonstrate that in Mexico, as in Colombia,
it is impossible to make a clear correlation between economic function and political affiliation.

Bazant finds it difficult to free himself, however, from the conventional conception of the two parties as economically distinct. Seeking to rescue this established view in the face of inconvenient data,
he suggests that liberal landowners were primarily urban-based
merchants whose investments in land were a sideline. And, by and
large, they exploited their land more capitalistically than the traditional landowners of conservative disposition.[18]

The often-used distinction between commercially oriented or export agriculture and the static hacienda is an attractive and seemingly
useful device for political analysis. In broad regional terms, one
thinks of the notable division between the conservatism of the high-
land areas and the liberalism of the plantation lowlands in Ecuador.
In Colombia the same pattern applies, in the same broad terms.
Tunja and Popayán, neither involved in exporting, remained bas-
tions of conservatism. The Caribbean coast and the Magdalena Valley tended to drift toward a liberal posture during the expansion of
agricultural exports of the middle of the nineteenth century. But the
Colombian case, as usual, presents anomalies. As one begins to look
more closely at the picture, it tends to lose clarity. The Cauca Valley
north of Cali fell under liberal dominion at least twenty years before

17 Bazant, *Alienation*, pp. 7, 43–44, 85–92.
18 Ibid., pp. 89–90, 116–117, 122.

it could effectively ship goods abroad or even to other parts of the country. And conservative Antioquia, while not in export *agriculture* until about 1880, was more heavily engaged in exporting, both as a gold producer and as the commercial organizer of other activities, than any other region.

If one looks seriously at the economic behavior of individuals, the matter may become even more complex. Discriminating between "capitalist" landowners and "traditional" ones may present as many problems as distinguishing between merchants and landowners. There are notable cases of men who on different holdings were engaged both in export agriculture and in more traditional production for the domestic market. And one cannot assume, as Bazant does, that producers of "commercial" crops, such as sugar in Mexico or tobacco in Colombia, necessarily operated more "capitalistically" than producers of locally consumed staples.

Assuming that one can distinguish between capitalists and economic traditionalists, it is still questionable that the cleavage correlates with party lines. Bazant sees a "union of commerce, industry, and liberal politics" in Puebla at least up to the middle of the nineteenth century. One might as easily identify a union of commerce, industry, and conservative politics, considering the proindustrial conservatism of Lucas Alamán and Esteban de Antuñano. And, as Bazant points out, even the liberals in Puebla gave only a conditional allegiance to that party. Between 1846 and 1853 a number of them evolved toward conservatism, in Bazant's view because the balance of their interests was shifting from commerce to manufacturing and thus from free-trade liberalism to conservative protectionism.[19] One gets the impression that the Puebla elite, having its eye on business, tended to be moderate or opportunistic politically.

In Colombia one finds a similarly mixed picture. In Bogotá between 1820 and 1860 most, though not quite all, men interested in manufacturing were conservatives and the export-import trade throughout the century was divided among liberals, conservatives, and men who strove to be entirely apolitical. There were a number

[19] Ibid., pp. 43–45.

of liberals who raised cattle in the traditional manner, while notable conservatives like Mariano Ospina Rodríguez played a leading role in promoting the cultivation of coffee for export.

Probably the most generally applicable statement to be made about economic categories and political affiliations in Mexico and Colombia is that capitalists could be found in either party but that they tended to hew to the center. And those who were most capitalistic, practically by definition, were those who attempted to shun any political identification and to find safety in the narrow interstices between the parties. One uncommon, but useful, way to look at the relationship of economic interests and politics is to view the truly bourgeois, the apolitical businessman, as opposed to the disruptive ideologies and ambitious politicians in both parties. For the true merchant-capitalist was disturbed less by the tenor of government policy, be it free-trade or protectionist, than by the violent upheavals, the changes in policy, the unpredictability with which politicians in both parties afflicted him. This resentment and distrust of politicians in both parties, documentable in the case of some merchants, may well have been characteristic of many landowners also.

What implications may this commentary have for the generally accepted picture of the dynamic of nineteenth-century politics? What general statements may one make? In a number of cases, most clearly in Mexico and Colombia, there was a conflict between one element that identified with colonial institutions and another that sought a new order. It seems doubtful, however, that one can identify the defenders of the colonial heritage as a landed group ("feudal" or not), the new wave as an urban capitalist one.

Conservatives did tend to be anticapitalist in some respects. Their belief in the necessity of a strong State and a strong Church (or Church-State) was such that they tended to resist, while liberals tended to promote, the alienation of the resources of either institution into private hands. Often conservatives found themselves defending mortmain, the tithe, and government monopolies, whereas liberals tended to attack these institutions as restraints on free exchange and efficient private capitalist exploitation of resources. On the other hand, it would be a mistake to characterize nineteenth-century conservatives in Mexico or Colombia as "feudal" or entirely backward-looking. Often they took the lead in creating modern capitalist institutions, particularly in the founding of banks and banking systems. Their differences with liberals tended to be not over the desirability of capitalism but over the role that State and Church might play in guiding capitalist development. Thus, while liberal movements of the era may be considered expressions of an upsurgent capitalism, they expressed only a particular version of capitalism. And they were opposed by conservatives less for their capitalist character than on other grounds (desire for order, religious piety, competition for public office).

One can say that the conservatives were an entrenched group, the liberals an emergent one. But conservative entrenchment was not localized entirely in the land; it was also represented importantly in government administration and in commerce. Nor did the liberals emerge entirely from urban areas and urban occupations; probably more of them came from landowning families in the provinces. In short, it seems much too simple to describe the conflict, at least in Mexico or Colombia, as one of *campo* versus *ciudad*.

The Venezuelan Variant

The case of Venezuela confirms at least one observation derived from Mexico and Colombia: in all three cases the opposing parties were clearly capitalist in orientation, only differing perhaps in their conceptions of the role of the state in capitalist development. Venezuela may have differed from the Mexican-Colombian pattern, however, in having a clearer demarcation between urban commercial interests and agricultural ones. (The urban interests in this case were represented by the "oligarchs" or "conservatives," and agricultural ones by the "liberals.") Further, in Venezuela as in Argentina, colonial economic institutions and privileged corporations were not principal issues, though the Spanish tradition in commercial law was a central question.

Venezuela's variations from the Mexican-Colombian pattern seem to be explainable in terms of the greater importance of the export

economy. In Venezuela an economy already markedly oriented toward export agriculture in the colonial period experienced a considerable expansion of coffee production in the 1830s. This development
appears to have contributed to the rapid removal of colonial economic institutions and the substitution of liberal capitalist ones. In
order to encourage the investment of foreign as well as domestic
capital, the Venezuelan oligarchy in 1834 instituted a freedom-of-
contract law, freeing interest rates, as similar laws did also at the
time in Mexico and Colombia. More importantly, the Venezuelan
establishment carried liberal capitalism further by removing colonial
constraints upon the auction of debtors' property and strengthening
judicial mechanisms for the collection of debts. Encouraged by such
measures as well as by the seemingly sunny prospects of the coffee
economy, British and Venezuelan interests established banks in
Caracas. The commercial laws and the privileged Venezuelan bank
provoked opposition from some planters, particularly during the
1840s, when a declining coffee market caught those who had borrowed to expand. Formally organized in an agricultural society, some
planters joined an emerging liberal party in attacking the oligarchy
for favoring the urban moneylending interests. The liberal-planter
alliance called for a return to colonial restraints on interest rates and
debt collection as well as for government low-interest loans to planters. Thus the "conservatives" in this case were economic liberals, the
"liberals" paternalists. The alliance between coffee planters and liberals did not outlast the 1840s, collapsing as soon as the offending
laws were expunged.[20] Nevertheless, the Venezuelan case suggests
that in countries most nearly affected by the vicissitudes of the export
economy, upper-class cleavages along lines of economic occupation or
roles (capital versus producer) may have been more evident than in
those, like Colombia or Mexico, whose economies still had a more
interior-focused, autarchic character.

Venezuela's export economy, by stimulating intensive capital in-

[20] Butler, in "The Origins of the Liberal Party in Venezuela," provides an orderly
description of the role of economic issues and interests in Venezuelan party divisions to 1848.

vestment in the land, may have produced a greater specialization of function among the upper classes than occurred in the more static, inward-turning economies. There is some evidence in Venezuela, however, of the kind of interpretation of urban and rural interests that Bazant describes for Mexico and I find in Colombia. It is conceivable that any tendency toward specialization was opposed by a counter-tendency to merchant investment in land, as occurred in both Mexico and Colombia. If such merchant investment represented the absorption of old planter land by urban creditors, however, this would be a fundamental factor in the evident merchant-planter tensions of the 1840s.

REGIONALISM
Regional Economic Interests

For many countries regional differences seem to be more relevant to political alignments than divisions among occupational groups. The two approaches, of course, are not mutually exclusive. Even where class or occupational divisions may have utility, they are used most accurately with reference to specific regions.[21]

As Joseph Love shows in his discussion of region in this volume, there are many different ways of approaching the subject. Economic approaches to regional conflict are probably the best known and most commonly used. One influential version of this approach is Miron Burgin's pioneering account of the conflicts among domestic producers in the Argentine interior, merchants in Buenos Aires, and diverse competing interests in the coastal region.[22] Harry Bernstein,

[21] In one of the best brief descriptions of the alignments of social groups in Mexico, for example, François Chevalier has deftly depicted a conservative coalition of Church hierarchy, professional military, and large proprietors, with strength primarily in the central plateau and the cities of Puebla, Querétaro and Guadalajara, and liberal forces on the periphery, composed of local caciques, professionals, merchants in the port cities and small towns, mestizo artisans and petite bourgeoisie in general, and all classes in the northern mining and ranching area ("Conservateurs et libéraux au Mexique: Essai de sociologie et géographie politiques de l'Indépendance à l'intervention française," *Cahiers d'Histoire Mondiale* 8 [1964]: 457–474).

[22] Miron Burgin, *Economic Aspects of Argentine Federalism, 1820–1852* (Cambridge: Harvard University Press, 1946).

among others, has applied a variant of Burgin's analysis to Mexico, emphasizing the conflict between the established Mexico City–Puebla–Vera Cruz axis and the rising new areas on the periphery.[23]

Regional economic conflict may provide a key to political differences in many cases. But the approach requires some refinement. In the first place, there is a tendency to think of regions or localities as behaving in a solidary manner. This tendency to view regions as undivided units leads to unnecessary obfuscation. For within most regions and even within many if not most localities, there are marked divisions.

The political importance of regional economic interests varies a good deal depending upon the geographies and economic structures of particular countries. The analyses of Burgin and Bernstein view economic differences in terms of directly conflicting economic interests (e.g., manufacturers versus importers) or in terms of similar but competing ones (competing commercial centers). This approach may be appropriate to nineteenth-century Argentina, whose geographical structure was conducive to a degree of national economic integration. In such a case, there might be relatively clear perceptions of conflicting or competing interests. In many other countries, however, the geographical-economic structure was much more diffuse. In much of Spanish America the combination of mountainous topography, poor roads, and tropical climate encouraged the persistence of more or less autonomous local economies, with almost all foods consumed being produced within a few miles of any particular municipal market. Such a lack of national economic integration was particularly evident in Colombia, which was divided into three or four regional economic agglomerations, each of which in turn included many substantially autonomous subregional economies. Peru, with its many economic pockets in the cordillera and its export enclaves strung along the coast, was in different ways economically invertebrate. Mexico, though with much more of a focus on the capital, also had many substantial regions that were not integrated into a national market.

23 Harry Bernstein, *Modern and Contemporary Latin America* (New York: J. B. Lippincott, 1952), particularly pp. 61–63.

In such unintegrated countries, even where potentially conflicting or competitive interests may be detected, they often have little political importance. There could not be much zeal to defend national manufacturing against commercial interests if manufacturers had no national market to defend. Nor were commercial centers likely to become galvanized into aggressive competition with only unsubstantial markets to vie for.

In the unintegrated countries perhaps the main object of regional economic interest would be the area's share of the national budget, in particular its share of funds for communications development. But in the first two-thirds of the nineteenth century a number of factors tended to reduce interest in the national budget. Ineffective revenue collection and the cost of supporting the military limited disposable government funds. Liberal ideology in the period further tended to limit the importance of the national budget. Internal improvements insofar as possible were handed to private enterprise. And in some cases, federalist influences also constricted the role of the central government.

Colombia's nineteenth-century history illustrates the thesis that the degree of economic integration, along with the national government's changing role in development, had an important effect in determining whether regional economic interests were reflected in political alignments. There are a few salient examples of competitive economic interests in pre-1870 Colombia—that is, of two regions vying to obtain the same ends—but their political consequences are not evident. After 1870, however, as projects to connect the highlands with the Magdalena River took the form of railroads and as the national government's role as guarantor of profits to railroad builders became critical, the stakes became higher. In the 1870s, coastal opposition to a major railroad project benefiting the interior (Ferrocarril del Norte) was translated into political division within the liberal party. Further fractures occurred among politicians of the interior who favored competing railroad routes from the highlands to the Magdalena River. Ultimately these divisions played a part in the downfall of the liberal party at the end of the 1870s and the emergence of a new coalition headed by Rafael Núñez.[24] The railroad-inspired cleavages of these years, however, provide another sort of confirmation of the point that regional economic conflicts are less likely to occur in unintegrated economies. The disputes of the 1870s occurred precisely because the country was moving toward economic integration and the national government's role in development was much more prominent.

It would appear, therefore, that the analysis of competing regional economic interests is likely to be fruitful primarily in those cases in which economic integration enlivens economic interests and in which the central government's power is of significance for local development.

Applying Dependency Theory to Politics

Regarding regional economic interests, one must consider the possibility of applying dependency theory to the analysis of developing political alignments. As elaborated by Andre Gunder Frank and others, dependency theory views as the principal feature of socioeconomic organization a chain of capitalist domination stretching from the metropolis (Western Europe for most of Latin America in the nineteenth century) through Latin American national economic centers to the economic peripheries (provincial towns, villages, etc.).[25] In some cases the dependency conception may highlight sources of political conflict within the upper class. Tensions between the national and provincial links in the economic chain may underlie the political drama in Argentina or Venezuela before 1850. But dependency theory does not everywhere provide the key to upper-class political divisions. In most cases the dependency relationship either failed to divide the economically dependent region from the center or actually served to strengthen interregional ties among the upper class.

For example, between 1820 and 1870 many in Bogotá's upper

24 Helen V. Delpar, "The Liberal Party of Colombia, 1863–1903" (Ph.D. dissertation, Columbia University, 1967), p. 290.
25 Andre Gunder Frank, *Capitalism and Underdevelopment in Latin America: Historical Studies of Chile and Brazil* (New York: Monthly Review Press, 1969).

class depended upon merchant-capitalists in Antioquia for the extension of loans. Most of the borrowers in Bogotá and the capitalists in Medellín were identified with political conservatism. Either the credit relationship between the two tended to strengthen their political alliance, or the tensions that may have risen between creditor and debtor had no appreciable effect upon the policies of the two groups. In general, dependency relations seem to have united rather than divided upper-class groups of different regions. This is demonstrated dramatically in the relationship between Bogotá, a center for distributing imported goods, predominantly conservative until the 1850s, and the province of Socorro, a weaving region that was overwhelmingly liberal. In the 1830s the Bogotá government attempted to provide moderate protection for the traditional home weavers of the Socorro region as well as for more modern factories attempted by upper-class entrepreneurs in the capital. During the 1840s, however, it became clear to both liberal and conservative members of the Colombian elite that neither form of manufacture was profitable to them, and in 1847 tariffs were lowered decisively. Hypothetically, one might have expected political resistance to this measure from the weaving province of Socorro. This did not occur, however, because the local elites in Socorro province formed part of a network extending from the metropolis to the national submetropolis in Bogotá to the provincial periphery. By the 1840s Socorro textiles had so declined under the pressure of foreign imports that the local upper class had less interest in protecting and promoting the local industry than in vending imported goods. Textile weavers were encouraged to devote themselves to the manufacture of palm-leaf hats, which could be exported and were not competitive with any important imported goods. Thus, the political leaders of the weaving region, rather than defending immediate local lower-class industry, took the lead in undermining or, at any rate, diverting it. Florentino González, the man whose name is most associated with the abandonment of moderate protection in Colombia, was born in and often represented the region, though by the time of the 1847 tariff he was a Bogotá merchant who had traveled to Paris and London. Later, in the 1850s, some of the leading merchant-politicians of the

Socorro-San Gil area collaborated with Bogotá wholesalers in the further demise of local looms by sending locally woven textiles to England for replication and importation into the Socorro market.[26] The tariff question never divided the upper class either along regional or along party lines, for, irrespective of the effect of the export-import trade on the lower classes, it bound the upper class together in a common interest.

As the upper classes of all areas collaborated in fostering the export-import trade, dependency analysis is of little use in understanding the creation of the country's two traditionally antagonistic parties. Yet upper-class administration of free trade to the hapless lower classes does permit one application of dependency analysis to the politics of nineteenth-century Colombia. The division, however, is not between center and periphery as *regions* but between commercial and artisan classes. The study of this class conflict, while highly interesting per se does not tell us much about the development of liberal-conservative alignments. The opposition between upper- and lower-class interests did find political expression in the alienation of Bogotá artisans after 1847, their support for the liberals in 1849, their temporary seizure of power in 1854 after continued liberal betrayal, and their continued political alienation from the dominant liberal regime through much of the period to 1880. But the conflict between the upper class and the artisans that emerged at the end of the 1840s had nothing to do with the division between liberals and conservatives that developed during the 1830s and was confirmed in the early 1840s. The artisans played a role in politics, sometimes a critical one, as in 1849. But for both parties they were a manipulated element. They did not provide the primary base for nor stimulate the creation of either party. During the twentieth century urban workers have tended to be identified with the liberal party. But at the end of the nineteenth century this identification had by no means been established: in the 1880s urban workers were appealed to by, and appear to have supported, the Nuñista-conservative regimes.

[26] Francisco Vargas, Bogotá, to Hermógenes Vargas, June 17, 1866, in Francisco Vargas y Hermanos Papers (in possession of Pedro Vargas, Bogotá).

Social Aspects of Regionalism

Aside from plotting regional economic interests, one may consider a variety of broader, more diffuse approaches, which focus on cultural variables or relate economic to social patterns. These broader approaches often present problems of verification, however; some of the social variables with which one may be concerned may not be easily measurable quantitatively—and may even be hard to document concretely in other ways. In discussions of cultural and institutional qualities, unsupported subjective judgments tend to be common coin. For example, towns with an aristocratic social climate tended to be conservative, those that were less aristocratic, liberal. But defining or measuring aristocratic tendencies is problematic.

Other aspects of cultural patterns, including racial differences, present similar problems. In most cases it is hard to tell whether racial or ethnic antagonisms, no matter how violently expressed, played primary causal roles in the development of political alignments or were more of a secondary reinforcing nature. In Argentina the famous mutual hostility between urban elites and caudillo-led gauchos reflected a fundamental cultural division that may have lain at the root of political alignments. Or the enmity may have been nourished carefully as an arm of combat for another cause. In Colombia upper-class *bogotanos* occasionally expressed fear of the *negros caucanos* as well as distaste for their darker compatriots on the Caribbean coast. But these sentiments did not determine party affiliations; they simply gave a fillip to political commitments already made on other grounds.

Such interregional racial or cultural tensions were unlikely to have much bearing on elite political allegiances because of the homogeneity of the upper sector in most Spanish American countries. While there might be considerable cultural or racial differentiation among the lower classes, the upper sectors for the most part were homogeneous racially and educationally, as well as in patterns of consumption and fundamental social assumptions. Political contenders among the upper sectors were quite aware that their real opponents in other regions were other members of the same sector, not the *populacho* that members of the elite might have mobilized in their respective regions. On all sides, then, racial and cultural questions were for the political elites an instrumental matter. By the same token, of course, political foot soldiers were often led to perceive political conflicts in terms of racial or ethnic divisions.

To suggest that regional ethnic differences were of minor importance to political elites is not to argue that the elites were unaffected by regional attachments. Most members of the elite depended on their native provinces as power bases. Politicians of particular regions naturally formed blocs, which were riven by internal rivalry but which also expressed some regional solidarity. There was a tendency for governments to be dominated by regional cliques, with politicians from excluded regions forming alliances to fight their way into power.

The question is whether these alliances were purely the fruits of opportunism or in some way expressed affinities rooted in the regions' social and economic structures. The evidences for mere opportunism is strong. But, in the interest of finding patterns in history, it is worth exploring various approaches to rationalizing political alliances among regions.

One might look to the character of the labor force as an element affecting elite politics. Where the labor force is docile and easily manipulated, the regional elite is likely to be seigneurial in social style and conservative in politics. The Indianoid peasant regions of central Mexico and the Colombian and Ecuadorian highlands, as well as the slave-based societies of Popayán and Cartagena, provide examples of this pattern. Where the labor force became politically mobilized, the elite may have been forced to become liberal in posture and rhetoric in order not to lose control. This schema would apply not only to the small holders of Socorro, already mobilized to some degree from the Comunero rebellion onward, but also to the former slaves of the Cali area, who became mobilized at the time of abolition and the liberal revolution of 1850. This approach might help to explain the conservatism of Antioquia, so puzzling from other points of view. Lower-class *antioqueños* remained politically immobilized, gripped by the fact and the myth of economic opportunity. The extraordinary religious piety of Antioquia may be seen as both a reflection of and an operative agent in this lack of political mobilization. While this approach is suggestive, like other social variables it presents problems of measurement.

SOCIAL LOCATION

The approach to the socioeconomic analysis of political alignments that I most favor looks at the relationship of individuals or regions to certain structures of economic, social, and political power as they existed at the end of the colonial period and the beginning of the republican one. This approach does not dismiss questions of individual or regional economic interest, but it looks at these in a somewhat different way than economic interpretations often do. The important question in such an approach is not an individual's occupation or a region's economic activity, but rather the access of individual and region to structures of power. Regarding the behavior of individuals, it assumes that social origins are more predictive of political attachments than social arrivals. It is therefore not the adult occupation that counts but formative factors such as family position, family relations, and access to education. The approach differs from regional analyses as they are sometimes performed in suggesting that it is not so much where an individual is from, territorially, that matters, but what that fact may imply about his relationship to dominant institutions. One is concerned, then, less about his physical location than about his social location. It is a class analysis in the Weberian sense of class as a definition of life chances. Those in the elite whose close early relationships to the structures of power gave them strategic advantages at the beginning of the republican epoch were likely to end up being termed "conservative"; those who stood at a greater distance were likely to become "liberal."

The approach that I am suggesting here involves discovering power centers in the society at the end of the colonial period and determining the relationships of individuals, groups, or regions to those centers. One may look at dominant power-holding institutions, such as the Church establishment or the civil bureaucracy. With this institutional approach should be integrated, however, the study of nodes of economic power, which may well not coincide with the formal institutional structures. One must deal with both economic and institutional power for the obvious reason that members of the upper class, in proportions varying with the individual, were concerned about both. Dependency theory, with its concern for the monopolization of power, is of some utility in this approach. It should be understood, however, that center and periphery in the context of this analysis refer to more than economic power.

The institutional aspects of this analysis are perhaps evident. Church hierarchies, for example, have long been recognized as the backbone of conservatism. There are also obvious family continuities between late colonial administrators and the first generations of conservative republican leaders.[27] But this type of analysis, emphasizing the relationship of individuals, families, and even regions to institutional structures, may be extended further. It is not merely a question of the Church hierarchy itself, but also of the families and clients of higher ecclesiastics. Similarly, even individuals who were not actually related to civil or ecclesiastical officials might enjoy central locations in the power structure by virtue of residing in established colonial administrative centers, where they had relatively easy access to government jobs or the people who controlled them. Perhaps, as a result of such advantages or perceived advantages, citizens of these established administrative cities may have identified with existing centralist institutions, which perpetuated a role of importance for their community.

One aspect of this institutional analysis is worth extended comment because it has not yet been much explored: the role of educational institutions. While residents of the established administrative centers enjoyed access to power in part because of family social connections, the structure of the educational system—the obligatory formal channel for entry into the political elite—reinforced this advantage. In the more important colonial cities the presence of royal administrators, the ecclesiastical hierarchy, and wealthy merchants and property owners in the colonial period had meant that these cities were well

---

[27] Glen Dealy, "Prolegomena on the Spanish American Political Tradition," *Hispanic American Historical Review* 48, no. 1 (February 1968): 49–50.

endowed with pious funds, which supported a variety of urban institutions, most importantly secondary schools and universities. For upper-sector residents of these cities it was relatively easy to take the first steps up the ladder of power. The universities prepared youths for government jobs and other upper-class roles, at the same time providing them with school connections that reinforced already-existing family associations. By contrast, towns of less significance in the colonial era, not having university instruction readily available, had much greater difficulty preparing their sons for entrance into the uppermost ruling sector. Residents of such towns did manage to send their sons to the university, but the cost was great and the chance of successfully completing the career much less.

At least in Colombia, members of the upper class, both in the established colonial cities and in the less favored provincial ones, were well aware of the strategic importance of universities in the making of careers. Provincial towns that lacked universities at the end of the colonial period sought in the republican era the right to create institutions that could grant law degrees. At every step these efforts were resisted tenaciously not merely by authorities in the national capital but also by the rectors of the universities in the important colonial towns, Bogotá, Cartagena, Popayán. One of the key issues of Colombia's liberal revolution of 1849–1853 was centralist restriction on professional education in the provinces. The liberals chose to resolve this problem by making university degrees unnecessary for practicing professions.[28]

The political analysis of strategic positions in institutions stemming from the colonial period has been applied to the economic sphere in at least one case. Ralph Woodward maintains that tensions in and about the Consulado of Guatemala played a key role in the development of early party alignments in that country.[29] It is not clear

---

[28] The role of higher education in Colombian politics is well discussed in John Lane Young's "University Reform in New Granada, 1820–1850" (Ph.D. dissertation, Columbia University, 1970). It is also touched upon in my forthcoming study on technical education in nineteeth-century Colombia.

[29] Ralph Lee Woodward, Jr., "Economic and Social Origins of the Guatemalan Political Parties (1773–1823)," *Hispanic American Historical Review* 45, no. 4 (November 1965): 544–566.

whether or to what extent his analysis can be applied more broadly to other *consulados* or other formally privileged economic groups in the colonial era. Most of these collapsed early in the independence era (unlike that in Guatemala). But the social ties and linked economic interests embodied in these institutions may well have remained for a time after the institutions themselves disappeared.

As the action of private economic power is usually less documented than the role of formal institutions, it is harder to track. But, at least conceptually and to a substantial degree in practice, it can be treated in a common analytical framework with the traditional institutions. In the case of the economic sphere one asks to what degree regional location and family position and relations affected an individual's access to capital and to perceivable ways of using that capital. In general one may expect to find those members of the educated elite who within existing structures possessed a high degree of economic access to be either conservative or moderate liberals in political attitudes. Those who were attempting new enterprises with high profit expectations (e.g., export agriculture, international commerce, land speculation), but with limited access to credit, were more likely to be "liberal."

Study of the organization of private economic power is particularly helpful for understanding the politics of countries in which the colonial inheritance did not weigh very heavily and of those countries that in the early republican era had relatively commercialized, export-oriented economies. Most obviously this approach may be applied to Venezuela and Argentina. It also may be used profitably in understanding the political commitments of commercially developed regions within otherwise static countries.

It is quite useful, for example, in explaining the anomalous political inclinations of Colombia's *antioqueños*. With regard to formal institutions, Antioquia was on the periphery in the late colonial and early republican periods. Until late in the colonial period it was administered ecclesiastically from Popayán and Cartagena; it lacked numerous and wealthy conventual establishments; it lacked a university and, except for brief periods, even a *colegio*. One therefore would expect Antioquia to have stood with Socorro and other institutionally poor provinces on the liberal side of the Colombian political equation. In fact, however, Antioquia by about 1840 was becoming markedly conservative, and by 1850 it was the most secure bastion of Colombian conservatism.

One possible explanation is Antioquia's extraordinary economic power in the nineteenth century. By the 1820s, *antioqueños* already predominated among the country's largest merchants. During the 1830s and 1840s, they engaged in gold mining and importing, lent substantial sums in Bogotá and elsewhere, dominated transportation on the Magdalena River, and were active in practically every notable enterprise in the country.[30] Antioquia probably had less strength in the political structure than Bogotá or even Popayán—though at least three men with ties to the region were among the top administrators between 1830 and 1845 and others were very influential in and out of Congress. But whatever the *antioqueños* may have lacked in political representation, they were amply compensated for by their position as economic insiders. Antioquia's businessmen in the first half of the nineteenth century were thus the Colombian equivalent of the *estanqueros* of Portales's Chile. Throughout the nineteenth century they remained conservative, and moderate in their conservatism, because their stake in order and the security of property was greater than that of anyone else in the country. The *antioqueños,* throughout the nineteenth century as well as in the twentieth, have proven to be among the most zealous defenders of religious piety. But this can be seen, at least in part, as a function of their economic position, which made them especially devoted to a cause that they perceived as the foundation of order.

Like the *antioqueño* elite, most of Colombia's other establishment groups were not tied to conservatism by a specific economic interest of the type usually brandished in economic interpretations of politics (e.g., free trade versus protectionism). Their conservatism can be explained in economic terms only or primarily as the desire of the propertied for order. There seems to be only one significant link

---

[30] Frank Safford, "Significación de los antioqueños en el desarrollo económico colombiano," *Anuario Colombiano de Historia Social y de la Cultura* 2, no. 3 (1965): 49–69.

between conservatism and specific economic interests—Popayán's conservatives could oppose liberals not merely as agents of general institutional disruption but also as the proponents of the more rapid extinction of slavery. This specific concern of Popayán, however, was of no importance to other conservative centers like Bogotá or Tunja and of rather little even to Cartagena or Medellín.

There appear to have been, in fact, significant divisions of economic interest within conservative coalitions. For example, in Colombia and Mexico the interests of landowners and the governing political elite diverged. For many conservative landowners some notable liberal causes may have had some appeal, the attack upon Church capital for example. Many centrally located, conservative landowners presumably benefited from easy access to loans from religious orders and pious funds. But this relationship could not have been unambiguous. As the century progressed, the Church's role as moneylender became relatively less significant as compared with that of secular sources. As landowners perceived the Church to be less useful as a source of capital, those with longstanding obligations to Church organization (*censos*) could well have viewed with complacency liberal laws that permitted the redemption of *censos* on easy terms. As the usually conservative proprietors of land clustered around important cities were precisely those most likely to be burdened with clerical encumbrances, they were the principal beneficiaries of these liberal measures. Similarly, landowners of conservative hue might well have looked favorably upon the abolition of the *diezmo* (collected on agricultural production), the abolition of the government tobacco monopoly, and even the *desamortización* of Church lands.[31]

Those conservatives whose base of power was the control of government office, however, looked at these matters quite differently. The state was their economic enterprise, so that they found themselves defending precisely those fiscal and other economic institutions that landowners may have found burdensome. In this regard conservative

[31] The probable ambiguity of conservative-landowner attitudes toward Church property, the collection of tithes, etc., is suggested by Bazant in *Alienation*, pp. 11–13, and by Arnold Bauer in "The Church and Spanish American Agrarian Structure: 1765–1865," *The Americas* 28, no. 1 (July 1971): 90–96.

politicians probably did not act as surrogates for landowners. When politicians objected to the elimination or reform of colonial revenue systems on grounds of fiscal responsibility, they were not merely articulating a general conservative principle but also defending their own particular interest as officeholders.

In Colombia, then, one can view the conservative coalition as composed of several groups, whose specific interests may have diverged, but who had in common various sorts of central location. Accumulated capital put the *antioqueño* elite close to the center of power; ownership of strategically located property (close to urban markets) was an advantage for others, particularly in Bogotá; still others, and these the most evident, through residence, social relations, and education in Bogotá and Popayán, were able to move to the seats of political power. All, because of their possession of power, had a stake in the present order, of which the Church seemed to be the most reliable guarantor. Significantly, when the Church seemed to be failing as a guarantor of social order in the mid-1850s, conservatives in Bogotá and Medellín alike seriously proposed the annexation of Colombia to the United States. Better political order and effective protection of property under Protestantism than social chaos under Catholicism.

If conservatives were from families controlling certain nodes of power at the beginning of the republican era, liberals by the same token were those who began their careers at a distance from these nodes. They generally were of provincial landowning or commercial families that had no connections with colonial administration or the Church hierarchy; they grew up in towns that were not administrative centers and that offered inferior opportunities for higher education; as entrepreneurs they did not have easy access to capital; nor could they inherit lands close to the most important markets. They had to journey to the capital city for university training, often a time of struggle and isolation. Less well connected to political potentates than youths from the established centers, they usually found themselve at the margins of political power. As the existing educational and economic structures in no way favored them, but rather constricted their opportunities, their dominant passion was to destroy these institutions—whether they were centrally controlled universities, presidentially appointed governors, government tobacco monopolies, restrictions upon the interest rate, taxes upon production and trade, or Church-controlled economic resources. As some conservatives agreed with liberals on some of these issues, the latter were able toward the end of the 1840s to chip away some of these institutional restraints. As the conservative coalition was temporarily undermined and thrown into confusion, liberal politicos were able to overpower the governing or political elite sector of the conservative grouping. They then proceeded to enact the remaining parts of the program, purposefully casting down fiscal responsibility and strong government and raising in their places economic liberalism and individual enterprise. Once ensconced in power, of course, the liberal counterelite sooner or later lost their outsiders' anti-institutional attitude. But it was at the heart of party differentiation in the 1840s and 1850s.

Evidently an approach dealing with both institutional arrangements and purely economic relations is quite complex. It not only incorporates regional identity and class position but also embraces the analysis of family networks and school associations. It cannot account for all possible influences on an individual's formation—e.g., accidental social relations or ideological influences derived through chance associations. But it is a sufficiently comprehensive and complex approach as to raise questions as to how one might utilize it in a systematic manner.

It would be desirable to test these hypotheses by using such standard quantitative techniques as collective biography and roll-call analysis. Richard Sinkin already has used these techniques to study nineteenth-century Mexican political elites.[32] Unfortunately, in most countries in Spanish America, unlike Mexico, roll-call votes on many questions are not available. Further, existing biographical materials do not provide the information that is most needed for the analysis of social location. As this analysis focuses more on origins than upon

[32] Richard N. Sinkin, "The Mexican Constitutional Congress, 1856–1857: A Statistical Analysis," *Hispanic American Historical Review* 53, no. 1 (February 1973): 1–26.

arrivals, it particularly requires precise information on the social and economic position of the parents or family of the individual being studied. Most biographical sources are woefully imprecise in this regard, referring to family background in such vague and general terms as "poor but honorable" or "a modest landowner" or the like. Fortunately, Spanish America's relatively ample genealogical materials help to compensate by providing substantial information on family connections. Such information may be used systematically,[33] though it may be less usefully adaptable to the computer than material on such categories as economic occupation.

As reliable, quantifiable information bearing upon these hypotheses is insufficient or unavailable, old-fashioned intuitive analysis, based upon fragmentary data, will remain a predominant feature of historical inquiry. Even where the data permits quantification, a subjective element continues—in the choice of categories, in coders' attempts to relate ambiguous data to fixed categories, and in the interpretations that must be made of the correlations that finally issue from the computer. While subjective error cannot be avoided entirely, it may be partially corrected and checked if the researcher is steeped in the raw materials of his subject in the traditional manner. With archival experience and an openness to that experience, he is likely to choose and use his categories in ways that are truer to the material. Even in the most skillful hands, moreover, computer categories necessarily strip the data of their qualitative nuances; at the end of the process these nuances must somehow be put back in. Finally, the correlations among the categories often do not point to obvious conclusions; a tactile sense of the subject may help to guide the scholar toward appropriate interpretations. For these reasons, intensive qualitative studies of the sociopolitical dynamic within key regions and of the patterns of behavior in those families for which records are available are at least as important as—indeed, are an

[33] See for example, Jacques A. Barbier, "Elite and Cadres in Bourbon Chile," *Hispanic American Historical Review* 52, no. 3 (August 1972): 416–435, and Samuel Stone, "Algunos aspectos de la distribución del poder en Costa Rica," *Revista de Ciencias Jurídicas* (Escuela de Derecho, Universidad de Costa Rica), no. 17 (June 1971).

indispensable companion of—effective quantitative analysis. Where data are sufficient to permit the use of quantitative techniques, they may serve as an auxiliary to, but hardly a replacement for, the imaginative scholar's sensitivity to the color and texture of the social fabric.

Political Power and Landownership in Nineteenth-Century Latin America

RICHARD GRAHAM

Historical works on nineteenth-century Latin America rarely question the generalization that large landowners, acting either alone or in concert with such other groups as the army and the Church, were politically dominant. It is not the purpose of this paper to argue a revisionist point of view. The reason for the longevity of this generalization, like that of many another, probably lies in the fact that there is a large degree of truth in it. Rather, what is proposed here is the need for a systematic comparative study of this allegation to elucidate variations in time and space. Such comparison will make possible the construction of hypotheses regarding two questions: what explains the differences and what was their effect? To illustrate the variations already implicit even in the conventional view, I here construct a crude typology of landed power; serious work on the hypotheses themselves must await a clearer delineation of different types than is now possible. Even the comparative survey, though, must

NOTE. Earlier versions of this paper were read by the other authors in this collection and by Carlos Guilherme Mota. I am grateful to all these colleagues for their useful suggestions. While writing this essay and editing this volume, I received financial support from the John Simon Guggenheim Memorial Foundation, the National Endowment for the Humanities, and the University of Texas Research Institute.

face some conceptual and methodological problems, and, after a few introductory considerations, it is to these that I will first devote attention.

One reason for the importance of such a study is that, if indeed landowners formed the dominant group in Latin America, explanations of political developments in the region must take them very much into account. Such an emphasis runs counter to a recent trend among some historians to concentrate their attention on the great masses of people rather than on the narrow layer at the top of society. This trend has gone furthest in the literature on those societies in which political leadership has already been much studied. The role of leaders in the French Revolution, for instance, has been examined by five generations of historians to the point of diminishing returns, and it is no wonder that new questions are now being raised about other sectors of the French population during those years of upheaval. One can only applaud the application of the techniques of the social historians, such as their use of police and other records that capture the day-by-day activity of common people, to the study of Latin America. But there are some basic questions that these studies too often ignore: what are the origins of the social changes they describe and what effect do these changes have on other aspects of a nation's history? Immigrants, say, are seen to rise in economic, social, or political spheres, but insufficient attention is normally paid to how this fact may or may not have changed the course of events. Although most of these historians avoid the merely antiquarian approach of being interested in the quaint eating habits of the workers as they were once fascinated by what the viceroy ate for breakfast, there is in much of the new social history a tendency to be more descriptive than explanatory. It is surprising how often even studies of historical demography or prices and wages are limited to description.

It may be granted that political leaders act in response to forces of change that sweep along the entire society and merely react to transformations taking place among the masses of people. But it is their decisions that shape, at least, the short- and medium-term course a nation will follow on such matters as tariffs, taxes, budgets, labor legislation, railroad building, land reform, and foreign relations. Although everyone makes decisions, the decisions made at the political and economic apex of society affect more people than decisions made by an equal number of people at other levels. From the point of view of the historian, then, there is a marked economy of effort in tracing the course of change by studying the behavior of those in the upper levels of the political structure. This is especially so for areas that, like Latin America, have not been thoroughly studied even by old-fashioned political historians. The verification or denial that landowners ruled Latin America, a precise notion of the variations in degree and method of such rule, and the construction and testing of hypotheses to explain these differences or to suggest their significance will be a major break-through for the understanding of that area's past.

Such a study will require, first, a precise notion of the relationship between socioeconomic position (landownership) and the exercise of political power and, second, for the comparison of one area with another, some sort of analytical frame within which their qualities can be examined.[1]

Some Marxists would say that major political decisions are always made by a "ruling class" until such time as a classless society is established. In Latin America they have often been quick to jump from this assertion to the conclusion that the landowners there formed the ruling class. Indeed, in many cases, landowners seem to have combined economic, military, and political power in a way approximating the ruling class as defined by Karl Marx and to have done so

---

[1] This part of the present essay has resulted from unsystematic reading over a period of years, and it would be unhelpful as well as tedious to recount the trajectory. Some may want to begin where I began with T. B. Bottomore's *Elites and Society* (London: Watts, 1964). Robert A. Dahl's article entitled "The Concept of Power," *Behavioral Science* 2 (July 1957): 201–215, proved valuable for the elaboration of the interest-group model discussed below, especially so when compared with his own attempt to carry it out in a pluralistic society: *Who Governs? Democracy and Power in an American City*, Yale Studies in Political Science, no. 4 (New Haven: Yale University Press, 1961). An excellent example of interest-group analysis for Latin America is Peter H. Smith's *Politics and Beef in Argentina: Patterns of Conflict and Change* (New York: Columbia University Press, 1969).

with obvious (although perhaps seriously misleading) similarities to what he considered to be the structure of feudal society.

One problem with this approach, as has so often been pointed out by others, is that the theory tends to be substituted for the evidence, leading to a certain circularity: The basis for the premise that the ownership of property was the key to power is the political dominance of landowners, but the primary evidence presented so far for this dominance has been their ownership of property. "They had economic power; so they *must* have had political power." Furthermore, although it may well be, as we have hinted above, that landowners did rule Latin America, it may not be that they did so *because* they owned the land. Such a conclusion will require still another, and difficult, verificatory step. In any case, no adequate methodology has emerged to facilitate the historian's task.

Another reason why a class analysis is difficult to adopt as a conceptual framework for a study of landed power in nineteenth-century Latin America is that the "subject classes," as some Marxists label them, were then so weak. Class conflict was at least partly submerged and concealed for most of the century and is thus not very useful as an analytical tool. This doesn't mean that the historical process does not reflect the emerging contradictions of the existing system, but, despite the effort of some historians to find the evidence of class struggle in Latin America, what seems most notable in the nineteenth century is the ability of the ruling class to dampen, cushion, and cover over the clash of class interests. Even in the twentieth century the subject classes have lagged in organizing themselves, in becoming politically or socially self-conscious, and in thus creating the basis for a struggle against the ruling class. When struggle did occur it is not easy to assert with any confidence that the challenging forces represented a class in the Marxist sense of the word. Presumably, a class would include and be limited to those persons who had the same function in the productive process, the same source of income— wages, profit, or interest—and the same relationship to other persons involved in the economy. Even if we consider the possible existence of "transition classes," "mixed classes," or those outside the productive system, it is hard to see the usefulness of a class-conflict scheme in breaking nineteenth-century Latin American reality down to meaningful units. The capitalist—be he landowner, industrialist, merchant, or all three in one—was often also a bureaucrat, a doctor, a lawyer, or a politician. The peon, the slave, and the industrial worker were only minor actors despite their numbers. The process of change is thus flattened out, and social reality remains undifferentiated. As a conceptual scheme, class analysis does not appear as useful as we might have hoped in sharply defining the subject of our study.

To avoid establishing an a priori link between socioeconomic class and political power, one could rely instead upon the concept of a "political elite," and then attempt to establish, without prejudgment, whether or not there was a link between it and the landowners. But to this course there are also objections.

It is not by accident that the term *political elite* may be contrasted with *ruling class*, for elite theory grew up at the turn of the century as an anti-Marxist effort. It was used at first to suggest that a classless society was a pipe dream, since all societies were and would always be ruled by an elite (a point that is irrelevant to our discussion) and that the basis of the elite's power had not been the control of the means of production but the elite's inherent virtue and superiority. The term *elite* itself originally meant "chosen" and implied the possession of superior qualities. Although it is probably needless to say that the use of this word in this essay is free of any presumption of virtue, this old allegation does serve to point out the value judgments that underlie conceptual formulations. I, for instance, am critical of any system in which political leaders are responsive only to a narrow layer of society and in which the great mass of the people are left powerless, although I am skeptical that a system characterized by representative democracy can give to each individual the maximum possible control over his life. Historians undertaking a comparative venture such as the one proposed here need not share the same values, but they should know where they differ in order to avoid talking past each other.

There are serious drawbacks to the use of elite theory in our present undertaking besides its historic conservatism. First, a discussion of a political elite implies the existence of other elites—religious elites, intellectual elites, labor elites, business elites—and thus bears within it the unstated allegation that there was not a single center of power; there would have been various power circles, each with its own center. The landowners who exercised direct power and formed the political elite are thus divorced, conceptually, from the landowners who may have exercised leadership in other spheres. What we began by discarding only for the nonce—the idea that the economic elite was also a political elite—can be readopted within this conceptual scheme only if there is a complete overlap of the various elites.

This concept also has the danger of suggesting that all elites are alike with regard to their most important characteristic, that is, their relationship to the rest of society. Their power over the nonelite may be stronger or weaker, but it is on one plane; it may differ quantitatively but not qualitatively. A failure to remain in power suggests the elite's morbidity or decadence. Worse yet, elite theory presumes that an elite loses power only to another elite and that no real change occurs in the power relationship between elites and nonelites, that is, in the social structure. The student of elites as elites does not study these structures, does not attempt to define them, does not differentiate between types of structures or examine how these structures have been altered over time. The end result may well be a curiously ahistorical account. Evidently, the particular historian may transcend this conceptualization, but as long as he remains faithful to it he will be blind to these other analytical dimensions. If we consider the landowners who may have exercised direct power merely as a political elite, the rise of military officers who displaced them or even the outbreak and victory of a revolutionary movement cannot be considered an evidence of class struggle, but only as an example of the circulation of elites within the unalterable structure of elites and nonelites. We have, that is, ruled out a priori the possibility of a class analysis as surely as we had previously a priori adopted it.

There is still another difficulty, a methodological one, with the use of this concept in attempting to determine the power of landholders in nineteenth-century Latin America: how to circumscribe the elite. Surely all large landowners (however defined in terms of size of holdings) did not participate in the political process even to the minimum extent of expressing an opinion. Even if we were to establish that indeed the decision-makers were all predominantly landowners, what will we do with the great bulk of landowners who were not decision-makers? Are they thus reduced to the same level as slaves and peons as far as decision-making goes? "Elite and nonelite" is a formulation that excludes the middle. Or are the decision-makers *representatives* of the landed class? How often is it not said without evidence that so-and-so was a "spokesman" for the landowners! Even among the landowners that are politicized and conscious of their political interests, some will actually participate in making decisions, while others will simply applaud their success or deplore their failure. Thus, we have to decide whether the political elite consists of all large landowners, whether it is formed instead by the politically active group of landowners, or whether it consists only of the dominant sector within this latter group. That is, we are once again faced with the difficulty of establishing the link between the political elite and a socioeconomic class.

A facile way to resolve this problem would be simply to define the political elite arbitrarily as those who occupy given political positions. There are two objections to this method, one minor and one major. The minor one is that it is difficult to establish comparability among officeholders. Were the members of Congress in Argentina in 1900 truly comparable to their contemporaries in Mexico, not to mention Nicaragua, or to their thirty-two predecessors at the Congress of Tucumán? It is hard to compare the Council of State in imperial Brazil, a life-term body of elder statesmen named by the king, without whose approval few measures could become law, with any group among the contemporary republics of Latin America.

The second and more significant objection is that to define the political elite in this way implies that the holders of political office made the key political decisions. It seems doubtful, though, in the light of what we know about human behavior, that it is always or even generally so. Are political officeholders a political elite or merely the creatures or representatives of the political elite? Establishing and describing this connection will be virtually impossible. Thus, from a methodological point of view as well as for conceptual reasons, it seems best to discard the political-elite model altogether.

An interest-group model provides still a third possible conceptual framework for a comparative study of landowners' power. Although it too presents problems, they are fewer than those encountered in the previous two and can often be circumvented. Furthermore, it has methodological advantages that outweigh its conceptual defects.

The point of view here is entirely reversed. Up to now we have been considering the problem from what might be called an internal perspective. We have assumed that certain people made decisions, and we wanted to find out who these decision-makers were and what the linkage was between them and the socioeconomic class of landowners. From an external point of view, however, we can instead limit our inquiry to just two matters: what do the landed, as opposed to other interest groups, want, and do they get it?

Society is here conceived as containing a variety of interest groups. For our purposes, an interest group may be said to consist of a number of individuals who express common desires regarding the outcome of a series of political decisions. An interest group could conceivably constitute a class or part of a class in the Marxist sense. A class analysis of interest-group behavior is perfectly possible but need not be assumed at the outset. As practiced so far, interest-group theory has had a much narrower focus, but it need not be so in the future. Interest groups may increase their ability to get what they want, or their success may lessen over time. With the alteration of the social structure they may even cease to make demands altogether and disappear as interest groups. Some groups may articulate their interests more clearly than others, some may be unable to successfully differentiate themselves and become self-conscious, and some may make temporary alliances with erstwhile rivals. Some may be formed by a small number of individuals, while others include a mass of people. Unlike the political elitists, we here assume that indeed there is a single center of power, but we consider it a black box into which we cannot see: groups place demands into it, and out of it come decisions that comply with or ignore those demands, but no effort need be made to know exactly what goes on in the box. An interest group is not a pressure group; the latter would be consciously organized for the purpose of working within the black box, and we are limiting our attention to those outside it who express a common desire for a result; at one extreme they may be unconscious of their commonality, while at another they may actually play a decision-making role. We presume that conflicting demands are presented to the political system by interest groups and that an effective measurement of the power of each group is their success or failure to win what they seek.

There are serious conceptual difficulties with this approach, but, in order to make them clear and evaluate their significance, it is preferable to consider first the method that would follow from such a conceptual scheme. To maintain that landowners were politically dominant in nineteenth-century Latin America we would have to show that (*a*) on a sizable number of issues they wanted something that other groups in society did not want, and (*b*) on a large proportion of these key political decisions the landowners got their way.

The first step will be to identify key political decisions. They may simply be defined as those governmental decisions over which there was some disagreement. Such a methodologically inspired definition rules out decisions (or nondecisions) on questions about which almost all groups were in agreement, such as the maintenance of the Church-State connection during most of the colonial period. It also eliminates from consideration those questions that, although vital to the land-owning class, were of no importance to other groups. There is no way of establishing the power of landowners (or any other group) to make a decision unless someone was opposed to it. For instance, it is impossible to argue that Brazilian landowners were powerful in the mid-eighteenth century by using as evidence the maintenance of the slave trade, since that trade was not under attack from any quarter. But once opposition to the slave trade began to grow within and without Brazil, one could safely assert that a key political decision was being made each time the issue came up. When, finally, the slave trade was ended, the historian can properly conclude that someone suffered a setback. Either the landed class was now weaker than it had been, or it had divided and the more powerful segment, for whatever reason (possibly to avoid British intervention) now preferred to end the slave trade. Similarly, since few nineteenth-century Argentines opposed dependence of the country on the cattle industry, the use of this issue for the measurement of landowners' power becomes possible only for the twentieth century. I will later return to some objections that may be raised to this definition of key political decisions.

From these examples we can also draw the conclusion that a study of the political power of interest groups demands the examination of a *series* of political decisions dealing with many issues in several areas of political activity. If it were established, to continue with Brazilian examples, that certain groups opposed slavery and that landowners supported it and that slavery was eventually abolished, this would still not show us that landowners had lost their power. "You can't win them all," a landowner might have said. Setting a precise point at which these victories become too few to establish political predominance would be a futile exercise at this point. The judgment of the individual historian will have to be used here, as it will in deciding the relative significance of gains and losses and the greater or lesser importance of some areas of decision-making.

It is also important to determine whether various interest groups are competing within the same arena. American importers may have had much more power than Hispano-Cuban planters in determining the price of sugar, but one cannot jump from that fact to the conclusion that the Americans were politically powerful in Cuba before 1898. The mere fact of an hacendado's power over his peons does not prove his political power. Key political decisions must be made within the political sphere, although evidently the connections between it and other areas of human activity may be close. Nor is it enough to say, to take another example, that during the first half of the nineteenth century the sugar planters of northeastern Brazil became weaker as the coffee planters of the Paraíba Valley became stronger, unless the scope of their decision-making is specified as being a national one. Surely in local politics the power of the northeasterners remained about the same as before, and the life of the humble *morador* in the Northeast, insofar as it changed at all, changed because of decisions made in Europe or the Caribbean and not because of the rise to political power of southern planters. Similarly, when one asserts that during the last twenty years of the nineteenth century Brazilian military officers increased their power at the expense of the landowners, one must do so by pointing to decisions of equivalent scope—elections or budgets—and not to questions of momentary interest that were not raised before or afterward, such as the right of officers to criticize the government.

Once the key political decisions have been enumerated, the next step is to determine what landowners wanted. But, it will be objected, landowners are not always in agreement with each other. What may benefit cattle raisers may damage sugar planters, and even the latter may disagree as to what measures will benefit their interests. Some landowners will ally themselves with other groups against their presumed fellows. This does not mean that landowners are not politically dominant; it only makes it harder to devise tests for that power. That is, it is not necessary to insist that power-holders must form a cohesive body. In fact, the more powerful they are, the more likely it is that they will feel free to disagree among themselves. In the latter case, one might either find one group of landowners regularly winning these decisions or find it splitting victories more or less evenly with another group. Finally, one may find that the positions of two groups, say landowners and foreign merchants, are consistently identical. The two groups may then be considered one, since their interests are the same. One real advantage of the interest-group approach is its flexibility: the historian is not locked into his initial premise that landowners ruled Latin America, but may refine, modify, or reject the hypothesis as he goes along.

There is also the problem of the silent majority of landowners. How do we know what their interests were if they were not stated? There is only one viable solution: if they did not express an interest, we define them as not constituting an interest group. An interest is always an expressed interest. Those who did not express an interest cease to be important for our study. The corollary of this statement is that it is unimportant to determine whether those who expressed preferences were only acting as agents for a smaller group that in reality decided the preferences to be advocated. There is no conceivable way of differentiating between *los que mandan* and those who speak out. If journalists, publicists, and professional politicians invariably shared expressed interests with landowners, we need not inquire whether the former were the creatures of the latter—a point usually impossible to prove—but only show that they formed part of the same interest group. Whereas the elite theorists must find the criterion by which to circumscribe their elite, within the interest-group model this is done by the historical actors themselves, albeit unconsciously. The historian need not posit a common set of values, a particular social status, or even a certain economic position; all he need do is find a commonality of demands. An interest group thus consists of those individuals who *expressed* the same interests and is not defined according to what interests the historian thinks they would or should have had.

Eventually he will want to describe the group with some precision. An interest-group approach will not require the analyst to rule out from consideration those landowners who were also industrialists and merchants. What the historian must do—and this is no small task—is attempt to know who and what those who expressed an interest were. If all of them have multiple roles, he will have to change the initial hypothesis: it is not landowners who ruled Latin America, but landowner-miner-industrialist-merchants. If only some had multiple roles, then one has to decide whether, in expressing a political preference, they were acting more in concert with other landowners than with other industrialists or merchants or miners. Finally, it does not matter whether or not they were absentee landlords who mingled with urban groups unless it is found that these landowners had interests distinct from those of the others.

It will be easier to pursue this method for some countries than for others. In Chile and Argentina, for instance, the landowners spoke through an organized lobby as well as individually. In other countries they were disorganized or, perhaps, so well organized in informal ways that no formal organizations were needed to speak for them or settle disputes among them. The former case will facilitate the study but will still require the examination of those who opposed the lobby to see whether they too were not large landowners. It could be

that the lobby represented the interests of a losing faction of landowners against the dominant faction occupying government positions.
In both cases, the full variety of historical sources must be drawn
upon, since positions taken in parliament or the press may be contradicted by those expressed in private even by the same persons and
much more so by members of the same group. Each country will also
differ in the amount of landholding used to define a large landowner.
But the principal difficulty that will be encountered in all Latin
America will be to discover whether or not those expressing desires
were indeed landowners and to discover the extent of regional or
economic diversification of their landownership.

Finally the question arises: Did the landowners get what they
wanted? By making this question central, one avoids the danger of
confusing potential power with real power. To return to our earlier
example of the slave trade to Brazil, it is clear that the British had
the necessary resources and could have put a complete stop to the trade
long before it ended by permanently occupying all the ports of Brazil
and by vastly increasing their slaving fleet so as to patrol the entire
coast. But they did not do this, and the slave trade flourished. Thus
for two and a half decades the British did not check the landowners,
even though they could have done so. The same distinction should be
kept in mind when discussing the power of the military in civilian-
run governments: they sometimes interfered in politics and got their
way, and they could have done this much more often. But they did
not do it all the time, and their great *potential* power cannot be used
as evidence of little power among landowners if the latter were victorious most of the time.

Victory may easily be confused with failure. Since to complain is a
universal failing, the victors may act and even feel as if they were
losers. Clashing interests may result in compromise, log-rolling, mid-
dle-term solutions, and only partial victories; both groups in conflict
may be more aware of what they lost than of what they gained. The
historian must weigh these propensities in drawing a conclusion.

In short, to resolve the question of how one establishes a connection between men of landed wealth and political decisions, one has
to find issues upon which men of landed wealth took positions op-

posed to those taken by others. Then, if the decisions were consistently made in their behalf, we may assert that they formed a politically
dominant group even if we cannot show by what process they influenced those decisions. It is not through a problematical chain of
influence that one will trace the power of the landowners, but through
the results of a series of decisions.[2]

The only way of testing the reality of a group's power is within
the context of conflict, confrontation, opposition, division, or variety
of preference. It is useless to protest that the resulting picture may
ignore powerful but silent groups. It is impossible to know what someone wanted if he did not express a preference. When the power of
landowners was most complete it cannot be measured or verified,
although evidently its real existence at moments of lesser strength
may be considered evidence of its existence at other times. Still, if no
key political decisions were made between, say, 1850 and 1880, we
should be cautious in drawing conclusions as to the extent of the
landowners' political power during that intervening period.

It is also true that, by defining our problem the way we have, we
have deliberately turned our back on many related questions of real
interest. For instance, we are not here concerned with the process
through which the power-holders come to that position. Only at a later
stage would it be possible to ask whether there is a steady renovation
of the landowning–power-holding group. We have also ignored two
questions that will always attract attention: did the landowners get
what they wanted *because* of their economic power, and were certain
decisions made *because* the landowners wanted them? These are
questions only a different methodology can resolve.

The major conceptual objection to this method is the presumption
that landowners as landowners will have interests in common, will

---

2 Officeholders now cease to be important, or, rather, are important only insofar
as they form a separate interest group. Some societies, such as that of Mandarin
China, are often described as being bureaucratic empires. A Brazilian author, Ray-
mundo Faoro, in his book *Os donos do poder: Formação do patronato político
brasileiro* (Pôrto Alegre: Globo, 1958) has alleged that in Brazil real power has
always been held by the bureaucratic corporation as against landowners. But he
fails to show that the bureaucrats were not also landowners.

recognize and express them, and will join together to secure them—
and that these interests will conflict with those of other groups. Is not
this presumption derived from pluralistic societies and inapplicable
to Latin America? Is it not possible, for instance, that all other groups
in Latin America were really clients of the landowners and will thus
never be found to have seriously challenged their interests? Or is it
not possible that landowners as landowners were not conscious of economic interests and that the real divisions were along family lines or
structures of personal dependence? The great political struggles may
turn out to be instances in which some merchants, miners, and industrialists side with some landowners against other merchants, miners,
industrialists, and landowners who belong either by blood, marriage,
or ritual kinship to opposing clans. That is, not all social structures are characterized by interest groups, and not all men see their
interests in economic terms. The possible role of ideology in defining
interests is also here ignored. And, finally, if a group's power cannot
be measured when it is unchallenged, does not the very power of
landowners in Latin America in the nineteenth century make this
method inadequate?

   If the observer is sensitive to these conceptual difficulties, the approach can still be used with profit. To begin with, when the method
is properly applied, if, for instance, the areas of dispute and the issues
of debate are wisely chosen, noneconomic interests will define themselves. All one seeks to establish is an alliance of desiderata. Subsequently one may assert or deny that landownership is what gave this
alliance its *raison d'être*. If family ties are predominant, the victorious
group will not consist exclusively of landowners, the initial hypothesis
regarding the power of landholders will have been seriously questioned, and the method vindicated. It may be more difficult, however,
for the historian to perceive diverging interests in a past society characterized by compromise and outward cordiality in personal relations.
That is, conflicts may be expressed in a way the historian does not
expect. It is certainly already clear that the formation of pressure
groups and organized lobbies is not the only way interests were expressed or solidarity confirmed. Differences may have been hashed

out and informal agreements arrived at without the use of public forums; but the historian's sources may give him access here even if contemporary groups were excluded. Finally, although the landowners in Latin America may have been powerful, it is difficult to believe that they ruled unchallenged and undivided for an entire century.

The labeling and grouping of those who expressed positions is both technically and conceptually the most challenging task. It is harder to define groups than interests, since the historian will, by the very nature of his role, impose categories not necessarily perceived by the actors themselves or by other historians. The very choice of issues will determine the resulting groups. The classifications into which historical actors are put (landowner, merchant; rural, urban; upper class, lower class; aristocracy, bourgeoisie; anticlerical, ultramontane; western, northeastern; Gallo family, Cavalcanti family) reflect the theory of the historian regarding the nature of human behavior. As with values, all that can be asked for is that theories be made explicit.

Another problem with this method is that, as we found with the Marxist approach, major challenges to landed power itself—as distinct from challenges to individual instances of its exercise—remain relatively scarce in Latin American history even in the twentieth century. Mexico from independence through its revolution can be considered to have experienced regular attempts, many aborted, others stillborn, some rachitic, and a few apparently successful, to challenge the power of large landowners. Who the challenging group was— whether small landowners, industrialists, landless peasants, urban middle classes, or foreign entrepreneurs—remains somewhat fuzzy in most of the literature. The elections of 1916 in Argentina and 1920 in Chile or the events in both countries in the 1890s could be considered serious challenges to a broad range of landed prerogatives. The rise of Juan Perón surely signaled a major shift of power away from Argentine landowners. The overthrow of the empire in Brazil in 1889 may eventually be seen as a blow to landed power, although the more usual date chosen for the landowners' decline is 1930, and their power remained strong at least until 1964. Only Cuba has effectively and definitively put an end to the power of private landowners, although the control of the economy by the government may be considered by some to have merely created a new class of "landowner"-bureaucrats.

Minor challenges to landed power, that is, challenges to landowners' specific desires at particular moments, seem to have been much more frequent. Perhaps here is our great opportunity. What is needed is a systematic attempt to examine these instances in as many countries as possible in order to determine more precisely how the power of the landowners fluctuated vis-à-vis other groups and how unified or disunited they were at these particular moments. Some of this work will merely call for a rereading of well-known political histories. At other times, however, original research will be necessary. In either case biographical dictionaries and other sources will have to be consulted to determine whether or not political actors were large landowners. The end result will make it possible to assert with some confidence the relative strength of the landowning group in each major country of Latin America at particular moments in their nineteenth-century histories and raise questions regarding the causes and results of any differences.

One advantage of pursuing this method is that, besides its quantitative dimensions, it places heavy emphasis on qualitative and even descriptive aspects of Latin American history without losing sight of explanatory goals. There are some cases in which a quantitative approach has been prematurely applied, since the historian often does not yet know enough about specific political decisions to be able to formulate significant quantitative questions about them. The sheer descriptive work has yet to be done, and in such circumstances the current vogue for quantitative studies threatens at times to impel historians toward the study of trivia that are easily measured and away from the essentials that are harder to marshal quantitatively. The approach I propose will tend to focus attention on political decision-making while simultaneously raising questions about the socioeconomic background. It reserves the quantitative techniques for use only on what emerge as truly significant dimensions of the political process.

A comparative study of the power of landowners in Latin America during the nineteenth century will, of course, reveal marked chronological and geographical variations. In order to suggest the hypothesis-producing possibilities of this variety, we may construct from the existing literature and out of the conventional wisdom a simplified typology of landowning power-holders as others have done with the caudillo.[3] Placing the types according to their relative apparent participation in the assumed decision-making process, we may identify at least four distinct but not mutually exclusive types, which I have named, with more attention to brevity than analysis: the Contemptuous Landowner, the Armed Landowner, the Bargaining Landowner, and the Aldermanic Landowner.

The Contemptuous Landowner did not deign to participate openly in the political process. Into the vacuum thus created stepped the ambitious caudillo, who was despised by men of landed property. The caudillo, in such cases, made up for his lack of wealth by using his cunning, his nerve, his weapons, and his charisma to win his way into the presidential palace. He relied upon the acquiescence of the landowners but not upon their active support and much less upon their respect. Either on the way up the ladder of power or after attaining its highest rung he might begin the process of acquiring the landed wealth with which his children or grandchildren could hope to buy their way into the social circle of the traditional landowners. But he could never be considered part of that circle, because its members sneered at his pretensions.

The landowners allegedly gave this kind of caudillo a free hand to run the governmental apparatus as he wished as long as he did not adopt measures that ran directly counter to their interests. They remained aloof from government, concentrating their attention on the direction of their landed estates or on the maintenance of an external class differentiation and an internal system of values from which they derived their principal satisfactions. They might privately deplore the despicable behavior of the caudillo, but they were unwilling

---

[3] Here too the literature is extensive. I especially remember the insights I derived from Merle Kling's "Towards a Theory of Power and Political Instability in Latin America," *Western Political Quarterly* 9 (1956): 21–35.

to take measures to overthrow or curtail him. A *caudillo bárbaro*, like Mariano Melgarejo in Bolivia, was not worth such effort, and the landowners considered government affairs beneath them.

It would be essential, in studying the Contemptuous Landowner, to see whether there were points at which such caudillos stepped out of bounds and, if so, whether indeed landowners then took steps to defend their interests. But only when such conflicts arose can the allegation that the caudillo dared not touch such matters be tested or proven. At some points, however, it may be that landowners specifically decried measures taken by the government, and the method we have outlined may here prove fruitful.

Next there is the case of the Armed Landowner. In this case the power of the caudillo was based on a pyramid of personal loyalties that had as its base the individual landowner commanding his peons armed with machetes. The peasants were bound to the landowner by bonds of loyalty and dependence so complete that he could command them unto death. Through a network of similar if less onerous ties the landowner owed allegiance, at least temporarily, to one of his fellows (who often owned more land), and the latter thus emerged as the political boss of the locality. Through similarly personal bonds, he was tied to a regional caudillo, also a landowner, and the latter was in turn linked to a national leader. When the stability of this line of command was shaken by the rising power of a regional caudillo, the peasants of the entire country might be mobilized under the leadership of Armed Landowners to support or oppose the challenger. The victor of the encounter might then rule with relative tranquility, counting upon the loyalty of those landowners who received benefits or the fear of those who had been defeated in battle, until such a time as another rival began to sense an opportunity to present a new challenge to the ruling caudillo. By definition, the new caudillo, like the old one, would be a landowner.

As with most ideal types, it is difficult to find any particular nation that conformed to this description over any significant period of time. Mexico and Argentina during the first half of the nineteenth century often appeared to resemble this type, although in Juan Manuel de

Rosas's Argentina the peasant armed with a machete was replaced with a gaucho and his *bolas*.

To what extent does a landowning caudillo defend the interests of landowners? Is he the representative of a class? According to the method we have indicated, this hypothesis can be tested only if there was opposition. It may be that he spoke for them entirely, but we cannot know this with certainty unless for any given policy there was also a contrary position defended by nonlandowners. Since this type of landed power almost presumes that contrary interests are weak if not nonexistent, the possibilities of the method may be exploited more effectively in measuring the relative strength of differing groups of landowners. Are there measures that were supported by coffee planters and opposed by the owners of sugar mills? Did cattle raisers oppose wheat farmers? Only by examining a series of decisions can this be determined. In effect, Miron Burgin did this for Argentina in the earlier part of the nineteenth century, although his conclusions need to be tested within a more systematic scheme.[4]

A third type is that of the Bargaining Landowner. His role became necessary when the caudillo emerged not from the land but from the army barracks. In principle, a formal structure of power, rather than personal loyalties or landed wealth, explains the leader's rise. But the landowners are not indifferent to his activity; they may even exercise their option to marshal military might of their own to overthrow or checkmate the power of the military leader. This seems to have been the process at work in Brazil, for instance, in 1894.

To what extent was the power of the landowners lessened by the occurrence of *cuartelazos*? The answer will depend on whether the army wanted programs to which the landowners were opposed, and, in general, the research has not yet been done with that question in mind. If there was no difference in what they wanted or if the scope of their interests did not conflict, then we may conclude that the power of landowners remained unchecked by army activity. If, on the

[4] Miron Burgin, *The Economic Aspects of Argentine Federalism, 1820–1852*, Harvard Economic Studies, no. 78 (Cambridge: Harvard University Press, 1946).

contrary, there were clashes, we will then have the means to measure their relative power.[5]

Still another type I have called the Aldermanic Landowner, remembering that the political units discussed here were no more populous than a modern city or an ancient shire. These landowners relied upon an apparent parliamentary democracy, in which they actively participated, to adjudicate internal differences among themselves and to preserve the legitimacy of their power in the eyes of defeated factions or of other groups. Elections were held with regularity, and the top officeholders succeeded each other with decorum. The same network of relationships used by the Armed Landowner to mobilize the peasants militarily could here be used instead to produce electoral victories: just as the number of peasants commanded (given limited military technology) gave the advantage to one Armed Landowner over another, so in the case of the Aldermanic Landowner, it was the numbers he commanded into the voting places that determined the victor. The military power of the landowners could thus remain more threat than actuality. Chile after the reign of Diego Portales may be said to come close to this type. Brazil during the Second Empire and Argentina after 1862 or 1880 are other approximations.

Again, it is only as the power of these landowners was opposed that it can be tested. The apogee of their power can only be suggested by the slant of the graph that depicts its decline. In Brazil in 1889 and in Chile and Argentina in 1890, overt political developments may already have reflected initial challenges. For the Aldermanic Landowner, as for the Armed Landowner, it may be that disputes did not revolve around "real issues" but only mirrored the struggles of great family clans or systems of personal loyalty. In any case an assessment of their power and the nature of their ties will depend upon a systematic study of those cases in which conflicting interests were expressed.

Finally, there are the hybrid types. Thus Brazil during the First

---

[5] It is to cover such cases that the army is often included in the triumvirate of power along with the landowners and the Church. The alleged power of the Church would have to be tested in the same way as that of other groups.

Republic, from 1894 to 1930 (and, if the truth be known, probably also during the Second Empire), was characterized by armed struggle at the local level in order to determine the local caudillo, while a parliamentary façade was used at higher levels to settle conflicts between regions. These could normally be bargained in the back rooms of state and national capitols. This system of *coronelismo* and the *política dos governadores* has already become a commonplace in Brazilian historiography and needs to be compared to that in other societies to determine in what way the Brazilian experience was different, why was this so, and what were the results of these differences. Another hybrid would combine the Contemptuous Landowner and the Bargaining Landowner. Perhaps Mexico at the apogee of the Porfiriato would show signs of such a mixture of ideal types.

It should be clear by now that, as far as the participation of landowners in government is concerned, the continuum of types begins at the extreme in which the landowners asked only to be left alone. By definition the interests of the Contemptuous Landowner in the direct conduct of the government, as long as his interests were not threatened, would be very slight. The Armed Landowner was directly involved in local politics at all times but would leave the direction of national affairs to his representative as chosen on the field of battle. The Bargaining Landowner would fall somewhere between these two and was listed after them only to facilitate description. Aldermanic Landowners, however, regularly took a direct and personal interest in running the government. They participated actively in the legislature, filled cabinet positions, worked hard as state governors, and occupied the presidency of the republic. Of all these types, the last is the easiest to examine for expression of preference among landowners, since their struggles took place within a somewhat more "open" political system. When the landowners' power was threatened by other groups, their active role in government may be considered a boon to the investigator.

A more sophisticated typology will emerge from a systematic and concerted comparative study. At the very least, instead of ranging the types according to active participation in governmental affairs, they will be ordered with reference to the success of landowners in getting what they wanted. For the time being, however, we may consider some questions that may be posed even within this limited scheme.

The explanation for the differences in type will require answers to several interesting questions. Was there any connection between the monopoly of landownership and the type of landed power? Did the presence of Armed Landowners depend upon the existence of a docile mass of peasants? Were they always found together? Was such a mass more common in areas of ancient Indian civilizations than elsewhere? Was there a correlation between the increasing means of rapid transportation or communication and the decline of the Contemptuous Landowner as a type, or was this decline more closely related to the growth of cities or the burgeoning of an export economy? Did the increasing size of the stakes produced by prosperity impel landowners to give up internecine struggles and devise methods for fooling the rest of the population? Or does the rise of the Aldermanic Landowner rather reflect the increasing importance of challenging groups that needed to be pacified by a change in style in the struggle for power? Did the legitimacy of governmental authority, as for instance in monarchical Brazil, facilitate the rise of the Aldermanic Landowner? If so, how does one explain his power in Chile and Argentina? Were professional politicians more prevalent in Brazil than, say, in Argentina in the 1880s? If so, why? Does the use of professional politicians correlate with increasing modernization or merely reflect the adoption of better mystifying techniques? Are the variations among Aldermanic Landowners and the methods they used to control elections to be explained according to degree of economic dependence, nature of land-tenure arrangements, type of labor supply, quality of foreign models, power and self-confidence of landowners, or some other category? These are some questions that comparative study can provoke.

Similarly, from this brief survey of types one could begin to draw up hypotheses regarding the results. Cannot this exercise tell us something, for instance, about political stability and instability? We could posit that the more regularly landowners took a direct and daily interest in the affairs of government at the national level, the more stable were the resulting regimes. Or, to revert momentarily to the language of elite theorists, we could say that political stability increased in direct proportion to the degree to which the political elite was responsive to the interests of the landowners: when the landowning elite and the political elite were coterminous, stability tended to be strongest.

To this hypothesis might be added a corollary to cover the exceptions: if the landowning class participated regularly and directly in government, it was virtually impregnable as long as it remained united. In the case of Brazil it could be argued, for instance, that the rise of a new group of landowners in São Paulo during the 1880s, impatient with the pace with which they were being admitted to the ruling circle, opened a breach into which the military and other nonlandowning groups drove a wedge of power in 1889. Once the *paulistas* marshaled the military strength of their agricultural workers under the direct command of the planters, won over the support of the landowners in other regions of Brazil, and thus reunited the landowners, the latter were able once again to exclude the military officers from the direct exercise of power. Aside from one occasion in 1910 when military officers were able to regain a momentary ascendancy through the support of one faction of landowners, the landowners were able to maintain their hegemony without real challenge until 1930. At that time, again, only the divisions of the landed sector allowed the participation of new interest groups in the power-sharing circle. The careful testing of this view in Brazil will depend upon its comparison with developments in other parts of Latin America— Chile and Argentina come to mind immediately—and could be based upon the application of the interest-group concept and its accompanying method of historical investigation.

Just as the comparative method can be used to study the stable-unstable dichotomy, it could also be applied to such categories as dependent–self-determined, modern-traditional, socially equal–unequal, rural-urban, agricultural-industrial, or other categories that might be explained by the degree of power held by landowners. Does mass political self-consciousness make any more progress under one type of landed power than another? Are the appeals of communal as against individual ties heightened or lessened by the nature and amount of the landowners' political power? Is the rate of urbanization dependent upon the transformation of landed power, or is it the other way around?

From the systematic comparative analysis of landed power, a new typology of that power can be derived. Using an interest-group model, it will be possible to pinpoint variations among concrete examples. And such an approach to the power of the landed classes will form a rich lode of hypothetical nuggets.

An Approach to Regionalism

JOSEPH L. LOVE

The problems of regional conflict—relationships of domination and subordination, the competition for scarce resources, and the tension between national integration and regional separatism—are of major importance in the history of Mexico, Brazil, and Colombia. Yet it is also true that some of the smallest of Latin American countries, such as Ecuador and Nicaragua, have been subjected to intense regionalist battles in the last 150 years. Although students of Latin American historiography have repeatedly pointed to the need for research on regionalism in the national period, few works have yet appeared.[1]

NOTE. I wish to thank Robert M. Levine of SUNY, Stony Brook, and John D. Wirth of Stanford University for their criticism of this essay. The three of us are engaged in a comparative regional history of Brazil (1889–1937), focusing on Pernambuco, São Paulo, and Minas Gerais, to be published in four volumes. In preparing this paper I have drawn heavily on the collective ideas of the team.

[1] Charles Gibson and Benjamin Keen, "Trends of United States Studies in Latin American History," in *Latin American History: Essays on Its Study and Teaching, 1898–1965*, ed. Howard F. Cline, 2 vols. (Austin: University of Texas Press, 1967), II, 539; Robert A. Naylor, "Research Opportunities: Mexico and Central America," in ibid., II, 554; Thomas F. McGann, "Research Opportunities: Southern South America," in ibid., II, 566–567; J. León Helguera, "Research Opportunities: The Bolivarian Nations," in ibid., II, 561–562. Cf. Stanley J. Stein's appeal to test generalizations "at the local level—village, municipal, state, provincial, or departmental" ("Latin American Historiography," in ibid., II, 591).

This fact is surprising, since territorial conflict—regional and urban-rural—is one of the five major types of intranational cleavage, according to two leading students of comparative politics.[2] Moreover, regional conflict seems to loom larger in nations with lower levels of economic and social development and is thus presumably more important in Latin America than in areas of the developed world.[3] Furthermore, regional analysis seems a fruitful way to approach the interplay between social development—that is, mobilization, structural differentiation, and functional specialization—and integration— a shift of loyalties and a transfer of decision-making and revenue-raising powers from regional to national levels. Regional cleavage is of course but one prism for viewing social reality—not more important than cleavages of class, race, or ethnicity, but certainly less frequently used in modern social research.

Region and *regionalism* are terms having a variety of meanings in the scholarly literature, and they are best defined within the context of a specific type of problem. Here we are concerned with the social and economic bases of politics over a period of decades. I therefore define a region as a unit with the following characteristics:

1. It is integrally related to a larger unit and interdependent with other regions that, together with the first, constitute the larger unit.

2. It has a definite geographic size and location, being politically bounded.

3. Each region has a set of component subregions, which are contiguous.[4]

---

[2] Stein Rokkan and Henry Valen, "Regional Contrasts in Norwegian Politics: A Review of Data from Official Statistics and from Sample Surveys," in *Cleavages, Ideologies, and Party Systems: Contributions to Comparative Political Sociology*, ed. Erik Allardt and Yrjo Littunen (Helsinki: The Westermarck Society, 1964), p. 166. The other four types of cleavage are sociocultural and religious cleavages, plus conflict in commodity markets (between buyers and sellers of agricultural goods) and conflict in labor markets.

[3] Robert R. Alford, *Party and Society: The Anglo-American Democracies* (Chicago: Rand McNally, 1963), p. 310. Regional cleavages are said to be more important in lesser-developed nations because of the absence or feebleness of more modern forms of conflict.

[4] Contiguity is not a theoretically necessary condition for defining regions in political sociology, according to Kevin R. Cox, if component units share other de-

4. The region generates a set of loyalties on the part of its inhabitants.

5. Loyalty to the region, however, is subordinated (nominally at least) to loyalty to the larger unit, e.g., the nation-state, among the politically effective sections of the region's population.

Regionalism is here defined as political behavior characterized, on the one hand, by acceptance of the existence of a larger political unit, but, on the other, by the quest for favoritism and decisional autonomy from the larger unit on economic and social policies, even at the risk of jeopardizing the legitimacy of the prevailing political system. Thus the emphasis is not on regional peculiarities per se (e.g., folklore, patterns of dress and speech), but on those factors that can be demonstrated to affect the region's political, economic, and social relations with the other regions and the larger unit of government, usually a nation-state.

Regionalization, the process of defining regions, is directly analogous to periodization in that the nature of the problem should define the regions. For the geographer or sociologist, the minimal territorial units for which one has relevant data are aggregated and defined as regions so as to minimize the internal differentiation of each region and to maximize the external differentation between the regions, given the number of regions required.[5] For the historian, the existence of pronounced regional loyalties may make the choice of regions more obvious. Yet it should be remembered that, if a region extends beyond (or cuts across) state or departmental boundaries, it is rarely defined

---

fining characteristics. (See "On the Utility and Definition of Regions in Comparative Political Sociology," *Comparative Political Studies* 2, no. 1 [April 1969]: 71.) Such latitude, however, would permit us to subsume the urban-rural dichotomy under a two-region framework, and I question whether so broad a definition of regions is useful for historians. Furthermore, Ira Sharkansky insists on contiguity as a pragmatic criterion in regional studies of the United States because ". . . the 'region' as an explanatory concept in political science is already an imprecise independent variable whose strength lies in its association with the historical experience and contemporary characteristics shared by neighboring states and the tendency of state elites to consult their counterparts in neighboring states" (*Regionalism in American Politics* [Indianapolis: Bobbs-Merrill, 1970], pp. 18–19).

[5] Cox, "On the Utility," p. 70.

identically in the scholarly literature (e.g., the American South). Furthermore, the historian must be careful to avoid accepting uncritically the boundaries defined by his sources. Ira Sharkansky warns that, "When an author fails to make a systematic comparison between his region and others, it is not possible to accept any claim that his region is peculiar," that is, that it truly constitutes a distinct region.[6] Finally, while we usually think of regions as mutually exclusive, it might be useful to define overlapping or telescoping regions for some problems; e.g., they could be used in determining broad similarities and achieving higher levels of generalization for more extensive areas, though at the cost of a looser use of defining characteristics. In such cases the smaller region simply becomes a component part or subregion of the larger one.

It is clear, then, that regionalization in historical studies will not correspond to the procedures set up in geographical theory. Geographers have defined two ideal types of economic regions—the *uniform* and the *nodal*. The former is homogeneous throughout, while the latter is organized around a central node, such as an urban-industrial complex, with diminishing characteristic qualities as one approaches the periphery. Nodal regions have the practical disadvantage of changing boundaries over time, as urban-industrial foci bring larger and larger areas into their orbits of supply and distribution. The uniform type is clearly more appropriate for describing a preindustrial (if not preurban) economy and is a poor representation of a modern one. Neither of these types is of direct use for most political and historical research, since the real subject for historians and political scientists is the behavior of the human population associated with a territorial unit.

Regions defined by historians have tended to be fixed political units.[7] One reason for the historian's preference for a fixed region

---

[6] Sharkansky, *Regionalism in American Politics*, p. 24.

[7] An exception to this trend, in a sense, is James J. Parsons' *Antioqueño Colonization in Western Colombia*, rev. ed. (Berkeley: University of California Press, 1968). This study in historical geography shows how the population of a culturally distinctive region, Antioquia, expanded into other areas of Colombia, while retaining its regional identity: "Thus Caldas has become a second Antioqueño department 'more Antioqueño than Antioquia'" (p. 9).

is its far greater convenience in the collection and interpretation of data; since the historian works with quantitative and qualitative data over time, the fixed territorial unit, which assures data continuity, is usually mandatory. Furthermore, political loyalties are often attached to a fixed unit or group of units—Antioquia, São Paulo, the Mezzogiorno, or Brittany. In the following discussion, I choose a fixed unit rather than a nodal one, though no assumption is made about uniformity within the region.

What advantages does a regional approach offer? One use of regionalized data, more familiar to social scientists than to historians, is in monochronic analysis, based on data collected at a given point in time, and another is in diachronic analysis, in which two or more points in time are used. Regional analysis has the advantage in both cases of moving beyond interpretations based on gross averages, inherent in using the nation-state as a unit of data organization.[8] Regional analysis allows us to compare subunits or regions against each other within given countries[9] and one region against another in different countries. The latter type of comparison might be instructive for analyzing leads and lags where regions in different countries have similar socioeconomic structures.[10] In underdeveloped countries, where the regional imbalance of leading and lagging sectors is often great, both internal and external regional comparisons may be even more revealing than among developed nations.

The "slice-of-time" approach, however, is clearly ahistorical. The historian qua historian must engage in dynamic or developmental

[8] For an example of the latter, see Charles Lewis Taylor and Michael C. Hudson, *World Handbook of Political and Social Indicators*, 2d. ed. (New Haven: Yale University Press, 1972).

[9] A good sociological analysis of contemporary Chile by regions is that by Armand Mattelart and Manuel A. Garretón, *Integración nacional y marginalidad (Ensayo de regionalización social de Chile)*, 2d ed. (Santiago: Icira, 1969). The authors do not use contiguity as a criterion for defining social regions.

[10] See the discussion of the merits of regional analysis by Juan J. Linz and Amando de Miguel, "Within-Nation Differences and Comparisons: The Eight Spains," in *Comparing Nations: The Use of Quantitative Data in Cross-National Research*, ed. Richard L. Merritt and Stein Rokkan (New Haven: Yale University Press, 1966), pp. 269–272. As in the Mattelart-Garretón study, in this essay contiguity is not a defining characteristic of social regions.

analysis, examining process rather than temporal cutting points. While the social scientist is concerned with levels of development of different regions at specific points in time, the historian traces the interplay of regions through time, and if he knows two nations well enough, he can compare regions in two countries over time.[11]

Despite the importance of regional interplay in the processes of economic development and social and political integration, relatively scant attention has been given these problems in the historical and social-science literature on Latin America. Regions are usually seen as self-contained "problem areas"; and this perspective ignores the interaction among regions as well as that between regions and the national government.

Let us look more closely at the ways in which a regionalist approach can be employed in writing Latin American history. In my view, there are four distinct (though not all mutually exclusive) types of regional analysis. They are as follows:

1. *The region per se.* This is of course the traditional "problem-area" approach. The region is viewed as a self-contained unit, with little or no consideration of the external influences on the region or its influence on other regions or on the larger unit to which it belongs. In the historical literature on Latin America, one might point to Ernani Silva Bruno's series on the regions of Brazil as an example.[12]

The remaining three types all deal explicitly or implicitly with a given region's relations with others (singly or in aggregate form), i.e., how a given region is like or unlike the others, or how it relates to them.

2. *The region (or subregion) as a representative case of the problem under study.* Stanley Stein's *Vassouras* is a monograph on a territorial unit presumably typical of the social system of the Paraíba River Valley, and the studies of Jean Blondel on the state of Paraíba

---

[11] An essay comparing a North American region in the colonial period with a Spanish colony in the same era is Herbert S. Klein's *Slavery in the Americas: A Comparative Study of Virginia and Cuba* (Chicago: University of Chicago Press, 1967).

[12] Ernani Silva Bruno, *História do Brasil—geral e regional*, 7 vols. (São Paulo: Cultrix, 1966–1967).

and of Eul-soo Pang on Bahia are presumably representative of the
political systems of northern Brazil in their respective periods.[13]

3. *The region as a variant case of a problem.* Two studies of Antioquia, Colombia, come to mind as examples of this type: those of
James J. Parsons and Everett E. Hagen.[14] Both deal with the entrepreneurial spirit of the *antioqueños*, allegedly atypical of inhabitants of
other regions of Colombia. Hagen argues that *antioqueños* achieved
economic pre-eminence because of status deprivation, and he thus implies that castelike distinctions can coincide with regional identities.
Another example—this time of a lagging rather than a leading region—is Brazil's Northeast, a major socioeconomic problem for the
rest of the nation; as such, it has generated a number of historical and
social-science studies.[15]

4. *The region as a dynamic component of the whole.* This class
has three subtypes:

a. *The whole analyzed in terms of competition or cleavage
among regions.* In this case, the historian sees regional cleavage as a

[13] Stanley J. Stein, *Vassouras: A Brazilian Coffee County, 1850–1900* (Cambridge: Harvard University Press, 1957); Jean Blondel, *As condições da vida política
no Estado da Paraíba*, trans. Alcântara Nogueira (Rio de Janeiro: Instituto de
Direito Público e Ciência Política, 1957); Eul-soo Pang, "The Politics of *Coronelismo* in Brazil: The Case of Bahia, 1889–1930" (Ph.D. dissertation, University of
California at Berkeley, 1969). Bibliographical items on Latin America here and
below are exemplary rather than exhaustive. Furthermore, some works would fit
under more than one category: I have cited examples for their relative emphasis,
since Pang's, for instance, has some aspects of 4b, below.

[14] Parsons, *Antioqueño Colonization*; Everett E. Hagen, *On the Theory of Social
Change: How Economic Growth Begins* (Homewood, Ill.: Dorsey, 1962), pp. 353–
384. Frank Safford reverses Hagen's argument by making pre-existing economic
achievement the cause of the *antioqueños'* reputation as Judaizers. See "Significación
de los antioqueños en el desarrollo económico colombiano: Un examen crítico de
las tesis de Everett Hagen," *Anuario Colombiano de Historia Social y de la Cultura*
1967: 49–69. Also see William Paul McGreevey, *An Economic History of Colombia: 1845–1930* (Cambridge: Cambridge University Press, 1971), pp. 190–194.

[15] E.g., Manuel Diégues, *População e açúcar no nordeste do Brasil* (São Paulo:
Comissão Nacional de Alimentação, 1954); Stefan A. Robock, *Brazil's Developing
Northeast: A Study of Regional Planning and Foreign Aid* (Washington, D.C.:
Brookings Institution, 1963); Josué de Castro, *Death in the Northeast* (New York:
Random House, 1966); Roger Lee Cunniff, "The Great Drought: Northeast Brazil,
1877–1880" (Ph.D. dissertation, University of Texas, 1970).

principal, even determining, aspect of historical development. A famous example is Miron Burgin's *Economic Aspects of Argentine Federalism.*[16]

b. Regional conflict seen from a given region's vantage point, with an analysis of subregional dynamics. My own study, *Rio Grande do Sul and Brazilian Regionalism*, is of this sort.[17] In a forthcoming multivolume study, Robert M. Levine, John D. Wirth, and I will attempt to analyze Brazilian regional conflict from the perspective of three important regions, and from the national perspective as well, thus combining types *a* and *b*.

c. The region considered either as center or periphery. While type *b* assumes at least a minimal degree of autonomy for each region, this type uses a dichotomous scheme of dominance and subordination. Within the nation-state of Brazil, Andre Gunder Frank views São Paulo as a metropolis, with Northeast Brazil as one of its satellite areas; in an international context, however, he sees São Paulo as a satellite (or submetropolis) of the developed capitalist world, cen-

[16] Miron Burgin, *The Economic Aspects of Argentine Federalism, 1820–1852* (Cambridge: Harvard University Press, 1946). For an analysis of regional cleavage in the following decade, see James R. Scobie, *La lucha por la consolidación de la nacionalidad argentina: 1852–1862*, trans. Gabriela de Civiny (Buenos Aires: Hachette, 1964). On nineteenth-century Mexico, see Harry Bernstein, "Regionalism in the National History of Mexico," in *Latin American History*, ed. Cline, I, 389–394. Bernstein's essay, originally published in 1944, has been superseded by François Chevalier's "Conservateurs et libéraux au Mexique: Essai de sociologie et géographie politiques de l'indépendance a l'intervention française," *Cahiers d'Histoire Mondiale* 8 (1964): 457–474. This study combines class and regional analysis in a sophisticated fashion. On recent political recruitment patterns in Mexico and the distribution of public works and patronage, see Paul W. Drake's "Mexican Regionalism Reconsidered," *Journal of Inter-American Studies and World Affairs* 12, no. 3 (July 1970): 401–415. On Colombia, see Frank Safford's "Social Aspects of Politics in Nineteenth-Century Spanish America: New Granada, 1825–50," *Journal of Social History* 5, no. 3 (Spring 1972): 344–370. Safford examines various theories of the origins of the Liberal and Conservative parties and finds that a sophisticated version of regional cleavage offers the least unsatisfactory explanation.

[17] Joseph L. Love, *Rio Grande do Sul and Brazilian Regionalism, 1882–1930* (Stanford: Stanford University Press, 1971). Another example is Winfield J. Burggraaff's "Venezuelan Regionalism and the Rise of Táchira," *The Americas* 25, no. 2 (October 1968): 160–173. Much of Burggraaff's analysis is based on Domingo Alberto Rangel's *Los andinos en el poder: Balance de una hegemonía, 1899–1945* (Caracas: Talleres Gráficos Universitarios, 1965).

tered in New York.[18] Even in studies where the emphasis is on the region within the nation, the external dimension of the region as a dependent area in an international complex seems fruitful, as I attempt to show in a recent article on São Paulo.[19] Another center-periphery or metropolis-colony study illustrates that sociological regions need not be defined as parts of nation-states: Harry Hoetink defines his Caribbean as the lowland tropical and subtropical areas with racially mixed populations from the American South to Bahia, all "colonial" in their culture, social stratification, and racial segmentation.[20]

Whatever type of approach is used, it is clear that many complex processes occur as the nation-state develops as a viable polity. The most relevant factors from the regional perspective are the processes of economic growth, social mobilization, and sociopolitical assimilation. The regional approach offers special insights into the relationship between social and economic development and the integration of dispersed populations into national political systems.

What sorts of regional disparities relevant to political behavior might be examined on a quantitative basis over time? In their study of Spain, Juan J. Linz and Amando de Miguel list as areas for investigation differences in (1) economic development; (2) social structure, especially in stratification and urbanization, including land tenure and unemployment; (3) education at various levels; (4) linguistic and cultural traditions; (5) "religious climate" (degree of religiosity as measured by number of baptisms, communicants, etc., per thousand population); (6) social mobilization (membership in

---

[18] Andre Gunder Frank, *Capitalism and Underdevelopment in Latin America: Historical Studies of Chile and Brazil* (New York: Monthly Review, 1969), pp. 190–201 and passim. A more general and more rigorous statement linking internal colonialism and international imperialism is Johan Galtung's "A Structural Theory of Imperialism," *Journal of Peace Research* 1971, no. 2: 81–117. Galtung's stages of imperialist domination parallel Frank's.

[19] Joseph L. Love, "External Financing and Domestic Politics: The Case of São Paulo, Brazil, 1889–1937," in *Latin American Modernization Problems*, ed. Robert E. Scott (Urbana: University of Illinois Press, 1973), pp. 236–259.

[20] Harry Hoetink, *The Two Variants in Caribbean Race Relations: A Contribution to the Sociology of Segmented Societies*, trans. Eva M. Hooykaas (London: Oxford University Press, 1967).

voluntary associations or in political and religious organizations, exposure to media, etc.); (7) political traditions; (8) recruitment into national functional elites (e.g., military hierarchies, high-level business leadership, national judiciary, cabinet posts); (9) values, norms, and "basic personality" (e.g., regional styles and myths); and (10) family patterns (size and importance of nuclear and extended families, etc.).[21] To such indicators we might add four others, namely, differences in (11) income transfers between various levels of government (in both amount and nature of the transfer); (12) degree and nature of foreign penetration in the regional economy; (13) child-rearing patterns; and (14) migration patterns.

The significance of these indicators depends on the specific problem under study, but numbers 1 and 2 seem to be most comprehensive and are also independent. All fourteen variables are themselves composite variables and are therefore subject to disputes about defining characteristics. Number 10 is a special aspect of number 2, and number 12 might be regarded as an aspect of number 1. The "traditions"—indicators 4 and 7—and the three other "cultural" variables—9, 10, and 13—are probably most difficult to quantify, especially given the fact that the historian, unlike the sociologist, cannot undertake survey research but must rely principally on the "ecological" data already collected by statistical agencies.

Such data are available in the (usually) decennial censuses of the Latin American nations, at least in the present century, as well as in the statistical yearbooks these countries publish. Quantitative data for some aspects of the first eight categories of Linz and Miguel are available for the study of Brazil, the country I know best, as well as for the additional items 11, 12, and 14.

One seldom lacks precision in Latin American data, but false precision is often embedded in them, and they thus invite pseudoscientific research. For example, in 1960 the Instituto Brasileiro de Geografia e Estatística (IBGE), the Brazilian government's main statistical service, published retrospective estimates of the national population back to 1851, and these figures often differ with con-

---

[21] Linz and Miguel, "Within-Nation Differences and Comparisons," pp. 279–280.

temporary estimates by the same agency or its predecessors. The overall results of the 1890 census stand up better than those for 1872 or 1920. Unfortunately, the retrospective data of the IBGE are not broken down by state and *município* (county). To make matters worse, the retrospective estimates were based on the preliminary results of the 1960 census, and the total population of Brazil for 1960 has been revised several times in the *Anuário Estatístico* in succeeding years. It requires little imagination to surmise that the 1970 census will bring about further re-estimates of the national population in previous years and decades. Thus the researcher faces a Kafkaesque shifting of digits, though each volume he examines will give no indication that the population tables therein are anything less than the results of the most rigorous scientific observation.

There are other problems. One is that the Brazilian *município*, for instance, is subject to frequent subdivision, and even *sedes* (seats) of *municípios* often contain a rural population. Consequently, urbanization would be a phenomenon exceedingly difficult to gauge accurately, even if population figures were accurate. Voting figures offer further difficulties. For the period 1889–1937 one seldom encounters complete official returns in Brazil. A more frustrating problem is that the establishment party until the 1930s won better than 90 percent of the vote, usually virtually 100 percent, even in a relatively developed state like São Paulo and even in urban areas there. Measuring interparty competition is thus a meaningless exercise. Still, voting figures are useful in three ways: (1) Since sections of some *municípios* are overwhelmingly urban, voting data give us a rough indication, at least, of the change in the size of the rural and urban vote, a shift that had consequences in the thirties and later. (2) If we regionalize and subregionalize voting returns over time, they may allow us to specify a moving locus of electoral strength and then (given heroic assumptions) allow us to say something about the regional and subregional shift in political power. (3) Measured against total population (or better, against total potential voting population), voting figures give us an indication of political mobilization by county, subregion, and region.

The historian of regionalism in Latin America can only look with envy on the variety and presumed accuracy of data available to analysts of regional political behavior in developed countries, especially in the contemporary period. For Sharkansky's systematic study of regionalism in the United States, he obtained a wide range of data on personal income, interparty competition, voting, taxation, characteristics of state legislatures, welfare payments, income transfers between levels of government, and education—a total of sixty-one variables for each of the forty-eight contiguous states. He found all his raw data in eight printed sources, and forty-three of his variables were derived from two sources.[22] We may also assume that the figures he used, collected and compiled by professional statistical staffs, are more reliable than those available to students of Latin American history.

Yet regional analysis in Latin America is far from hopeless. To illustrate some of the possibilities, I shall briefly describe a cooperative study of Brazilian regionalism now in progress. In Brazil we can generally equate political regions with the nation's component states;[23] this is especially true for the South, where political power has been concentrated since 1889. Minas Gerais, São Paulo, and Rio Grande do Sul all constitute political "regions" in that their leaders operated autonomously from 1889 to 1930 and did not consistently seek alliances with political forces in contiguous states. In the Northeast, a case could be made for a multistate area as a political region— at least for some issues—because of concerted action and similar responses to common problems, notably the recurrent drought.

In the three-author study in progress, referred to above, Levine, Wirth and I hypothesize that decisions made at the state level have played a major role at a critical phase of national political integration. More concretely, from 1889 to 1930 the Brazilian state governments served as regional centers of power; they assumed decision-making responsibilities in the areas of social and economic services before the federal government was willing or able to accept such burdens. Between the First World War and 1930, and then in an accelerated

---

[22] Sharkansky, *Regionalism in American Politics*, pp. 185–187.

[23] From 1889 to 1930, Brazil had no enduring national political parties; each state had its own political organization. Even in the 1930s, new political parties were essentially confined to one or a few states.

manner from 1930 to 1937, these powers devolved upon the national government—in part because investments spilled over state lines (especially in the case of São Paulo) and because the Great Depression forced the highest governmental authority to assume the obligations of the states in a debt-consolidation program.

Thus two of the main problems under study are the degrees to which the states served as foci of social mobilization and of integration of their populations into a national polity—two distinct and potentially conflicting processes. The research team's initial hypothesis was that the states functioned as "halfway houses," pioneering in areas of social and economic legislation and slowly ceding responsibilities to the federal government between the First World War and the centralizing revolution of 1930. It is now clear, however, that the southern state governments (and that of São Paulo in particular) continued to innovate down to 1930, even when the federal role was growing. Thus government responsibility at *both* levels was increasing down to 1930. The team has discovered many contrasting instances of autonomy and dependence, growth and decline, initiative and acquiescence. We expect to develop a series of qualifications and amendments for center-periphery models as they apply to Brazil and other countries.

In the period of the First Republic (1889–1930) state governments rather than the Union pioneered in such social areas as wage regulation and the organization and regulation of functional associations (*sindicatos*). In the economic sphere the states' most notable venture was the attempt to control international commodity supplies (coffee and rubber) and thereby to control international prices for those goods. In addition, the states experimented in the control of the supply of domestically consumed commodities (e.g., jerked beef and beans); they constructed and maintained transportation networks and public utilities; and they provided public credit for the agricultural and pastoral industries. Even as late as the 1930s, the state of São Paulo pioneered in welfare assistance and innovated in public education.

One reason for the long-term failure of state leadership was the pronounced inequality of the revenue-generating power among the several state and regional economies. Many states were in fact dependent on some form of federal financial assistance. Another reason was the tendency of decision-makers in the viable regional economies to rely on foreign loans to finance state government initiatives, coupled with a dependence on agricultural export markets. Disruptions and dislocations in the regional, national, and international economies ultimately forced the states to yield their powers to the federal government—initially at a gradual pace, then, after 1930, in an accelerated fashion. The first major step in this direction was São Paulo's cession to the national government in 1921 of the coffee valorization program. The transfer of this responsibility was a *paulista*-sponsored measure in response to the economic dislocations of the First World War and its aftermath and in response to the fact that by then fewer than half of Brazil's coffee trees were located in São Paulo.

Changes in economic structures and flows are only one dimension of the study of regional behavior, however. Another element in the story is the behavior of various elite groups directly and indirectly affecting politics. For the concrete case of Brazil, many of the quantitative indicators listed above can be related appropriately to political, social, and economic elites; as we move backward in time, analysis of the behavior of elites is not only a convenient way of limiting the scope of research, but also the most realistic way to look at the Brazilian political process.[24]

The Brazilian political elite is a multipurpose group, in which a given actor fills a variety of roles with little functional specialization. Three major hypotheses on elites now being tested for the three-author project are (1) that in Brazil both state and national political elites were held together by extensive kinship and personal ties and that the national elite was a function of the state elites; (2) that these elite networks acted as a brake on social mobility, even when

[24] Elite control of politics could be demonstrated in an extended treatment, but let it suffice here that only 2 to 6 percent of the national population voted in federal elections between 1889 and 1930, and only 13 percent of the population did so by 1945, in which year the majority of the Brazilian people were still illiterate and consequently disenfranchised.

economic growth was rapid (as in the case of São Paulo); (3) that Brazil's national elite has been fairly homogeneous and has interacted dynastically, professionally, and affectively as a limited universe of decision-makers to provide the nation with leadership that limited modernization and yet provided a basis for integration from locality to nation.

One of the ways to approach these problems from the regional perspective is to examine the interaction and composition of the functional elites (category 8 of Linz and Miguel). Discovery of skewed recruitment patterns among such elites by region might throw light on the ways in which economically dynamic regions can "exploit" or "be restrained by" more retarded areas. Let us again cite the Brazilian case: At the end of the period under study (1889–1937), São Paulo supplied more than one-third the value of Brazil's industrial output and more than half her exports (mostly in agriculture). Yet in certain decades—and especially after 1930—São Paulo supplied less than its "share" of leaders in functional political elites. Therefore, it is plausible to suppose that economic and political power occasionally tend to be at odds. Broadly speaking, this seems to be true for São Paulo after 1930. Prior to 1930, economic and political power tended to be more congruent—for example, São Paulo supplied more presidents than any other state between 1889 and 1930. After 1930, São Paulo's regional economic priorities seem to have been sacrificed to national ones, partly because São Paulo lost control of the federal government.[25]

Economically, São Paulo was a region overshadowing all the others in the period under study, as it does today. Imbalance in the social and economic development of regions is a phenomenon found throughout the world, as the cases of Italy, the United States, and Brazil illustrate. We can therefore regard some degree of leads and lags within nations in the process of development as a normal process. Yet it seems probable that these disparities are greater in underdeveloped countries.[26] The mere acknowledgement of the existence of

[25] Love, "External Financing," p. 259 and passim.
[26] Linz and Miguel, "Within-Nation Differences and Comparisons," p. 271. J. G. Williamson argues that regional income disparities increase in early decades of

technological (not necessarily sociological) dualism would seem to support this contention, because modern technology is usually unevenly diffused among the regions of underdeveloped countries.

To conceptualize the problem of imbalance among urban areas, the term *primate city* was developed; it seems useful to extend this notion to regions. Thus we might speak of São Paulo as a "primate region" in Brazil, whether defined as a metropolitan region[27] or as a fixed territorial unit to which a resident population owes cultural and political allegiance. The "locomotive pulling twenty empty boxcars" (as the *paulistas* like to compare their state to the others) is a half-truth, but that half is worth remembering. Likewise, it seems appropriate to apply the notion of "internal neocolonialism" to a primate region as well as to a primate city, as Rodolfo Stavenhagen has for the capital of Mexico.[28]

The exploitation of some regions by others is, however, only part of the story. The more backward regions, as indicated above, might also have a restraining effect on the more developed regions, however much they might be drained of skilled labor and capital by the "exploiting" areas. We might hypothesize that vastly divergent economic development patterns among regions tend to place limits on the modernization of the advanced areas (for example in rationalizing

---

economic development, then level off, and finally diminish as an economy reaches maturity. See his "Regional Inequality and the Process of National Development: A Description of the Patterns," in *Regional Analysis: Selected Readings*, ed. L. Needleman (Baltimore: Penguin, 1968), pp. 99–158.

[27] On the definition of the metropolitan region, see Donald J. Bogue, "The Structure of the Metropolitan Community," in *Studies in Human Ecology*, ed. George A. Theodorson (Evanston, Ill.: Row, Peterson, 1961), pp. 524–538.

[28] Rodolfo Stavenhagen, "Seven Erroneous Theses about Latin America," in *Latin American Radicalism: A Documentary Report on Left and Nationalist Movements*, ed. Irving Louis Horowitz, Josué de Castro, and John Gerassi (New York: Vintage, 1969), pp. 102–117. Also see Pablo González Casanova, "Internal Colonialism and National Development," *Studies in Comparative International Development* 1, no. 4 (1965): 27–37. Concerning Spain, Linz and Miguel note that two provinces "approach the social and economic structure of some colonies—producers of raw materials, agricultural goods, and mining for absentee owners and corporations" ("Within-Nation Differences and Comparisons," p. 294).

economic production) because of lifestyles, particularistic associations derived from the traditional elite, and national political compromises.[29]

Such a scheme requires the assumption that regional cleavages are greater than urban-rural cleavages. With respect to São Paulo, there are a number of reasons for suspecting that this was the case for the era in question. One salient consideration here is the extent and importance of *panelinha-clientela-parentela* networks, which tied urban and rural branches of the same *paulista* family or peer group together. Another is the fact that colonization on the frontier of São Paulo and beyond was undertaken largely by branches of extended families (*parentelas*) moving westward, always with connections in the state capital and more established agricultural regions. Still another reason for hypothesizing a minimum of urban-rural cleavage among the elite stratum is the fact that agricultural investments retained an important place in the portfolios of the state elite, even after industry had begun its rapid ascent. Finally, historical and mythical factors have played a role in regional cohesion. Identification with the state as an entity (as opposed to metropolis versus hinterland) has been reinforced by twentieth-century political events, especially the civil war of 1932, which pitted the state of São Paulo against the rest of the country. In addition, the myth of the *paulista* or *bandeirante* personality (serious, adventurous, hard-working, materialistic) is in part a self-fulfilling prophecy, because it has to be lived up to.[30] Such

[29] The negative effect of traditional lifestyles on *paulista* industrialists' ability to act as rational capitalists is noted by Fernando Henrique Cardoso in "The Structure and Evolution of Industry in São Paulo: 1930–1960," *Studies in Comparative International Development* 1, no. 5 (1965): 45. Also see Warren Dean, *The Industrialization of São Paulo, 1880–1945* (Austin: University of Texas Press, 1969), pp. 44, 72–73, 124–128, 179. Cf. Barrington Moore, Jr.'s judgment that, if the plantation system of the American South had taken root in the West by the middle of the last century and had been permitted to surround the Northeast, then the United States would have developed "a latifundia economy, a dominant antidemocratic aristocracy, and a weak and dependent commercial and industrial class, unable and unwilling to push forward toward political democracy" (*Social Origins of Dictatorship and Democracy: Lord and Peasant in the Making of the Modern World* [Boston: Beacon, 1966], p. 153).

[30] On the self-fulfilling regional myth, see Albert O. Hirschman, *The Strategy of Economic Development* (New Haven: Yale University Press, 1958), pp. 185–186.

"myth obligations" are presumably accepted not only by the elite but also by members of lower social strata, especially when dealing with non-*paulistas.*

The case of São Paulo as developed here provides an interesting opportunity for testing Robert Alford's hypothesis that industrialization and urbanization tend to produce class polarization in politics and to diminish regional and other types of cleavages.[31] I suspect that the hypothesis would hold for São Paulo in the 1970s, but the considerations in the previous paragraph would lead me to believe it is not valid for the 1930s and earlier. In fact, my research to date has tended to confirm the absence of the classical political effects of urbanization and industrialization in the period down to 1937. That is, class-based political parties did not displace traditional liberal-democratic parties, even though the number of voters in São Paulo more than doubled in the thirties and fascist and Marxist groups had liberty of action. The "nineteenth-century liberal" parties (the Partido Republicano Paulista and the Partido Constitucionalista) won overwhelming electoral majorities, even in São Paulo City, despite the rapid growth of extremist parties in other states. Given the inchoate nature of many new urban groups, I hypothesize that a partial explanation can be found in the absence of a truly urban ethic among the upper and upper-middle classes, which tended to define the ground rules of politics. These groups (whether primarily planters, merchants, or industrialists) were closely knit by family links and continually renewed their rural ties by investing in lands on the coffee and cotton frontiers. Export- and rural-oriented, they successfully resisted polarizing movements based on mobilization of the urban sector.

Despite the generally recognized importance of elites in the Latin American political process, few historical studies have dealt with them. In particular, the networks that hold state and national elites together are central to the Brazilian political process, and yet they have received almost no attention in the existing histories of modern Brazil. The Levine-Wirth-Love study defines state political elites in

[31] Alford, *Party and Society*, p. 310.

a uniform manner, and data collected on several hundred members of the political elite are being examined for each of the three states and organized in a uniform fashion. At a later stage, interstate comparisons will be made, along with an examination and analysis of national functional elites.

In conclusion, let us note that regionalist studies about areas of the world other than Latin America are alive and well, even for such a developed and economically integrated nation as the United States.[32] In areas more culturally heterogeneous than Latin America—Europe, Africa, and Asia—regionalist studies in a variety of disciplines are probably considerably more numerous than those on our area. But in the historiography of Latin America, and especially Brazil, regionalist research by North Americans has mounted rapidly in the last decade.[33] The trend seems to reflect a new maturity in Latin American studies in this country, as scholars look beyond national and local frameworks in defining historical problems.

[32] See the bibliography in Sharkansky, *Regionalism in American Politics*, pp. 163–183. On the interdisciplinary nature of regional studies, see especially the dated but still useful work by Howard W. Odum and Harry Estill Moore, *American Regionalism: A Cultural-Historical Approach to National Integration* (New York: Holt, 1938).

[33] On the republican era alone, note Love, *Rio Grande do Sul and Brazilian Regionalism*; the Levine-Wirth-Love project described above; Dean, *The Industrialization of São Paulo*; Pang, "The Politics of *Coronelismo* in Brazil"; Ralph della Cava, *Miracle at Joaseiro* (New York: Columbia University Press, 1970); Carlos E. Cortés, *Gaucho Politics in Brazil: The Role of Rio Grande do Sul in National Politics, 1930–1964* (Albuquerque: University of New Mexico Press, 1973); and Linda Lewin's dissertation on the politics of Paraíba in the Old Republic (forthcoming at Columbia University).

Comparative Slave Systems in the Americas:
A Critical Review

JOHN V. LOMBARDI

In recent years the history of black slavery in the Americas has attracted increasing attention from the historians of the United States and Latin America alike. In the generation now drawing to a close, a host of monographs and syntheses appeared that have radically altered the accepted notions about Anglo-American and Latin American slavery. Before the debates of the 1960s focused our attention and pushed graduate students into intensive research, scholars interested in understanding slavery in Latin America felt secure in citing Frank Tannenbaum's *Slave and Citizen* for the legal and institutional structure of slavery and Gilberto Freyre's *The Masters and the Slaves* for a practical view of life on the slave plantation.[1] Outside a small core of specialists, no one before the 1960s much challenged the widely held view of Latin American slavery as a relatively benign and

---

[1] Frank Tannenbaum, *Slave and Citizen: The Negro in the Americas* (New York: Alfred A. Knopf, 1946); Gilberto Freyre, *The Masters and the Slaves: A Study in the Development of Brazilian Civilization* (New York: Alfred A. Knopf, 1946). In the notes to this paper I will make no attempt to survey the vast literature on slavery in the Americas. By and large that task has been admirably performed by Mangus Mörner's outstanding analysis, *Race Mixture in the History of Latin America* (Boston: Little, Brown, and Company, 1967). For those interested in more detailed reviews of the literature, see the notes to the works mentioned throughout this essay.

paternalistic slave system.[2] Then in 1959 we received one of the most influential and controversial studies of the servile institution from the pen of Stanley M. Elkins, whose book, *Slavery*, has helped define the debate for over a decade.[3] Elkins explained the contrast between an apparently benevolent slave system in Latin America and a harsh restrictive system in the American South as a product of differing cultural norms and social institutions. According to this conception, the American Negro slave lived under the control of an almost absolute master, whose power brooked no interference from man or government. In Latin America, however, Elkins saw a slave system in which the master's authority over his slaves was diminished by institutional restraints. The Church and the State had important roles to play in regulating the Latin American slave system, providing the slave with institutionalized protection against the master's excesses. The primary examples of this sort of benevolence were the frequent manumissions characteristic of Latin American slavery and the possibility of a slave's buying his own freedom. Presumably, then, the Latin American slave system resulted in a radically different kind of institution that had less drastic effects on the black man's psyche than did the United States version of slavery. This theory of slave systems proved very popular in the United States in the early sixties and quickly became the standard view of things accepted by the educated public, by many historians, and by scores of students.[4]

2 Indicative of this genial acceptance of what has come to be called the myth of the friendly master was Carl N. Degler's original attempt to use the Latin American experience to provide comparative insights into the uniqueness of the United States slave arrangements in his article "Slavery and the Genesis of American Race Prejudice," *Comparative Studies in Society and History* 2 (1959): 49–67. The small core of specialists included among others Stanley J. Stein (*Vassouras: A Brazilian Coffee County, 1850–1900* [Cambridge: Harvard University Press, 1957]) and Sidney Mintz ("The Role of Forced Labor in Nineteenth Century Puerto Rico," *Caribbean Historical Review* 2 [1951]: 134–141). For an example of the "friendly-master" advocates before 1960, see Mary W. Williams, "The Treatment of Negro Slaves in the Brazilian Empire: A Comparison with the United States," *Journal of Negro History* 15 (1930): 313–336.

3 Stanley M. Elkins, *Slavery: A Problem in American Institutional and Intellectual Life* (Chicago: University of Chicago Press, 1959).

4 Elkins, *Slavery*, pp. 52–80, 134–139. Of course only part of Elkins's thesis rests on his Latin American material. Nevertheless, the Latin American control case re-

In spite of this popularity, however, some Latin Americanists refused to accept the Elkins thesis. Almost as if in direct answer to Elkins's popularization of Tannenbaum and Freyre, Marvin Harris produced his influential book, *Patterns of Race in the Americas*. Possessed of monumental courage and a great talent for synthesis, Harris, in a few short pages, delivered a full analysis of race and class for all of Latin America. Where Elkins had seen the Church and State intervening in the master's operation of his plantation, Harris found rural plantation masters a law unto themselves. Where Elkins saw manumission as clear proof of the master's sympathetic paternalism, Harris found manumission a device to create a necessary class of free colored people to do the work the masters would not do and slaves could not be permitted to do. Where Elkins stressed cultural heritage and institutional stability, Harris emphasized economic needs and material conditions.[5]

With the appearance of Harris's work, then, the two poles of the debate were planted, and since that time scholars have oscillated between these positions, trying to find a place where the contradictions could be resolved. Although the arguments have yet to produce a

---

mains crucial to his entire argument. If the data and interpretation of Elkins's analysis of Latin America can be proved false, most of the rest of the Elkins thesis will necessarily collapse. This helps explain, in part, the exceptional virulence of the attacks on Elkins's Latin American comparison. But the strength of the Elkins thesis can be measured by its acceptance into the conventional wisdom of textbooks. John E. Fagg, in *Latin America: A General History*, 2d ed. (New York: The Macmillan Company, 1969), pp. 145–146, and Hubert Herring, in *A History of Latin America from the Beginnings to the Present*, 3d ed. (New York: Alfred A. Knopf, 1968), p. 230, both hew rather closely to the Elkins-Freyre-Tannenbaum version, as do August Meier and Elliot M. Rudwick in their *From Plantation to Ghetto* (New York: Hill and Wang, 1966), pp. 63–64.

[5] Marvin Harris, *Patterns of Race in the Americas* (New York: Walker, 1964). Harris's tremendous influence on the debate over the nature and significance of slavery in the Americas stems from the timeliness of his work as well as from its exceptionally clean, concise, and schematic presentation. For students and scholars dissatisfied with Elkins, Freyre, or Tannenbaum, Harris's book provided a ready-made, plausible, and simplified structure that could be set in opposition to the exponents of the friendly-master school of thought. However, the virtues of Harris's book when used in debate become liabilities when it is used as an analytical tool.

consensus, their nature and focus have greatly contributed to our understanding of the problem.

Each participant in this festival of scholarship has focused on one aspect or another of comparative slavery, and each has contributed to our knowledge without resolving the controversy over the nature of Latin American slavery. For example, one of the easiest criticisms of the Elkins or of the Harris thesis is that they both work on too grand a scale. The task of saying anything meaningful about comparative slave institutions in over twenty countries during more than four hundred years is next to impossible. A student runs the risk of generalizing his subject to the point of irrelevance. In the attempt to include Brazil, Chile, and Mexico within a Latin American slave system, the fabric of history is stretched too thin. In hopes of narrowing down the field and thereby getting better control of the generalizations, Herbert S. Klein produced *Slavery in the Americas: A Comparative Study of Virginia and Cuba.*[6] By confining his analysis geographically, Klein hoped to avoid the errors of his predecessors while at the same time clarifying the problem of comparative slavery. If Klein had visions of resolving the question, the disillusionment must have been quick. Part of Klein's problem came from his conclusions, which seemed to support the Elkins-Tannenbaum end of the controversy precisely at the time when it was coming increasingly under attack. But there were substantial criticisms of Klein's work too. The limitation by geographic area appeared to raise as many problems as it solved. For one thing, many scholars thought the choice of Virginia poor, because Virginia hardly represented the American South, nor did it provide a reliable picture of slave life in Anglo-America. Klein also heard from some Latin Americanists who questioned his assertions about the effectiveness of Church and State and his concentration on pre–nineteenth-century, preplantation Cuba.[7]

[6] Herbert S. Klein, *Slavery in the Americas: A Comparative Study of Virginia and Cuba* (Chicago: University of Chicago Press, 1967).

[7] Although not written specifically to challenge Klein's interpretation, Franklin W. Knight's *Slave Society in Cuba during the Nineteenth Century* (Madison: University of Wisconsin Press, 1970) presents a different view of Cuban slavery.

Most students of slavery recognized David Brion Davis's *Problem of Slavery in Western Culture* as a major contribution to the literature.[8] Unfortunately for our purposes, Davis's book did not resolve the controversy or offer guidance on methodology. His survey of the literature on slavery in the Americas concluded wisely that most participants in the debate had made important contributions but that none of them had arrived at a usable, definitive synthesis.[9]

A final effort to resolve the controversy and revive the discussion came from Carl N. Degler, whose *Neither Black nor White* surveyed the structure of race relations in Brazil and in the United States.[10] Degler did not really focus on slavery but rather on the history of race relations, for his major concern was with the future of race relations in the United States. Even so, he too had to take on the problem of comparative slavery, which he did with considerable skill. The immensely greater sophistication evident in Degler's comparison over that in Elkins's pays tribute to the importance of such controversies in improving our approaches to historical problems. Degler's solution to the dilemma, nevertheless, was no better than those of his predecessors. While his review of the literature showed careful research and excellent synthetic talent, the result failed to add much new to the discussion. Degler concentrated on the "mulatto escape hatch" as a device that distinguished race relations in Brazil from those in the United States.[11] This is an attractive thesis, but neither

[8] David B. Davis, *The Problem of Slavery in Western Culture* (Ithaca, N.Y.: Cornell University Press, 1966).

[9] For a fascinating review of Davis's work see Moses I. Finley, "The Idea of Slavery: Critique of David Brion Davis' *The Problem of Slavery in Western Culture*," *New York Review of Books* 3, no. 1 (1967): 7–10.

[10] Carl N. Degler, *Neither Black nor White: Slavery and Race Relations in Brazil and the United States* (New York: The Macmillan Company, 1971).

[11] Degler, *Neither Black nor White*, pp. 205–264. Degler's use and interpretation of the "mulatto escape hatch" is one of the controversial tenets of his essay. Many scholars have noted the greater apparent mobility experienced by mulattoes in Latin America, and Marvin Harris showed that one function of this mobility was to create an intermediate class of free workers. But Degler carried this idea much farther than many of his predecessors to make the mulattoes' greater chance of success the key to the difference between United States and Latin American slave and race relations. For an earlier version of this kind of explanation see Harry Hoetink, *The Two Variants in Carribbean Race Relations: A Contribution to the Sociology of*

Degler nor his scholarly predecessors have managed to show convincingly how the mechanism of manumission worked or to what extent it functioned.

In the generation from Tannenbaum to Degler, then, what have we accomplished, and where are we headed? Clearly the most important advances in the field have come in two areas, international aspects of slavery and microhistory. One only need mention the work of Leslie M. Bethell, whose book on the abolition of the Brazilian slave trade is very close to definitive, to understand the solidity and progress of scholarship in this area.[12] Arthur F. Corwin's study of Spain and the abolition of slavery in Cuba brought a wealth of new detail into the discussion of international influences on American slavery.[13] Although less likely to stand the test of time, Philip D. Curtin's survey of the statistics of the slave trade also broadened our understanding of the magnitude of the forced migration that created the topic of comparative slavery in the Americas.[14]

On another level, scholars have gradually been working away at the task of dispelling our phenomenal ignorance about some of the

---

Segmented Societies, trans. Eva M. Hooykaa (London: Oxford University Press, 1967).

[12] Leslie M. Bethell, *The Abolition of the Brazilian Slave Trade* (Cambridge: Cambridge University Press, 1970). For those interested in pursuing the subject of the Brazilian slave trade from another perspective, see Robert Conrad's excellent work, "The Struggle for the Abolition of the Brazilian Slave Trade" (Ph.D. dissertation, Columbia University, 1967).

[13] Arthur F. Corwin, *Spain and the Abolition of Slavery in Cuba, 1817–1886,* Latin American Monographs Series, no. 9 (Austin: University of Texas Press, 1967). Corwin's book should be supplemented by Knight's *Slave Society in Cuba* (n. 7 above).

[14] Philip D. Curtin, *The Slave Trade: A Census* (Madison: University of Wisconsin Press, 1969). Curtin's book has performed an extraordinarily useful service to scholars by bringing order to the chaos of slave-trade statistics. He, of course, runs the risk of incurring the wrath of numerous scholars whose microcosmic view of the trade in particular places or at particular times may be more accurate than his. If Curtin's work helps us get better figures, then it will have served its purpose admirably. The relative solidity of the recent slave-trade studies, when compared with the slave-system analyses, should not surprise us. The historiography and methodology of slave-trade scholarship, being branches of diplomatic history, have had many generations in which to develop and mature, while comparative slavery is a hothouse flower but a generation old.

basic characteristics of slavery in the Americas. Most of these works have focused on one country or even a region within a country in order to gain a depth of understanding not readily accessible on a grander scale. A model of this genre is the now classic work of Stanley J. Stein on Vassouras, a Brazilian coffee county.[15] Unfortunately, too few of us have had the courage, ability, or opportunity to focus our work this closely, and thus most of the new approach tends to concentrate on national entities, particularly with reference to the abolition of slavery.

Abolition, of course, provides a natural topic for dissertations or research projects. For most Latin American countries no solid, reliable work existed on the topic before the mid-1960s, but because of the official and usually controversial nature of the process, documentation proved relatively easy to find. Even more importantly, the topic of abolition seemed to provide an ideal vehicle for a general examination of the slave systems of the countries involved. As a result of this reasoning we have today full-scale studies of abolition in at least three important slaveholding countries: Brazil, Cuba, and Venezuela.[16]

For Brazil, the literature on abolition grows larger daily, but the most comprehensive analysis of the whole topic I have yet seen is in Robert Conrad's recent book. Although Conrad's sections on the slave system and the dynamics of abolitionism are the most convincing discussions available, they will not resolve the controversy. One has only to read the analyses of the same situation by Richard Graham

[15] Stein, *Vassouras*. This fine book was not conceived as a slave-system analysis and encompassed far more than the slave element of the population. Indeed, the very comprehensiveness of Stein's universe gives his book a usefulness and a validity far beyond that offered by most slavery studies. Stein is also among the select few whose awareness and comprehension of the reality of slavery in Latin America predates the 1960s.

[16] On Brazil see Robert Conrad's study, *The Destruction of Brazilian Slavery, 1850–1888* (Berkeley: University of California Press, 1972), in which he makes an excellent analysis of the movement in all parts of the country. For a somewhat different perspective see Robert B. Toplin's *The Abolition of Slavery in Brazil* (New York: Atheneum, 1972). On Cuba we have Knight's superb *Slave Society in Cuba* and Corwin's *Spain and the Abolition of Slavery*. Venezuela is covered by my book, *The Decline and Abolition of Negro Slavery in Venezuela, 1820–1854* (Westport, Conn.: Greenwood Publishing Corporation, 1971).

and Robert Brent Toplin to appreciate the complexity of the argument.[17] The Cuban case, however, emerges a bit more clearly from the pages of Franklin Knight's outstanding study of slavery and abolition in nineteenth-century Cuba and Corwin's work mentioned earlier. Yet, while we may feel reasonably confident of Knight's analysis of abolition, his description of the Cuban slave system does not completely settle the issues raised earlier by Klein. Whether the striking differences between Klein's picture of slavery and Knight's picture can be reconciled remains to be seen, and, although at this writing Knight's account would appear correct for the nineteenth century, Klein's version of slavery in the earlier period has not yet been replaced.[18] Finally, for Venezuela, my own work on abolition in that country has only validated my uneasiness with the use of abolitionism as a tool for understanding slavery.[19]

What all this literature indicates is a confusion of aims, goals, and functions within the profession. Students of slavery seem to have divided themselves into two large groups. One group, the Synthesizers, spin elaborate theories of comparative slavery, taking the whole world as their domain. They evaluate the components of slave systems,

---

[17] Conrad, *Destruction of Brazilian Slavery*; Toplin, *Abolition of Slavery in Brazil*; idem, "Upheaval, Violence, and the Abolition of Slavery in Brazil: The Case of São Paulo," *Hispanic American Historical Review* 49 (1969): 639–655. Richard Graham's views on Brazilian abolition can most easily be seen in his "Causes for the Abolition of Negro Slavery in Brazil: An Interpretive Essay," *Hispanic American Historical Review* 46 (1966): 123–137, and "Brazilian Slavery Re-examined: A Review Article," *Journal of Social History* 3 (1970): 431–453.

[18] While Knight's book can be taken as a refutation of Klein's conclusions, that is not necessarily the case. It is quite possible that both scholars are substantially correct, Klein for the early period and Knight for the nineteenth century. Of course, the question cannot be resolved by remote control. We need an investigation based on Cuban archival sources, which is regrettably rather difficult for North American scholars today.

[19] Among the major slaveholding countries of Latin America, Venezuela possessed a number of characteristics that set her apart. Although she maintained a significant investment in slave property and showed a stubborn reluctance to do away with the institution, Venezuela's slave population comprised a small percentage of the population and the labor force. As a result Venezuela serves as a control case for generalization about Latin American slavery and abolition based on the experience of Brazil or Cuba, where slavery tended to have a much more dominant role in the economy and social structure.

describe the ideologies and motivations of slave-owning classes, and castigate each other for lapses of vision, scholarship, or methodology.[20] This is a most seductive kind of history, to which most of us fall victim at one time or another. And certainly these synthetic works have tremendous importance in guiding and formulating research designs and theoretical conceptions. But one of the curious features of the Synthesizers' debate is its circularity.

After having read the major books and the important articles of the controversy, a student begins to experience a strange feeling of *déjà vu*. Each new article, each re-evaluation of the themes of comparative slavery interprets the same material and reaches the same sets of unsatisfying conclusions.[21]

On another level of scholarship stands the second group, which, for lack of a better term, I shall call the Diggers. These hardy souls spend long and tedious hours digging out the raw material that will be used by the Synthesizers in constructing elaborate theories. The Diggers tend to focus their work rather narrowly and, as a result, get good, solid, reliable information. Yet because of the specificity of

[20] One of the best introductions to the entire controversy can be found in a collection of essays edited by Laura Foner and Eugene Genovese, *Slavery in the New World: A Reader in Comparative History* (Englewood Cliffs, N.J.: Prentice-Hall, Inc., 1969). Crucial sections from most of the works mentioned in these remarks are included: Tannenbaum, Elkins, Mintz, Harris, Davis, Klein, and Finley are all there in addition to other essays of considerable importance. One of the more fascinating items in the group is Genovese's dissection of Marvin Harris's *Patterns of Race in the Americas*. Genovese, a master of polemical writing, demonstrates the brilliance and imaginativeness that are his hallmarks in this piece as well as in "The Treatment of Slaves in Different Countries," also included in the collection. The most recent review of the United States–Brazilian comparison can be found in Thomas E. Skidmore's "Toward a Comparative Analysis of Race Relations since Abolition in Brazil and the United States," *Journal of Latin American Studies* 4 (1972): 1–28.

[21] This reaction is not to imply that the recurring conclusions are unimportant or that there are few significant points separating the various debaters. On the contrary, many of the issues raised during the recycling of comparative slavery have vital significance for our understanding of slaves and slavery. Although some of the discussion may have turned on relatively trivial points, most of the energy has been well spent. My only objection here is to the circularity and repetitiveness of the debate, which indicates to me a serious problem in our formulation of the parameters of the problem.

their work the Diggers' contributions also fail to answer the vital questions of comparative slave analyses.

Under normal conditions, the symbiotic relationship existing between Synthesizers and Diggers would be a healthy one, but in this case this relationship is under severe stress. The main problem stems from the inability of the Diggers to supply new data fast enough for all the Synthesizers to use, as a result of which the Synthesizers find themselves forced to keep reworking and rearranging the bits and pieces that slowly emerge from the Diggers' efforts. Because the data from the Diggers is so scarce and fragmentary, the Synthesizers never seem able to give us satisfying answers to our questions about comparative slavery.[22]

In spite of the frustrations inherent in the work of Synthesizers and Diggers, their efforts have not been wasted. Thanks to the persistence of the Synthesizers in reworking and re-examining the problem of comparative slavery, we can point with some confidence to the methodological and conceptual shortcomings plaguing our discussion. Surely the repetitiveness and circularity of much of the literature on comparative slave systems should encourage us to review our assumptions and question our approaches to the topic.

One of the most striking features of the debate among the Synthesizers has been their strong methodological debt to the historiography of slavery in the United States South. Such a dependence on United States models and approaches comes as no great surprise,

[22] The inability of Diggers to keep pace with the hothouse flowering of the Synthesizers derives in a large part from the underdeveloped state of research on Latin America. While Latin Americanist pioneers of the first half of the twentieth century produced some admirably researched work on Latin American themes, consistent, systematic, and large-scale research has been a byproduct of the Cuban Revolution. When we compare the kind of information available to scholars interested in Modern Europe or the United States with the bits and scraps the Latin Americanist must contend with, the data gap appears wide indeed. Furthermore, the more solid research we begin to acquire from scholars in Latin America, in Europe, and in the United States, the less tenable our earlier generalizations become. With the structure of Latin American history so incompletely revealed, it is no wonder the Synthesizers have a hard time answering questions on comparative slavery. An excellent way to appreciate the pioneering character of Latin American history is through the comprehensive and stimulating review of Latin American social history in the *Latin American Research Review* 7 (Spring 1972): 5–94.

since most of the Synthesizers are primarily North American historians who have turned to Latin America for comparative insights. In spite of their imaginative hypotheses and herculean researches in the secondary literature of two or three languages, the Synthesizers have proved unable to break out of the mind-set placed on them by students of the Old South.[23]

These scholars refuse to conceive of slavery as anything other than a system. A system implies a central ethic and driving force that unifies the condition of slavery. The Synthesizers, with all their complexity of thought and sophistication of concept, must necessarily be able to encompass all of the Latin American black slaves within the confines of a coherent and reasonably rational unity. This occurs because, without a Latin American slave system, there can be no comparison with an Anglo-American slave system. And an intellectually satisfying comparative construct is what the debate is all about.[24]

If there were any validity to the notion of a Latin American slave system, the Synthesizers would not have to become involved in the gradual narrowing of the field for comparison, and, particularly, there would be no need to do most of the narrowing in Latin America. With the exception of Klein's book, which restricted both sides of the comparison, all the Synthesizers of note have either implicity or explicitly narrowed the Latin half of their comparison to Brazil and Cuba, or, even further, to just Brazil.[25] Now, does this not imply that

[23] Many of our great Synthesizers come from backgrounds and training in United States history, Elkins, Genovese, and Degler being the prime examples. Equally important in explaining the application of the United States model has been the already developed methodology and historiography focused in minute detail on the Old South, ready and waiting to be reapplied to the Latin American case.

[24] Anyone who doubts the importance of elegance in the debate over comparative slavery need only read Eugene Genovese's critique of Marvin Harris, cited in n. 20 above. Probably the most sophisticated version of slave-system synthesis is offered by Genovese in *The World the Slaveholders Made* (New York: Pantheon Books, 1969). By focusing on the slaveholding class he manages to construct a more coherent explanation than most Synthesizers. But even Genovese's creative mind cannot dispose of the contradictions inherent in the Latin American slave-system idea. By separating mainland Spanish America from Cuba and Brazil and by concentrating on the slave masters as a class, he goes a long way toward rejecting the slave system as an analytical tool.

[25] Elkins, Degler, Klein, and Genovese among others are forced to rely almost

the comparative generalizations worked out for Brazil and the United States South have no validity for Cuba, let alone for Venezuela or Colombia? Perhaps, then, there is more than one Latin American slave system? Yet, as we have noted above, even the narrowing process, to Brazil for Degler and Cuba for Klein, fails to solve the dilemmas of our traditional conceptual framework. Clearly our notion of a Latin American slave system needs an overhaul.

The root of this problem goes back into the most easily accepted notion of the entire topic: the concept of the black slave. We have created our own historiographical dilemma by tacitly assuming that being black and being held in legal bondage imposed a common condition on Negro slaves that sufficiently set them apart from their social context to justify analyzing their historical experience as an autonomous system. To be sure, this notion of Negro slavery as an identifiable and commensurable entity has not produced total confusion. For students of legal and intellectual history the concept of slave systems makes eminently good sense, and the proof of the utility of the concept in these areas can be seen, for example, in Davis's *Problem of Slavery in Western Culture.* In like fashion, the students of diplomatic and commercial history have found Negro slavery a useful conceptual tool. Here, too, the proof exists in the satisfying studies by Bethell and Corwin, which concentrate on diplomacy and legality. Even Curtin's controversial numeration of the slave trade stimulates comment not so much on conceptual grounds as on statistical ones.

The error of our ways becomes evident only when we step out of diplomacy, away from the legalists and ideologues, and into the social reality within which the black slave existed. Here we find our carefully drawn distinctions blur, our elaborately built legal structures crumble, and our precisely ordered concepts become confused.

---

exclusively on Cuba and Brazil for their examples and illustrations, simply because those countries have the best developed historiographies on slavery and race relations. Nevertheless, the lack of hard data on the other Latin American countries does not justify lumping them in with Brazil and Cuba. Many of them had slaves, some in large numbers, and, if there is a Latin American slave system, they too must be a part of it.

Perhaps the best example of this condition comes from the definition of slave status. If the concept of "black slavery" means anything, we should be able to define the characteristics of slave status in
such a way as to include all those legally enslaved and generally exclude those legally free. Although scientific precision would be ideal,
we can settle here for a working definition that could be used with
reasonable ease by Synthesizers and Diggers alike. For the sake of
this discussion let us hold that the essential quality of slave status is
the loss of basic personal freedom to another person who holds more
or less absolute dominion over the slave's life and action.[26] From
time to time and place to place, the State, the Church, or custom may
restrict the master's control over the slave, but the essence of slave
status still remains the loss of personal freedom of action. For the
sake of argument, let us accept this definition for the moment, although it lacks a certain elegance.

One would expect such a definition or one somewhat like it to play
a prominent role in our discussions of comparative slave systems.
Curiously enough, few Synthesizers or Diggers actually concern themselves with or make use of such a definition. For all of us black slavery
is a self-defining institution and a self-generating concept. When we
go to analyze the conditions of black slavery in the Americas, the
test by which we exclude individuals from the scope of our research
is solely the publicly recognized status of slave. We rarely inquire as
to the degree of personal freedom enjoyed by an individual or a class
of individuals in determining whether they belong within or without
the slave system.[27] Such a procedure leads us to some rather strange
conclusions.

[26] This definition, a sort of man-in-the-street, common-sensical definition, cannot
stand the careful scrutiny of the philosophers among us. A more precise, although
less wieldy, set of distinctions is drawn by Moses I. Finley in his review of Davis,
cited in n. 9 above. An excellent discussion of the meaning of the term *slave* is in
Arnold A. Sio's "Interpretations of Slavery: The Slave Status in the Americas,"
Comparative Studies in Society and History 7 (1965): 289–308.

[27] This is true even of such complex arguments as those presented by Davis in
The Problem of Slavery in Western Culture and Genovese in his various articles.
While Davis spends a good deal of time and effort on the defining characteristics
of slavery in ancient and modern times, he too ends up using the same kind of crude
formula as the rest of us.

For example, the rubric *slave system* lumps together the *bozal* or newly landed African field hand and the *ladino* or *criollo* town artisan. It includes both rural coffee pickers and semi-independent urban *negros de ganho*.[28] At the same time, our principle of exclusion rejects the free black *agregado* and the free mulatto artisan; it also excludes nonslave stevedores and free coachmen. No wonder we cannot make much sense out of a comparative social history that tries to blend all the disparate elements of a population called *slaves* into a semihomogeneous whole called *slave system*.

Fortunately, a growing number of scholars have seemed to sense this problem and have taken various stratagems to get around it. Perhaps nowhere can this be better seen than in Franklin Knight's concluding chapter in his outstanding study of Cuban slavery and abolition. In an effort to place the Cuban experience in proper perspective Knight elaborates on the theme of plantation America first popularized by Charles Wagley.[29] Without going as far as I have in rejecting the concept of slave systems, Knight nevertheless clearly shows the importance of plantations as the central institution for determining the social conditions of black slaves. His entire work implies, if it does not explicitly state, that the lifestyle and expectations of black slaves depended much more on their mode of employment, their location, the profitability of their economic endeavor, and the degree of mechanization of their plantation than on their slave status.[30] While Knight's work is not the first to develop this theme, his book refines it and carries it out more fully than most of its predecessors.[31]

---

[28] The failure of the slave-system concept to encourage meaningful distinctions makes it extremely difficult to appraise the role and significance of these *negros de ganho*, practically free slaves who worked independently and only fulfilled the obligation of paying a stated sum to the master.

[29] Charles Wagley, "Plantation America: A Culture Sphere," in *Caribbean Studies: A Symposium*, ed. Vera Rubin (Jamaica, B.W.I.: Institute of Social and Economic Research, University College of the West Indies, 1957), pp. 3–13. See also Sidney M. Greenfield, "Slavery and the Plantation in the New World," *Journal of Inter-American Studies* 11, no. 1 (1969): 44–57.

[30] Knight, *Slave Society in Cuba*, pp. 179–194.

[31] Both Harris and Genovese have made these points or suggested this approach, as has Sidney Mintz. But so far this concept has had little development except for the study of the plantation itself. See Pan American Union, Cultural Affairs Depart-

What this suggests is that we should shift our attention from the comparative history of slavery and slave systems. Such a focus has served its function and should now be de-emphasized in favor of social history more broadly conceived. Our first task is to reorganize our system of categories or, more properly put, our classification system. Instead of talking about slaves, let us talk, say, about artisans; let us concentrate on the lifestyle, the material conditions of work, the financial rewards, and the coercions applied to all artisans, whether slave or free. Slave artisans will live and work under certain restraints not experienced by free artisans, but the crucial distinction is that slave artisans should be studied as a subset of the general category of artisans, not as a subset of the general category of slaves. This approach will permit us to discover the dynamics of plantation society without being restricted by an artificial distinction between slave plantations and nonslave plantations. More important, as books like Knight's show, will be the distinction between mechanized and unmechanized plantations, the distinctions between highly profitable, expanding plantations and stagnating, marginally profitable operations.

It may be argued that this approach ignores the inhumanity and the oppression suffered by black people in slavery. But this objection is a foolish one. By lumping the black experience in America under the general term *slave system* we end up homogenizing a wholly unhomogeneous situation. Some blacks were brutally exploited on plantations, and other blacks lived better materially than many freemen. By putting these two types of experience together we end up with a deceptive statistical average for slavery that softens the brutality of some plantations while denying the advantageous position of urban black slaves. Such a confused means of assessing the import of black history does no one any good.

ment, *Plantation Systems of the New World*, Social Science Monograph No. 7 (Washington, D.C.: Pan American Union, 1959); Eric R. Wolf and Sidney Mintz, "Haciendas and Plantations in Middle America and the Antilles," *Social and Economic Studies* 6 (1957): 380–412; and especially George L. Beckford, *Persistent Poverty: Underdevelopment in Plantation Economies of the Third World* (New York: Oxford University Press, 1972).

Nor does the rejection of the slave-system idea mean the rejection of slave-centered topics. Not at all. Stuart B. Schwartz's excellent article on the *mocambos* of colonial Bahia provides a fine example of a social topic focused on slaves that can be carried off successfully.[32] And should someone want to compare outlaw and renegade communities throughout the Americas, such work would be welcome. The only danger to be avoided is the temptation to see runaway slaves and the slave system as the only elements in generating and maintaining such communities. If Schwartz's work and the investigations of R. K. Kent on Palmares teach us anything, they show the complexity of the relationship existing between the *quilombo* and the host society.[33] They show the important role played by nonslaves in the successes and failures of these communities, and they stress the variety of influences that create and maintain these bands of *cimarrones*. Runaway communities may require slavery, but they certainly cannot be understood as some part of a nonexistent slave system.

On a broader scale, we can look back almost to the beginning of this debate for a model to imitate. Stein's *Vassouras* is an excellent example of the socioeconomic history that offers so much promise. By restricting his focus to the *município* of Vassouras, Stein could talk about the totality of the slaves' universe and he could place those slaves within their social context. From Stein's book we can discover the functional relationship of all the people, slave or free, to each other and to their physical environment. It is this emphasis on explaining all the functional relationships within a social universe that gives this approach its strength. Although community studies are somewhat out of style among historians, that fact does not preclude us from approaching these subjects from such a perspective. For those who like their social history on a broader scale, there is James A. Lockhart's fascinating analysis of colonial Peru.[34] Free of the conceptual restrictions of a "slave system," Lockhart ends up telling us

[32] Stuart B. Schwartz, "The Mocambo: Slave Resistance in Colonial Bahia," *Journal of Social History* 3 (1970): 313–333.

[33] See R. K. Kent, "Palmares: An African State in Brazil," *Journal of African History* 6 (1965): 161–175.

[34] James A. Lockhart, *Spanish Peru 1532–1560: A Colonial Society* (Madison: University of Wisconsin Press, 1968), especially Ch. 10 (pp. 171–198).

more about slavery in Peru through his functional approach to the social universe than we could hope to get from traditional slavery studies.

Acceptance of the reorientation I have suggested here will have a major impact on the analyses and work of both Synthesizers and Diggers, although I suspect the Diggers will be the less affected. Rejection of the comparative slave-system methodology will severely disturb many Synthesizers whose greatest stretches of logic have been made in the futile effort to reconcile the contradictions inherent in any effort to compare Anglo-American and Latin American slavery. Yet, before we write off these fine minds and send them into a premature retirement, let us preview the kinds of topics available for grand synthetic schemes in the new approach.

One obvious area where the incisive criticism of the Synthesizers can be applied to good effect lies in the field of plantation analyses. Our Synthesizers have yet to thoroughly test the notion of plantation America. By the same careful analytical methods they brought to the field of comparative slavery, the synthetic masters can now refine and orient the comparative study of plantation economics and society in the New World. They can test the proposition that all plantations of a given size, profitability, and crop operate in much the same fashion whenever and wherever they occur.

Similarly, we need methodological and theoretical guidance from the Synthesizers for further progress in the historical analysis of the urban masses. Did the artisan groups, the domestic groups, and the menial workers of urban environments live and work amidst the same conditions and under the same handicaps throughout Latin America? Did the role of the urban poor, the vagabonds, and the marginal classes change from time to time and place to place?

Should our synthesizing friends refuse to give up on the notion of slave systems, they might well focus their comparative endeavors on such specific themes as the function, purpose, and frequency of manumissions throughout the Americas. Or perhaps a study of comparative abolition movements might be in order, although this topic offers less excitement than many others.

For the Diggers of our profession, the task remains much as before: mine the data, analyze its significance, and place it in its context. But they can focus their efforts on topics more likely to provide good test cases for the Synthesizers' new theories. Local social history and microeconomic studies must provide the understanding of the functional relationships in social reality so necessary for useful comparison. Family history and the analysis of kinship networks need to be carried out, as do historically oriented collective biographies.[35] Diggers can analyze individual plantations and recreate the social and economic structure of the elites. Demography must become a more frequent topic: how little we know about marriage patterns, or birth and death rates! How crude are our figures on population distribution![36] For Diggers fascinated with the slave status, many topics remain. Peter Eisenberg's study of the transition from slave to free labor in Pernambuco provides a fine example of this kind of work.[37] In short, the rejection of the notion of slave systems in no way restricts the field but rather releases us to emphasize more valuable topics.

[35] Some of the possibilities of this genre can be seen in Stephanie Blank's study of the Caracas colonial elite, "Social Integration and Social Stability in a Colonial Spanish American City: Caracas (1595–1627)" (Ph.D. dissertation, University of Wisconsin, 1971).

[36] There is a considerable literature on the populations of various areas within Latin America, but much of this work has been done as spin-offs from other topics. If all the available data on Latin American populations before 1850 could be brought together and systematized, much in the manner of Curtin's work on the slave trade, we would stand a better chance of making reasonable generalizations about Latin American populations. For some examples of recent population work of interest to the social history of slavery, see Dauril Alden, "The Population of Brazil in the Late Eighteenth Century," *Hispanic American Historical Review* 43 (1963): 173–205; Edgar F. Love, "Marriage Patterns of Persons of African Descent in a Colonial Mexico City Parish," ibid. 51 (1971): 79–91; and the forthcoming demographic compilation by John V. Lombardi and Trent M. Brady, *The Population of the Bishopric of Caracas, 1780–1838*. Indicative of the lack of coherent development in the field of Latin American historical demography is the durability of Wilbur Zelinsky's "The Historical Geography of the Negro Population of Latin America," *Journal of Negro History* 34 (1949): 153–221.

[37] Peter Eisenberg, "Abolishing Slavery: The Process on Pernambuco's Sugar Plantations," *Hispanic American Historical Review* 52 (1972): 580–597. This is by no means to ignore the work done by Knight, Conrad, and others on slave occupations as part of their studies but only to recommend that these topics deserve to be the central focus of analysis rather than peripheral to other subjects.

Once comparative history is focused on the whole of Latin American social and economic institutions rather than on some abstract notion of slave systems, the level of historical discussion will rise and the possibilities for important and satisfying results will greatly improve. With the decline of the idea of comparative slave systems, we will be freed to comprehend the real significance of the captive black man within the context of Latin American society. We will no longer need to speak of a disembodied abstraction inhabiting the statistical limbo of a slave system, but instead can find the *negro de carne y hueso* who worked in cities and on plantations, whose possibilities of life ranged from the most dismal to the very hopeful, and whose experience in America is rich with variety and meaning.

Approaches to Immigration History

MICHAEL M. HALL

Immigration can profoundly affect not only the lives of the migrants involved, but also the economic and social structure in the areas of their departure and arrival. Not surprisingly, a phenomenon with such far-reaching implications has attracted the attention of scholars from a number of disciplines. All of the social sciences have dealt to some extent with migration, and, while the results have thus far not been especially satisfying for those who hope to be able to discover significant general laws of human behavior, the literature is sizable and growing.[1]

Except for recent work on internal migrants, however, Latin America has been the subject of very little study in this area.[2] Neglect by

[1] J. J. Mangalam, *Human Migration: A Guide to Migration Literature in English, 1955–1962* (Lexington, Ky.: University of Kentucky Press, 1968); Brinley Thomas, *International Migration and Economic Development: A Trend Report and Bibliography* (Paris: UNESCO, 1961).

[2] A good introduction to internal migration is to be found in the *International Migration Review* 6, no. 2 (Summer 1972), which is an issue devoted to "Internal Migration in Latin America." In addition to the items cited elsewhere in the present essay, useful historical studies are Carl Solberg, *Immigration and Nationalism: Argentina and Chile, 1890–1914*, Latin American Monograph Series, no. 18 (Austin: University of Texas Press, 1970); Torcuato S. Di Tella, et al., *Argentina, sociedad de masas* (Buenos Aires: EUDEBA, 1965); and Juan Antonio Oddone, *La emigración europea al Río de la Plata* (Montevideo: Ediciones de la Banda Oriental, 1966).

historians is particularly unfortunate since, in the great migrations from Europe during the nineteenth and early twentieth centuries, Latin America was one of the major destinations. Although the total number of immigrants entering Brazil and Argentina was far smaller than the comparable statistic for the United States, the South American figures are still substantial. Between 1821 and 1932, some thirty-four million people emigrated from Europe to the United States, six and a half million to Argentina, four and a half million to Brazil.[3]

Such numbers seem especially significant in relation to the total population of the areas involved. While immigrants never represented more than 15 percent of the population of the United States, the comparable figure for Argentina was almost 30 percent in 1914, and the proportion remained as high as 23 percent until 1930. In certain important parts of Argentina, the concentration of immigrants was even greater. For over sixty years, some 70 percent of the adult population of Buenos Aires was composed of foreigners, and the figure was near 50 percent in several major provinces.[4]

Immigrants to Brazil were somewhat similarly concentrated in certain regions. About 55 percent of them went to São Paulo, which was economically by far the most important state in the republic. There they represented roughly 20 percent of the population from the 1890s to about 1920. At the latter date, some years after the period of heaviest immigration, the foreign-born still formed a majority of the adults in the city of São Paulo. Immigrants and their Brazilian-born children, it has been calculated, comprised over half the population of the state in 1934.[5]

The historical significance of Latin American immigration, however, does not derive simply from the numbers of people involved or

[3] Alexander M. Carr-Sanders, *World Population* (Oxford: The Clarendon Press, 1936), p. 49.

[4] Gino Germani, "Mass Immigration and Modernization in Argentina," in *Masses in Latin America*, ed. Irving Louis Horowitz (New York: Oxford University Press, 1970), pp. 289, 306.

[5] Samuel H. Lowrie, *Imigração e crescimento da população no estado de São Paulo* (São Paulo: Escola Livre de Sociologia e Política, 1938), pp. 8, 11, 42–43; Brazil, Ministério da Agricultura, Indústria e Comércio, Directoria Geral de Estatística, *Recenseamento do Brasil realizado em 1 de setembro de 1920*, IV, pt. 4, pp. 18–19.

from the fact that it is an important instance of a world-wide phenomenon. To take the Brazilian case, the one with which I am most
familiar, immigration seems to have had a major role in most of the
important historical transformations of the last hundred years: the
abolition of slavery, the expansion of the coffee economy, urbanization, industrialization, the formation of a proletariat. Immigrants
were not less important in the historical development of Argentina
or Uruguay. Granted the potential value of investigating the part immigration has played in such immensely complex matters, how one
proceeds in outlining a social history of the subject is far from clear.

The problem is one not so much of techniques as of conceptualization. Should the historian, for instance, use the categories of the sociologist? It is difficult, perhaps even impossible, to specify any altogether satisfactory distinctions between history and sociology—in
respect either to subject matter or to strategies of explanation.[6] There
has, however, clearly been something of a division of labor. Sociologists who study migration have generally focused either on the process
itself—primarily on questions about who migrates and why—or on the
problems related to assimilation in the host society. Some of the
techniques used in such studies are obviously not applicable to situations in which one can no longer interview or directly observe the
people involved. Even so, there are sometimes ways of collecting historical data that allow scholars to answer many of the same questions
about migration for past societies as for contemporary ones.

A more serious methodological problem is to be found in the
nature of the questions one asks. Some sociologists have sought to
formulate universal laws about migration, while others have regretted
the relative lack of success in such attempts and have urged their colleagues to redouble their efforts in search of general rules that would
be valid for migration at all times and in all places.[7] Historians have

[6] For a particularly lucid discussion of this question, see Philip Abrams, "Sociology and History," *Past and Present*, no. 52 (August 1971): 118–125. Cf. the quite
similar remarks by T. B. Bottomore in *Sociology: A Guide to Problems and Literature*, 2d ed. (New York: Random House, 1972), pp. 76–78.

[7] J. J. Mangalam and Harry K. Schwarzweller, "General Theory in the Study of
Migration: Current Needs and Difficulties," *International Migration Review* 3
(Fall 1968): 3–17; idem, "Some Theoretical Guidelines toward a Sociology of Mi-

customarily limited themselves to the description and explanation of rather specific cases, and their generalizations have applied at most to particular historical epochs and more commonly to individual groups or societies. As Eric Hobsbawm has put it, social history is "a collaboration between general models of social structure and change and the specific set of phenomena which actually occurred."[8]

One possible framework for examining immigration history in a way useful to both sociologists and historians has been suggested by Herbert J. Gans. In 1967 the editors of the *International Migration Review* asked Gans, a sociologist who has done important work on immigration, to suggest what seemed to him to be some of the crucial questions that historians should try to answer.[9] His specific questions, several of which will be examined at length below, are perhaps not too different from those that good immigration historians normally use, but they have not been systematically asked by scholars about Latin America. Moreover, they do help somewhat to focus historians' attention on some of the fundamental issues and to frame historical research in such a way as to make the results more readily useful to other disciplines. Gans also issued an intimidating challenge to historians to concentrate on "analytic historical research which addresses itself to fundamental questions of change and social process" and to make their discipline "*the* dynamic social science par excellence, synthesizing the methods and concepts of all the individual disciplines."[10]

gration," ibid. 4 (Spring 1970): 5–21; Everett S. Lee, "A Theory of Migration," *Demography* 3 (1966): 47–57.

[8] Eric J. Hobsbawm, "From Social History to the History of Society," in *Historical Studies Today*, ed. Felix Gilbert and Stephen R. Graubard (New York: W. W. Norton, 1972), p. 10. Pertinent examples of how two immigration historians deal with the question of generalization are found in Oscar Handlin's *The Uprooted* (Boston: Little, Brown, 1951) and Rudolph J. Vecoli's "*Contadini* in Chicago: A Critique of *The Uprooted*," *Journal of American History* 51 (December 1964): 404–417. Vecoli argues quite persuasively that Handlin has mistakenly taken the case of Eastern European immigrants in the United States to be characteristic of all immigrants.

[9] Herbert J. Gans, "Some Comments on the History of Italian Migration and on the Nature of Historical Research," *International Migration Review*, n.s. 1 (Summer 1967): 5–9.

[10] Ibid., pp. 8–9.

The remarks that follow attempt to combine some aspects of the sociologists' emphasis on general theory with the historians' interest in specificity and to suggest in the process several of the ways in which an understanding of immigration can illuminate more general concerns in Latin American social history. To keep matters within a reasonable compass, the discussion will be centered on the Italians in São Paulo—the largest and most important group of immigrants in Brazil—though an attempt will be made to see some aspects of their experience in comparative perspective. Unfortunately, research on many of the questions raised is still entirely lacking for most of Latin America, and it seems much too early for any satisfactory comparative synthesis—desirable as that would certainly be. Perhaps a discussion focused to a large extent on one important case, with a fairly specific survey of some of the technical and conceptual problems facing researchers in the field, can at least suggest the usefulness of additional and broader studies.

Mass immigration in Brazil was largely the result of a boom in world coffee prices that began in the late 1880s and continued for a decade. During this period, the São Paulo planters organized an elaborate system of importing families of Italian immigrants at government expense to work on the coffee fields. The treatment they received was harsh, and the bulk of them left either for other countries or for the city of São Paulo, only to be replaced by successive waves of Spaniards, Japanese, and internal Brazilian migrants—all contributing to the planters' goal of a cheap and abundant labor force. Yet, whatever the original reasons for their presence, the approximately one million Italians who came to São Paulo made it one of the major areas of world immigration, and the question of their subsequent history has implications not only for Brazil but also for the broader field of migration studies.

The first question Gans poses is "What kinds of people migrated from Italy?" The readily available historical data in the Brazilian case are unfortunately not very helpful in several important respects. For example, statistics on the occupations of arriving immigrants are quite useless because, in order to be eligible for the Brazilian subsidy, everyone had to declare himself an agricultural worker even though it was widely recognized at the time that many who did so were in fact not from such backgrounds. Further confusion arises because of a purported distinction made for certain years in the São Paulo statistics between "subsidized" and "spontaneous" immigrants. This was sometimes taken to imply that substantial numbers of artisans and urban workers were paying their way to São Paulo and that only the "subsidized" immigrants were agricultural workers. The "spontaneous" classification, however, appears to have been to a large extent a way of getting around a 1902 Italian ban on *prepaid* passages to São Paulo. A "spontaneous" immigrant could get his passage refunded *after* arrival, and a substantial number of such individuals were destined for work on the plantations.

Fortunately, the Italian government did collect data and conduct inquiries of various sorts about its departing citizens, and, in addition, there are other, more impressionistic Italian sources that can provide at least partial answers to questions about who the migrants were.[11] Preliminary research indicates that, especially during the fifteen years of heaviest emigration to Brazil (1887–1902), the current was made up largely of Northern Italian, especially Venetian, tenant farmers and casual agricultural laborers plus their families. After 1902, those destined for Brazil were more frequently from Southern Italy and, perhaps, more often urban in origin than their more numerous compatriots had been in the 1890s.

We know relatively little about the culture and social organization of nineteenth-century rural Northern Italy, which has been less well studied in these respects than has the South.[12] Skeptical as one may be about the general helpfulness of cultural explanations in history, it seems clear that more knowledge about the society from which the immigrants came would be useful in trying to understand their experience in the New World.

[11] The most extensive bibliography is in Grazia Dore's *La democrazia italiana e l'emigrazione in America* (Brescia: Morcelliana, 1964), pp. 381–493.

[12] An excellent bibliographical essay on recent Italian work is to be found in Fernando Manzotti's *La polemica sull'emigrazione nell'Italia unita*, 2d ed. (Milan: Società Editrice Dante Alighieri, 1969), pp. 186–194.

Might not some features of Northern Italian rural culture have been transferred to Brazil and decisively affected the immigrants' assimilation, say, or their economic behavior? Eunice Ribeiro Durham has, in fact, sought to account for the successes of Italian immigrants in São Paulo in terms of their prior experience with market economies, the organization of the "traditional Italian family," and the attitudes toward work and saving that they are said to have brought from their homeland.[13]

Professor Durham presents no evidence for her contention, and certainly research in the United States makes one wary of accepting explanations of immigrants' behavior that are based on intuitive notions about the culture and social structure of the places from which they came. Humbert Nelli, for example, in a recent book about Italians in Chicago, rather persuasively argues that, "ironically, the old-world community intimacy that Italians in America 'recalled' so nostalgically originated in the new world as a response to urban surroundings."[14]

At the very least, one needs to know a great deal more about such matters as the role and composition of the family in rural Venetia, the immigrants' prior political and economic experience, and their familiarity with collective action before generalizing very confidently about the sources of their behavior in Brazil. The argument, apparently accepted in Brazilian historiography, that the Italian immigrants' previous experiences explain their success—relative to the native Brazilian population at least—in the new industrial society that arose in São Paulo needs to be carefully studied.[15] Similarly, Gino Germani's assumption that, in Argentina, immigrants served as "agents of modernization" because of their European origins could probably benefit from closer examination of the particular historical reality.[16]

[13] Eunice Ribeiro Durham, *Assimilação e mobilidade* (São Paulo: Instituto de Estudos Brasileiros, 1966).

[14] Humbert S. Nelli, *The Italians in Chicago, 1880–1930* (New York: Oxford University Press, 1970), p. 6.

[15] Such an argument, for example, underlies Florestan Fernandes's explanation of why immigrants and not blacks formed the early São Paulo proletariat. See his *The Negro in Brazilian Society* (New York: Columbia University Press, 1969).

[16] Germani, "Mass Immigration and Modernization."

To take a very specific example of this problem, how is one to explain the presence of the Mafia in North America and the absence of anything resembling it in Brazil—in cultural terms, by the smaller Southern Italian emigration to Brazil, or by differences in the host countries and the immigrants' place in them (wider access, perhaps, in Brazil to other sources of wealth and power)?

While no one can deny that additional knowledge about the characteristics, culture, and previous history of immigrant groups is highly desirable, it may well be that such matters are far less important in determining what happens to newcomers than is the economic and social structure of the recipient countries. Careful comparative history could obviously advance our understanding of this whole complex subject.

Gans' second set of questions deals with the immigrants' initial motivations: "For what reasons did Italians migrate?" "How did they choose the country to which they emigrated?" Once again, the sources available to the historian who attempts to answer such questions for Brazil are far from satisfactory. There has been no systematic effort to collect and preserve primary documentation about the Italians in São Paulo. While such material probably still exists, research in Italy and Brazil has turned up no sizable collections of the sorts of letters, diaries, and other accounts that have so enriched our understanding of the history of various immigrant groups in the United States. Without such documentation, the inquiries into the psychological motives behind emigration that researchers who study contemporary migrations are able to make remain very inferential indeed.[17]

In general terms, however, it seems evident that the "push" factors were overwhelmingly more important than the "pull" in the São Paulo case. The planters were quite fortunate in that their labor crisis coincided with what Gino Luzzato has termed "the most critical years of the Italian economy."[18] The disastrous competition of cheap

[17] For examples of the sorts of questions one might want to ask, see Gino Germani, "Migration and Acculturation," in *Handbook for Social Research in Urban Areas*, ed. Philip M. Hauser (Paris: UNESCO, 1965), pp. 159–178.

[18] Gino Luzzato, "Gli anni più critici dell'economia italiana (1888–1893)," in *L'economia italiana dal 1861 al 1961* (Milan: Dott. A. Giuffrè, 1961), pp. 420–452.

American grain in Italian markets, when added to the long-standing malaise of Italian agriculture and other factors, created a ready supply of desperate emigrants. Italian sources of the period leave little doubt that those who departed were fleeing an increasingly hopeless situation for themselves in Italy and that they ended up in Brazil in most cases largely because the country provided free passage from Genoa.[19] Certainly the emigrants had only the foggiest of notions about what to expect in their new country, and when knowledge of the fate that had befallen the migrants on the Brazilian coffee plantations became widespread in their homeland, the Italian government was eventually compelled to place an outright ban on subsidized emigration to São Paulo.

What the dominance of "push" over "pull" meant in this case, however, remains obscure. One could hypothesize, for example, that in such a situation immigrants would be more apt to reject identification with their homeland and would thus assimilate more readily in their new surroundings. It might also seem plausible, however, to argue that, since the newcomers had made little commitment in choosing Brazil and had little knowledge about it, their adjustment there would be different, perhaps more difficult, than in other countries and that they might be more inclined to leave in the face of adversity.

Direct evidence for such propositions is very hard to come by, and attempts at explanation along the lines suggested rapidly become enmeshed in immense complications. For example, support for various "patriotic" Italian causes and organizations was notoriously weak in São Paulo, but class and regional divisions within the colony seem to have had far more to do with the matter than any lingering resentments over the circumstances under which mass immigration had taken place. It is likewise difficult to attribute the exceptionally high rate of departures (almost 50 percent) from São Paulo to a lack of "pull" in the original immigration. The departure rate is significant when compared to that prevailing in the United States and Argentina,

[19] Some of the most conclusive evidence on this score is to be found in the detailed reports of local officials printed in Italy, Ministero de Agricoltura, Industria e Commercio, Direzione Generale della Statistica, *Statistica della emigrazione italiana avvenuta nell anno 1888* (Rome: Aldina, 1889).

especially since Brazil saw virtually none of the seasonal migration that took place in those two countries, but economic realities quite unconnected with the original decision to migrate could easily provide a sufficient explanation for the differences.

Historical research in the third area of investigation suggested by Gans seems more promising. "What happened to the Italians in their new country?" "What social and economic roles did Italians play in the host country?" "What social, political and cultural institutions did they develop?"

Economically, immigrants served as the "reserve army of the unemployed" in the development of Brazilian capitalism. They provided cheap labor for export agriculture and later for industry, though the extent to which they may have contributed to economic growth by holding down wages and maintaining high rates of profits, investments, and expansion remains to be studied. Their presence certainly facilitated the transition from slavery to free labor in the São Paulo coffee industry in the 1880s, and they provided at least a somewhat better market than slaves had for domestically produced consumer goods.

Detailed investigations by various researchers into the social history of rural São Paulo are just beginning. Analysis of local and plantation records will undoubtedly help deepen our understanding, but the Italian consular reports on Brazil and the Italian-language press already allow the historian to reconstruct at least the main features of immigrant life in the rural areas.[20] It seems clear that the turnover of plantation workers was rapid, that most suffered quite extraordinary exploitation, and that the immigrants served essentially as a rural proletariat, only rarely managing to buy land.

The lot of the immigrants who came to the city of São Paulo either directly from overseas or after a period on the coffee fazendas is more complex. We do know that the first generation of the urban working

---

[20] In addition to the Dore bibliography cited earlier, see Giorgio Mortara, "Bibliografia sôbre a emigração italiana para o Brasil," *Revista Brasileira de Estatística* 7 (1956): 308–323, and Guido Manzini, "Studi e pubblicazioni italiane sul Brasile dal 1900 al 1940: Saggio bibliografico," typewritten (Florence, 1945). I have used the copy of the Manzini bibliography at the Library of Congress.

class in São Paulo was almost wholly foreign-born, but its history remains to be written. Questions of class consciousness, labor militancy,
and working-class culture have heretofore been debated on a rather
a priori basis.[21]

The most promising single source for the history of urban immigrants is the working-class press of the period, of which few traces
are to be found in public Brazilian repositories. There are several important collections still in private hands, often in circumstances that
make both consultation and future preservation quite precarious.
Sizable holdings can also be found in Europe, including an extraordinarily extensive collection at the International Institute for Social
History in Amsterdam. There seem to be virtually no surviving union
records, which, given the ferocity of state repression, is not too surprising. The Brazilian government did not collect systematic data on
labor disputes until recent years, and the usefulness of trying to reconstruct such information from the press seems problematic on account of censorship and other obstacles.

Perhaps the central question for our purposes concerns the significance for the history of the São Paulo proletariat of its immigrant
origins. While foreign-born workers may have perceived themselves
as more isolated from society than they would have, had they not been
immigrants, this factor probably limited their influence by helping prevent what was, after all, a rather small part of the total population
from seeking allies among discontented Brazilians. Moreover, while
nationalism—the frequent solvent of class sentiments—was not too
effective in that capacity for the immigrant generation, it seems to
have had considerably more influence among their Brazilian-born
children during the 1920s. Similarly, such questions as the effect of
the workers' immigrant origins on the extent and meaning of repression or on the real influence of revolutionary ideologies within
the São Paulo proletariat are still to be answered.

Not all Italians were workers; a handful were successful entrepreneurs, and their fame has long confused popular perceptions of

---

21 The best account, and one which is more a history of the labor movement than
of the working class, is Azis Simão's *Sindicato e estado* (São Paulo: Dominus Edi-
tôra, 1966).

Brazilian immigration history. Virtually all the well-known entrepreneurs were from impeccably petit-bourgeois backgrounds, and their careers tell us little about the social mobility of the Italian-born population.[22] In addition, recent research has tended to deny that any special "entrepreneurial" qualities, of either local or immigrant origins, are of significance in explaining early São Paulo industrialization.[23]

The specific role of Italians is unclear in any case. One study found that 34.8 percent of São Paulo entrepreneurs in 1962 either were Italian-born or had fathers or grandfathers born in Italy (compared to 15.7 percent who were third-generation Brazilians), but this says nothing about the importance of Italians in the earlier stages of economic development.[24] There is some scattered evidence that such immigrants were less significant in the beginning of Brazilian industrialization than were their compatriots in Argentina.[25]

Oscar Cornblit has argued that the industrialists' immigrant origins in Argentina and the hostility of various powerful groups toward them prevented such entrepreneurs from working out political al-

[22] Warren Dean, *The Industrialization of São Paulo, 1880–1945*, Latin American Monograph Series, no. 17 (Austin: University of Texas Press, 1969), pp. 49–66. A critical study of the most famous entrepreneur of them all is José de Souza Martins's *Empresário e emprêsa na biografia do Conde Matarazzo* (Rio de Janeiro: Instituto de Ciências Sociais da Universidade Federal do Rio de Janeiro, 1967).

[23] This is one of the major themes of Warren Dean's *Industrialization*. See also his article, "The Planter as Entrepreneur: The Case of São Paulo," *Hispanic American Historical Review* 46 (May 1966): 138–152.

[24] Luiz Carlos Bresser Pereira, "Origens étnicas e sociais do empresário paulista," *Revista de Administração de Emprêsas* 4 (June 1964): 83–106. The results are not especially surprising in view of the heavy foreign population in São Paulo. Bertram Hutchinson found in 1956 that only one-quarter of the adult population had been born in Brazil of Brazilian-born parents and grandparents. See his "Structural and Exchange Mobility in the Assimilation of Immigrants to Brazil," *Population Studies* 12 (1958–1959): 112.

[25] Italians owned 1,446 of 2,966 individually owned firms in São Paulo in 1920. See *Recenseamento*, V, pt. 1, pp. lvii, lxi. But foreigners (not just Italians) controlled only 68 of 428 corporations listed for Rio and São Paulo in 1914 (Luciano Martins, "Formação do empresariado industrial no Brasil," *Revista do Instituto de Ciências Sociais* 3 [1966]: 105). The preponderance of immigrants in the ownership of Argentine industry is discussed by Roberto Cortés Conde in "La expansión de la economía argentina entre 1870 y 1914 y el papel de la inmigración," *Cahiers du Monde Hispanique et Luso-Brésilien* 10 (1968): 81–82.

liances to advance their long-term interests.[26] Their counterparts in Brazil seem not to have faced isolation and obstacles of that sort, but, on the other hand, they made no more progress in securing governmental policies favorable to industrialization.[27] Given the rather different political systems of the two countries, the meaning of the comparison is ambiguous, though perhaps it suggests that the alleged spirit of industrial entrepreneurship among São Paulo immigrants has been somewhat overrated.

Systematic studies of the social and geographical mobility of the Italians in São Paulo are also lacking. In fact, it seems unlikely that research of the sort associated with Stephan Thernstrom and other "new urban historians" in the United States can be duplicated for São Paulo.[28] The city does not have, for the late nineteenth and early twentieth centuries, the manuscript census returns, directories, and tax records that would allow researchers to trace the histories of large numbers of individuals over time.

However, from impressionistic evidence and the high rate of departures, one suspects that geographical mobility in São Paulo took place on a scale comparable to that in the United States, and it seems to have had a similarly devastating effect on working-class consciousness.[29] Residential segregation of a sort existed in São Paulo, or at least identifiable Italian districts did—some of which were based on regional origins. However, the real extent and significance of such ethnic neighborhoods remains to be studied. Perhaps parish or notarial documents, or even records from the Italian regional associations, in lieu of manuscript census returns, would enable researchers to investigate the matter in a systematic way.

[26] Oscar Cornblit, "European Immigrants in Argentine Industry and Politics," in *The Politics of Conformity in Latin America*, ed. Claudio Veliz (New York: Oxford University Press, 1967), pp. 221–248.

[27] Dean, *Industrialization*, pp. 72–73.

[28] For an introduction, see Stephan Thernstrom, "Reflections on the New Urban History," in *Historical Studies Today*, ed. Felix Gilbert and Stephen R. Graubard (New York: W. W. Norton, 1972), pp. 320–336.

[29] See Stephan Thernstrom and Peter R. Knights, "Men in Motion: Some Data and Speculations about Urban Population Mobility in Nineteenth-Century America," *Journal of Interdisciplinary History* 1 (Autumn 1970): 7–35.

The one available major survey of social mobility was conducted by Bertram Hutchinson in 1956.[30] He found that, in a sample of the adult population of the city of São Paulo, the rate of upward mobility declined, while that of downward mobility increased, the greater the Brazilian ingredient in the subject's ancestry. For example, of those who were born in Brazil of foreign-born parents and grandparents, 49 percent were of higher status than their fathers, 39 percent were the same and 12 percent were lower; for the group whose parents and grandparents were Brazilian, the figures were 28 percent, higher, 50 percent, the same and 22 percent, lower. Hutchinson also found that the upwardly mobile were not ejecting Brazilians from their positions but were occupying new ones that formerly did not exist. Some three-quarters of all upward mobility among immigrants and their children was only possible because of the emergence of new status positions.

Hutchinson further suggests that the relatively small danger to the native population of socioeconomic competition from immigrants may partially explain "the good relations which on the whole have marked the process of immigrant absorption in São Paulo." Certainly one can hardly exaggerate the importance of the Italians' having arrived in Brazil and Argentina during an early stage of economic development in both countries and thus having been able readily to take advantage of opportunities arising from economic growth. The Italians' entry at a much later phase in the history of the North American economy has decisively marked their experience in the United States.[31]

The largest body of research on Italians in Brazil has dealt with assimilation. The emphasis for São Paulo has generally been on the rapidity and completeness of the process. "What normally happens in three

[30] Hutchinson, "Structural and Exchange Mobility." While a number of questions could be raised about the definitions and methodology of the study, the greatest problem for historical purposes is that it includes only those immigrants and their children who were still around to be interviewed in 1956—a major difficulty indeed for a city, such as São Paulo, with a high rate of out-migration.

[31] Hutchinson, "Structural and Exchange Mobility," p. 120; Humbert Nelli, "Italians in Urban America," in *The Italian Experience in the United States*, ed. Silvano M. Tomasi and Madeline H. Engel (New York: Center for Migration Studies, 1970), p. 101.

generations, happened here in two," José Arthur Rios has exclaimed.
"It is incredible the rapidity with which assimilation proceeds."[32] The
evidence for such remarks—and they fill the literature—is less overwhelming than one might expect, but the contrast with the United
States is striking. Here, as Gans and others have maintained, Italian
immigrants "acculturated but were not assimilated."[33]

The simplest explanation for such a contrast is based on differences
in culture. Italians going to Brazil, the argument runs, found another
Catholic country that also spoke a Romance language and supposedly
shared a "Latin" culture. Immigrants would adjust more readily in
such a situation than in the United States. So far as I know, no historian has ever systematically investigated the matter. It is far from
obvious, however, that the similarity of cultures was as great as one
might suppose. Whether family structures, say, or belief systems were
in fact nearly the same in both societies is surely an empirical question.
The scattered bits of evidence now available are inconclusive. Carlo
Castaldi found that immigrants and native Brazilians rate the prestige
of various occupations similarly, but Thales de Azevedo and Marialice
Foracchi reported for widely separated regions of Brazil that Italians
have notably different attitudes toward work from those of the host
society.[34] Altiva Pilatti Balhana found additional evidence of cultural
differences between the two groups.[35]

Other explanations for the differing patterns of assimilation must,
after all, be taken into account. For one, massive Italian immigration

---

[32] José Arthur Rios, "Aspectos políticos da assimilação do italiano no Brasil,"
Sociologia 20 (1958): 338.

[33] Gans, "Comments," p. 6. See Milton Gordon, *Assimilation in American Life*
(New York: Oxford University Press, 1964) for a thoughtful presentation of this
general point of view. Gans's own book, *The Urban Villagers: Group and Class in
the Life of Italian-Americans* (New York: The Free Press, 1962), has been one of
the most influential studies of the subject.

[34] Carlo Castaldi, "Nota sôbre a hierarquia das ocupações segundo os imigrantes
italianos em São Paulo," *Educação e Ciências Sociais* 1 (1956): 118; Thales de
Azevedo, "Italian Colonization in Southern Brazil," *Anthropological Quarterly* 34
(1961): 65; Marialice Foracchi, "A valorização do trabalho na ascensão social dos
imigrantes," *Revista do Museu Paulista*, n.s. 14 (1963): 311–319.

[35] Altiva Pilatti Balhana, *Santa Felicidade: Um processo de assimilação* (Curi-
tiba: João Haupt, 1958), p. 243.

ended in Brazil almost as it was starting in the United States, and the São Paulo colony received new members on a very reduced scale after the 1902 ban. The Italians in the United States may for some time have remained closer in many respects to their European origins than did their counterparts in Brazil. The relative proportion of Italians and the stage of economic development at the time of their arrival might also prove on careful investigation to be as important in the assimilation process as cultural similarities.

The specific evidence on various aspects of assimilation in Brazil also leaves something to be desired. The use of the language of the host country is probably one of the better indicators of acculturation, and the most widely cited Brazilian statistics on the subject come from the census of 1940. They show only 13 percent of the Italians in São Paulo preferring to speak their native tongue and only 8.7 percent unable to speak fluent Portuguese. Such figures are usually hailed as evidence of remarkably rapid acculturation and, if true, they certainly would be.[36]

However, the date of the census (September, 1940) followed a period of intense agitation in Brazil over the question of unassimilated foreign minorities, and such extraordinary figures on linguistic acculturation are quite likely the result of an understandable reluctance of the respondents to identify themselves as unassimilated. Other research clearly suggests that the 1940 figures are misleading. Carlo Castaldi, for example, in a study of an Italian neighborhood in São Paulo conducted in the mid-1950s found that 49 percent of the residents between the ages of eighteen and forty (only 12 percent of whom had been born in Italy) normally still spoke an Italian dialect in their homes.[37]

Statistics on intermarriage can be equally misleading. Giorgio Mortara cites figures for the 1930s showing Italians marrying Bra-

[36] Giorgio Mortara, "Immigration to Brazil: Some Observations on the Linguistic Assimilation of Immigrants and Their Descendants in Brazil," in *Cultural Assimilation of Immigrants* (supplement to *Population Studies* 3 [March 1950]), pp. 39–44.

[37] Carlo Castaldi, "O ajustamento do imigrante à comunidade paulistana: Estudo de um grupo de imigrantes italianos e de seus descendentes," in *Mobilidade e trabalho*, ed. Bertram Hutchinson (Rio de Janeiro: Centro Brasileiro de Pesquisas Educacionais, 1960), p. 292.

zilians in São Paulo at a rapid clip, and he infers that this is evidence for a high "index of assimilation."[38] Actually, what was going on is a process Hutchinson has termed "disguised endogamy," since Italians were marrying largely the Brazilian-born children of Italians. Such marriages appear in the statistics, however, as taking place between Italians and Brazilians. In some 88 percent of such so-called mixed marriages involving Italians, the parents of the Brazilian-born spouse were also Italian.[39]

Such figures are obviously influenced by the high proportion of second- and third-generation Italians in São Paulo and it is difficult to know how to interpret them. Especially in the post–World War II period, there seems to be virtually no evidence of prejudice against Italians.[40]

The immigrants' feelings toward the Brazilians varied so much with period and class that generalizations are difficult. It does seem clear, however, that Italians in São Paulo were rather less intimidated by the host culture than were their compatriots in North America. Nelli reports that Italian-language newspapers in the United States often provided their readers with "advice regarding behavior and modes of expression acceptable to Americans."[41] This was hardly a common practice in São Paulo. The famous Italian-language daily *Fanfulla*, in fact, was often inclined to reverse the procedure and lecture the Brazilians on suitable behavior.

The whole process of assimilation was also obviously influenced by the absence of strong and organized antiforeign sentiments in São Paulo. With a few ambiguous exceptions in the 1890s, nativism in the state was neither very strong nor particularly directed against the Italians. This fact doubtless had a great deal to do with the absence of a Brazilian working class for the immigrants to compete with, but it is

[38] Giorgio Mortara, "Pesquisas sôbre populações americanas," *Estudos Brasileiros de Demografia* 1 (1947): 198–199.

[39] Bertram Hutchinson, "Some Evidence Related to Matrimonial Selection and Immigrant Assimilation in Brazil," *Population Studies* 11 (1957–1958): 155.

[40] Manuel Diégues and Arthur Hehl Neiva, "The Cultural Assimilation of Immigrants in Brazil," in *The Cultural Integration of Immigrants*, ed. W. D. Borrie (Paris: UNESCO, 1959), p. 195.

[41] Nelli, "Italians in Urban America," p. 92.

also probably related to the weakness of Brazilian nationalism. Brazil was a peripheral and dependent country with a small, ineffective, and quite cosmopolitan bourgeoisie. Nationalistic pressure directed against Italians was very limited before 1920 and probably had more to do with social class than with nationality after that date.

Italians did not play much of a role in São Paulo politics before 1945, but then neither did the bulk of the Brazilian population. The elite hardly encouraged mass political participation, and the apathy of the Italian colony toward the rather meaningless elections of the Old Republic (1889–1930) is understandable. Rios maintains that the Italians were too divided by class and region to participate effectively as a group in politics, and perhaps he is right, though it is difficult to see how even a unified colony would have worked its political will on the São Paulo oligarchy in any case.[42]

It is hard to understand assimilation until we have detailed historical studies of how the process went on. What was the role of the school system? Of housing patterns? How did Italian societies and associations affect assimilation? To such questions we have, thus far, almost no answers. And yet it is primarily by means of thorough comparative investigation of these and related matters that Latin American history can make important contributions to our understanding of such significant phenomena as assimilation. Comparative studies are generally the nearest historians can come to laboratory tests for their hypotheses, and Latin America in this field provides a vast laboratory indeed.

Ultimately, I think, the case of the São Paulo Italians strikes one as paradoxical. Why did such a vast group exert so little influence on the host culture? It would be quite difficult to argue, for example, that the Italians moved Brazilian, or even *paulista*, society in directions it might not otherwise have gone. Mass immigration in Brazil left the essential structures of power unchanged. In fact, by providing a readily exploitable labor force at a key period, immigration may have even strengthened such structures. Interestingly, Roberto Cortés

---

[42] Rios, "Aspectos políticos," p. 332.

Conde has reached quite similar conclusions about the significance of immigration for Argentina.[43]

Those Latin American countries, such as Mexico, in which cheap labor was more readily available than in Argentina and Brazil and which have thus had little recourse to large-scale European immigration since independence hardly seem to have suffered from the fact. In any case, the performance of the Mexican economy over the last thirty or forty years certainly compares favorably with that of countries that did receive heavy immigration, and it would be hard to argue that differences in, say, political culture—which may not be very substantial in any event—have a great deal to do with the presence or absence of large numbers of immigrants.

São Paulo does provide evidence to support the proposition, which Gans has suggested for the United States, that what happens to migrants is ultimately "less a function of their characteristics and culture than of the economic and political opportunities which are open to them when they arrived [*sic*] and subsequently." As he points out, such a proposition, if empirically demonstrated, "would move the burden of adjustment from the shoulders of the individual immigrant and lay it at the feet of the economic power structure and caretaker elements in the larger society who determine how the immigrant will be treated and what he will be allowed to do."[44]

The implications of such a hypothesis are almost as substantial for Brazil as for the United States, and its investigation should be high on the agenda for Brazilian social history. Not only can the study of immigration illuminate important aspects of the national histories of several Latin American countries, but such studies can also make useful contributions to more general theoretical concerns.

[43] Cortés Conde, "La expansión," pp. 78–79, 86–88.
[44] Gans, "Comments," p. 8.

Psychoanalysis and Latin American History

MARGARET TODARO WILLIAMS

Latin American historians employ psychologically laden concepts such as *caudillismo*, *machismo*, *personalismo*, *caciquismo*, and *paternalismo* all the time. It seems strange, therefore, that almost no Latin American historian has attempted to use the techniques of psychoanalysis to understand these phenomena. As long ago as 1958, William Langer devoted his presidential address to the American Historical Association to urging that historians avail themselves of the theoretical riches of psychoanalysis in order to study man and his motivations on yet another level.

Americanists, Europeanists, Sovietologists, and students of other historical branches responded to his challenge, producing a long bibliography of psychohistorical studies.[1] Latin Americanists con-

NOTE. I wish to thank Bruce Mazlish, James Wilkie, and the editors of this volume for their careful reading of the manuscript and for their valuable suggestions. I owe a special debt of gratitude to Peter Loewenberg, not only for critically commenting on the essay, but also for awakening my interest in psychohistory several years ago.

[1] A few recent studies include: Anne Jardim, *The First Henry Ford: A Study in Personality and Business Leadership* (Cambridge: MIT Press, 1971); Carl Binger, "Conflicts in the Life of Thomas Jefferson," *American Journal of Psychiatry* 125 (February 1969): 1098–1107; Alan Beckman, "Hidden Themes in the Frontier Thesis: An Application of Psychoanalysis to Historiography," *Comparative Studies in Society and History* 8 (1966): 361–382; Arnold Rogow, "Private Illness and Public Policy: The Cases of James Forrestal and John Winant," *The American*

spicuously ignored the new field. Although our area of specialization has its economic historians, its intellectual and social historians, its military and political historians, I know of not one of us who might legitimately qualify as a psychohistorian.

Gilberto Freyre talked about sex. Philosophers and psychoanalysts, including Samuel Ramos, Octavio Paz, Carlos Octavio Bunge, and Ancieto Aramoni, have provided us with fascinating interpretations of the collective psychology of their countries.[2] However, only Ramón Menéndez Pidal, in *El padre Las Casas, su doble personalidad*, persistently utilized some of the concepts and techniques of psychoanalysis, albeit in an intuitive and untrained fashion, to give us a startling and revisionist view of the savior of the Amerindian.[3]

Journal of Psychiatry 125 (February 1969): 1093–1097; John Demos, "Underlying Themes in the Witchcraft of Seventeenth Century New England," *American Historical Review* 75 (June 1970): 1311–1326; Peter Loewenberg, "The Unsuccessful Adolescence of Heinrich Himmler," ibid. 76 (June 1971): 612–641: idem, "The Psycho-Historical Origins of the Nazi Youth Cohort: 1928–1933," ibid. 76 (December 1971): 1457–1502; Rudolph Binion, "Repeat Performance: A Psychohistorical Study of Leopold III and Belgian Neutrality," *History and Theory* 8 (Spring 1969): 213–259; William Blanchard, *Rousseau and the Spirit of Revolt: A Psychological Study* (Ann Arbor: University of Michigan Press, 1967): E. Victor Wolfenstein, *The Revolutionary Personality: Lenin, Trotsky, Gandhi* (Princeton: Princeton University Press, 1967); Susanne H. Rudolph, "Self Control and Political Potency: Gandhi's Asceticism," *American Scholar* 35 (Winter 1965): 79–97.

[2] See Gilberto Freyre, *The Masters and the Slaves*, trans. Samuel Putnam, 3d ed. (New York: Alfred A. Knopf, 1967); Samuel Ramos, *Profile of Man and Culture in Mexico* (New York: McGraw-Hill, 1963); Octavio Paz, *The Labyrinth of Solitude: Life and Thought in Mexico* (New York: Grove Press, 1961); Carlos Octavio Bunge, *Nuestra América: Ensayo de psicología social* (Buenos Aires: Vaccaro, 1918); Ancieto Aramoni, *Psicoanálisis de la dinámica de un pueblo* (Mexico City: Universidad Nacional Autónoma de México, 1960). Recently, psychoanalysts Erich Fromm and Michael Maccoby have turned their attention to Latin America in *Social Character in a Mexican Village* (Englewood Cliffs, N.J.: Prentice-Hall, 1970). They raise some interesting questions regarding the interrelations between the emotional attitudes of the Mexican peasant and his socioeconomic situation.

[3] Ramón Menéndez Pidal, *El padre Las Casas, su doble personalidad* (Madrid: Espasa-Calpe, 1963). The historical works of the Spanish physician and humanist Gregorio Marañón, while rich in psychological insight, do not utilize explicitly psychoanalytic concepts. See, for example, his *Antonio Pérez, Spanish Traitor* (London: Hollis and Carter, 1954). Similarly, Ezequiel Chávez's *Ensayo de psicología de Sor Juana Inés de la Cruz* (Barcelona: Araluce, 1931) is more an interpretive literary essay than a psychological analysis of the subject's life and works, despite

This methodological gap in the field of Latin American history seems all the more curious in light of events of recent history that cry for explanation on the psychological level. Frequent references to "personality cults" and "*-ista* parties" emphasize this dimension. Revolution, radicalism, and the appeals of mass political movements from Integralism to Castroism invite interpretation in terms of individual and group psychology.

Similarly, many long-functioning systems for regulating social and economic relations in Latin America have yet to be approached from the psychoanalytic perspective. Commonly observed phenomena indicated by the words *palanca, parentela,* and *pistolão* appear susceptible to explanation in terms of dependency needs or identity conflict as well as in socioeconomic terms. The study of master-slave, *patrón-peón* relations surely falls as much within the purview of the psychohistorian as of the social historian. The role of women in Latin American society, like the problem of race relations, might fruitfully be explored from the psychosexual viewpoint.

Colonial and neocolonial relationships inevitably involve psychological confrontations and interactions. Latin Americans from Bolívar to Rodó to Arévalo to Castro have understood as much in their defenses of "Nuestra América." Psychohistorical investigation of the Latin American wars from the Paraguayan to the Chaco—all launched on waves of patriotic sentimentality—can reveal much about the origins of aggression.

Finally, a psychohistorical approach to Latin American history does not exclude work on earlier, prenational themes. Many Iberian concepts, such as *hidalguismo* and *limpieza de sangre*, can best be comprehended in psychocultural terms. Inquisition records on the trials of Jews, homosexuals, prostitutes, blasphemers, and sexual aberrants, viewed from the psychoanalytic perspective, may enable us to recon-

---

the book's title. The psychologist Roberto Agramonte examines the historical figure of Gabriel García Moreno in *Biografía del dictador García Moreno, estudio psicopatológico e histórico* (La Habana: Cultural, 1935). This work succumbs to the lure of reductionism. Agramonte views the Ecuadorean caudillo entirely in psychopathological terms and, in his eagerness to prove the common root of "genius and criminality" in "degeneracy," abjures all semblance of historical balance.

struct the morality and mentality of early Hispanic America. The possibilities seem limitless, yet little has been done.

This essay, then, is addressed to historians of the Latin American area. Its general purpose simply is to interest Latin American historians in psychohistory, that is, in the use of psychoanalysis as a historical tool. It rests on the assumption that the past eighty years have proven the validity of psychoanalysis as a theory of human psychology and a methodology for the study of human motivation and behavior as well as a technique for the treatment of emotional disturbances. Specifically, the essay will attempt: first to answer arguments against and clarify misconceptions about the field of psychohistory, particularly as it relates to Latin American history; second, to demonstrate the "how-to" of psychohistory through use of a Brazilian case study in psychobiography; third, to indicate the interpretive possibilities of such investigations; and, fourth, to suggest some useful starting points for the interested Latin American historian.

What accounts for the peculiar hesitancy on the part of Latin American historians in exploring the theoretical and empirical possibilities of a psychoanalytic approach?

At least part of the answer seems to rest on the mistaken (but popular) notion that psychohistory means the mechanical application of Freudian theory to the Latin American area and its historical figures. Thus, psychohistory seems little more than a documentary search for evidence of individual or national neuroses and psychoses for the purpose of formulating monocausal historical interpretations. The psychohistorian, perceived in this inappropriate manner, seems to lay false claim to possessing *the* true explanation for historical causation.

A second misconceived argument against psychohistory focuses on the irrelevance of studying deviant personalities and behavior. What possible use can Latin American historians make of knowing that the Brazilian *pensador* Jackson de Figueiredo exhibited severe symptoms of schizophrenia or that identity conflicts have plagued the political careers of certain mulatto and Negro politicians? Some will contend that, while such knowledge may possess an inherent fascination, the neuroses of individuals can tell us nothing about Latin American society.

A third and related misconception probably has its origin in our own notion of the Latin American field as "underdeveloped." Although most historians would admit the utility of psychoanalytic technique in explaining manifestations of social pathology, many Latin Americanists would argue that such aberrations hardly deserve priority in a field in which basic studies of institutions and political processes have hardly begun. Antonio Conselheiro, messianic cults, and *voodún* do not represent the Church. Gabriel García Moreno does not represent the Ecuadorean people. The antisemitism of the Integralists does not characterize Brazilian political ideology. The historians of an underdeveloped field view psychohistory as a luxury in which they cannot afford to indulge until the constant, the representative are known entities.

Finally, reflecting the sometimes maddeningly difficult job of doing any kind of research in Latin America, many historians will insist that the documents needed for psychohistorical investigation simply will not be found. This, they may assert, is particularly true because psychoanalytic theory focuses on infancy and childhood, periods for which we have the least written evidence. And, since most of the personages whom we would investigate are dead, no possibility for this type of inquiry remains open to us.

These four arguments stem from a basic confusion as to the nature of psychoanalytic methodology. Although psychoanalysis has had pretensions to being a science, in fact its methodology is historical.[4] The psychoanalytic covering law of overdetermination recognizes that there are multiple explanations for a single manifest psychic phenomenon. This law forces the analyst to operate exactly like the historian: both must seek and expect a variety of explanations for unitary occurrences. Both must reconstruct history from their different sources. In the analyst's case, the sources are the patient's dreams, as-

---

[4] John Klauber discusses psychoanalysis as science and psychoanalysis as history in "On the Dual Use of Historical and Scientific Method in Psychoanalysis," *International Journal of Psycho-Analysis* 49 (1968): 80–88.

sociations, and recollections of his early history. In the historian's case, the sources are written documents.

In both cases only a part of the total history can be reconstructed at any time. Yet, on the basis of their reconstructions of the past, both analyst and historian will formulate interpretations. These interpretations must take the wider social contexts into strict account. Thus, the analyst's judgments interrelate complex personal psychological motives with external forces, i.e., with the "life history" of the patient. Concomitantly, the historian's monograph derives conviction from its "fit" with the total picture of the dynamics of a society. Neither can make interpretations in isolation from the whole body of evidence. The analyst's interpretation of a dream cannot proceed independently of the total picture of the patient's personality. The historian reconstructs the activities of a *cabildo* of the Río de la Plata and makes his interpretations on the basis of knowledge of the dynamics of Hapsburg and Bourbon institutional policies.

Once we admit the historical methodology of psychoanalysis, we begin to clarify the first misconception. Psychoanalysis can then become a technique for posing and answering new kinds of historical questions and a new methodology for textual explication. The psychohistorian will consider his documents much in the same manner that the analyst listens to his patient. The analyst directs his attention "less to what the patient is saying than to echoes evoked by his speech."[5] Similarly, the psychohistorian does not search his sources for manifestations of neurosis and psychosis in order to provide demonstrations of pat, predetermined theory. Rather, he will listen to the texts for correspondences, similarities, and relationships that previously have been ignored.

For example, the psychohistorian might look at the letters of Simón Bolívar, the edicts of Diego Portales, the *pronunciamentos* of Juan Manuel de Rosas, the decrees of Gabriel García Moreno, the speeches of José Manuel Balmaceda, and the poetry of Rafael Núñez. But his purpose would not necessarily entail analyses of nineteenth-century caudillo obsessive-compulsive behavior. That is to say, his work would

[5] Alain Besançon, "Psychoanalysis: Auxiliary Science or Historical Method," *Journal of Contemporary History* 3 (1968): 152.

not stop with personal analyses. The neuroses of Rosas *of themselves* tell us nothing about Latin American society. But the psychohistorian can proceed from readings of these various texts to an interpretation of nineteenth-century Latin American culture. By treating these texts and their symbolic content as though they were of one piece, the psychohistorian will be able to pose new questions regarding the special characteristics of Latin American symbols of authority, power, and leadership and the manner in which men conformed to the cultural model reconstructed through the texts.[6]

This, however, need not be the end of psychohistorical study. Even the interpretation of symbols cannot carry our study far. In the words of Alain Besançon:

... although there are thousands of symbols, the things symbolized are very few. Interpretation, if there were no more to it than that, would seem dismally monotonous. Behind all the riches of all the cultures always to find mother, father, child, castration, death—what a lamentable reduction! But the correct interpretation of symbols is no more than the first stage of the work, whose concern is with the specific symbolic pattern of a culture. . . . Once the symbolic pattern has been brought to light, there remains the task of demonstrating its function and of showing how it con-

---

[6] It may be argued that one cannot glibly lump together Latin Americans from different countries to produce such a study, since the Argentine personality will differ from the Chilean, and these will bear little resemblance to the Colombian. However, I would argue with the psychohistorian Bruce Mazlish ("Group Psychology and Problems of Contemporary History," *Journal of Contemporary History* 3 [1968]: 163-177) that the concepts of *national character* and *modal personality* are purely hypothetical ones, which describe entities that may or may not exist empirically. A serious challenge to the concept of national character emerges from the psychological studies conducted thus far. These give evidence of intranational psychological differences that exceed observed *international* differences. I tend to think that international groups, for example nineteenth-century national caudillos, have more in common psychologically with individuals of the same status of other nations than they have with their compatriots of different status (and thus warrant investigation within a single framework). This is not to say that national character studies do not offer valuable insights. For a thorough and clear exposition of what is being done in this area, the reader should consult Alex Inkeles and Daniel Levinson's essay, "National Character: The Study of Modal Personality and Sociocultural Systems," in the *Handbook of Social Psychology*, ed. Gardner Lindzey, 5 vols. (Reading, Mass.: Addison-Wesley Publishing Co., 1954) IV, 415–506.

tributes to the general equilibrium of the culture. The latter is a purely historical task.[7]

Both Church and State in Latin America since colonial times have availed themselves of potent and vivid symbols to impress their claims upon the individual. The interpretation of characteristically Latin American symbols and their relationship to the general pattern of social life will give insights to the culture that common sense alone cannot provide.

Such a psychocultural approach to history cannot be deemed mechanistic. It does involve a strong psychological conception of cultural patterning, but this operates in conjunction with and supported by knowledge of institutions, rituals, and societal organization. Individual personality configurations will enter in, where sufficient documentation exists. However, the resultant societal analysis is not a projection of psychoanalytic theory onto culture. Rather, it is attention paid to the configurations within which Latin American society attempts to synthesize unconscious concepts and conscious ideals through culture.

Psychohistory works in a variety of ways. Its most common usage lies in the field of biography. And, it is true, most published psychobiographies treat of "deviant" subjects, those who have exhibited paradoxical behavior, phobias, suicidal urges, work problems, discordance between self-image and idealized image, and other disturbances. This is simply because human nature can best be studied in a state of conflict. It is not likely, however, that the lives of troubled individuals differ *essentially* from those of normal persons, except in the intensity and clarity of the phenomena involved. In most cases, the subject's psychic imbalance bears an inextricable relationship to the development of his work and ideas. However, the psychohistorian does not look for single clues to the nature of the subject's conflict as in the dynamic process of psychoanalyzing. He approaches the task of psychobiography incorrectly when he looks for "symptoms," as of a disease. Rather, the basis of his interpretation rests on documentary evidence of *Gestalten*, of consistent, repetitive, observable, uncon-

[7] Besançon, "Psychoanalysis," pp. 158–159.

scious patterns.[8] He constructs his interpretation not from a single passage but from a wide range of confirming and reinforcing materials.

Moreover, psychobiography does not fixate on the aberrant elements of personality. Rather, it aims at moving from the microstudy to the macrostudy, from individual to collective psychology. It is no longer valid to view psychoanalysis as relatively "encapsulated"' within the individual's instinctual-unconscious processes to the neglect of cognitive-conative adaptive processes and social factors. The past two decades of psychoanalytic development have witnessed an increasing concern with ego processes and the social forces that contribute to personality formation. Erik Erikson emphasizes this tendency when he centers his psychohistorical works on the interaction between the individual (soma, ego) and the group (social context).

Thus, a psychobiography of Balmaceda would have to focus on the conflicts and motivations of a peculiarly egotistical man. But it also would have to deal with the political and economic issues at stake during his presidency, the socioeconomic composition both of his followers and of his opposition, and *their* motivations. The psychohistorian errs, as did Sigmund Freud and William Bullitt in their study of Woodrow Wilson,[9] when he reduces his subject to his oral, anal, and genital aspects. But the investigators can move from personal conflict to historical complexity when he relates private motivation to a concrete sociopolitical analysis.

The psychohistorical study of the individual must proceed in conjunction with empirical studies of the society that influences him and that he in turns acts upon. This "binocular vision" operates throughout the psychohistorical process. Its operation serves to clarify the third misconception, which views the psychohistorical approach as a luxury that Latin Americanists can ill afford. This notion presupposes a set of historical priorities. It considers that psychohistory neither can nor should be done until the groundwork for it is laid in institu-

<hr>

[8] Fritz Schmidl, "Psychoanalysis and History," *Psychoanalytic Quarterly* 31 (October 1962): 539–543.

[9] Sigmund Freud and William Bullitt, *Thomas Woodrow Wilson* (Boston: Houghton Mifflin, 1967).

tional, economic, and political history. The assumption is that, when these more basic areas have been surveyed, one can justify entry into the more glamorous (and, implicitly, less substantive) realm of psychohistory.

A failure to appreciate the inexorable connections between personality and the sociocultural matrix seems to lie at the bottom of this misunderstanding. Personality does not develop in isolation from society. A whole host of sociocultural factors, including child-rearing practices, accepted cultural values, and religion, affect the formation of adult personality. Furthermore, the individual's participation in society occurs through membership in a series of groups: family, church, occupation, class. And each of these positions demands an expected pattern of behavior from the individual, thus influencing his personality.[10] Changes in society, such as those produced by urbanization, industrialization, mass communication, the destruction of old political orders, and the emergence of new elites, are also likely to exert an impact on personality patterns.

In short, the study of personality and behavior, even of aberrant personality and behavior, does not proceed either before or after the study of other aspects of society, but in conjunction with them. It cannot be otherwise. Furthermore, if the personalities or behavorial patterns we study have attained the status of historical personages or phenomena, it is likely that this is so because of the influence they have exerted on their milieu. The interactions work both ways. Thus, psychohistorical studies will illuminate the "impact of personality on the currently evolving social structure,"[11] the nature of the changes made (or impeded) in a society, and the reasons for the persistence of some institutional forms in one society and not in others. Far from representing an unnecessary luxury, this work seems rather directly concerned with our common task of understanding the dynamics that underlie Latin American society.

Latin American history can use psychoanalysis in many and varied

[10] Wilbert E. Moore, "Social Structure and Behavior," in *Handbook of Social Psychology*, ed. Gardner Lindzey, 2d ed., 5 vols. (Reading, Mass.: Addison-Wesley Publishing Co., 1969), IV, 294.

[11] Inkeles and Levinson, "National Character," p. 491.

ways. The possibility of all psychohistorical studies, however, depends absolutely on the amount of material extant. Since the purpose of psychohistory is not therapeutic, it will not matter to us that our subjects are dead. Moreover, since psychohistory aims at historical understanding, we will not be greatly concerned if certain intimate data are missing from the records. Consistent with modern personality theory, which sees critical developmental experiences occurring throughout the life cycle rather than just in infancy and childhood, the Latin American psychohistorian need not search *Ulises Criollo* for clues to José Vasconcelos's toilet-training. Rather, in the existentialist style of ego psychology,[12] he will direct his attention to stages of Vasconcelos's life for which there is documentary evidence, for example, his adolescent years as a *pocho* in a Mexican border town. He will, moreover, utilize Freud's theories of defense mechanisms without necessary reference to his theories of libidinal energy or the Oedipus complex. People at all stages of their lives commonly employ various psychological strategies, such as projection, displacement, repression, and sublimation to protect themselves from external and internal threats. Their verification need not rely on occurrences buried in the subject's prehistory. Therefore, the psychohistorian can make use of memoirs, private papers, autobographies, diaries, letters, essays, literature, government edicts, and even medical reports.

In the matter of useful sources, it would seem that Latin American psychohistorians have some edge over their counterparts in other branches of the discipline. In many ways the history of the region is the history of key families. Since the colonial period, enduring familial ties to the national power structures characterize the area's history. Often this factor of generational continuity works to the advantage of the historian. Many Latin American families zealously maintain valuable private collections of papers, documents, and letters belonging to their prominent ancestors. Sons, daughters, and other relatives often write interpretive or clarifying studies of the ac-

---

[12] See Ch. 7, "The Eight Ages of Man," in Erik Erikson's *Childhood and Society*, 2d ed. (New York: W. W. Norton and Co., 1963), pp. 247–284, and his book *Identity and the Life Cycle* (New York: International Universities Press, 1959) for a fuller understanding of psychoanalytic ego psychology.

tions of a renowned, and generally "misunderstood," parent. Almost all enjoy talking at length of their deceased and distinguished forebears. The psychohistorian of Latin America, therefore, frequently will have at his disposal not only the written production of his subject(s) but also the written (and, in some cases, verbal) testimony of families, friends, and enemies. "The result is a check, and double check, on the psychohistorian's interpretation of the general character pattern of his subject, from outside sources. . . . [Thus] we find ourselves quite comfortably esconced with the historian's traditional task of reconciling and interpreting conflicting and confirming evidence. The only difference in psychohistory is that the interpretation and confirmation of evidence must be done in terms of informed awareness as to the meaning and application of psychoanalytic theory. But then, what would one expect?"[13]

The "how-to" of psychohistory will be illustrated by sketching the evolution of a psychobiographical study. The subject of this study, Jackson de Figueiredo (b. Aracajú, Sergipe, 1891; d. Rio de Janeiro, 1928) was a Catholic journalist and political theorist. In the last decade of his life, Jackson performed the feat of almost singlehandedly wrenching the Brazilian Church from the position of static equilibrium in which it had lain suspended since the days of the empire. Proselytizing and polemicizing through such diverse mechanisms as *A Ordem* (his literary journal), the Centro Dom Vital (his institutional counterpart), political campaigns, and polemical writings, he transformed the Church ("revitalized" it, he would say) into a lively and controversial intellectual and political force. Because of the decidedly conservative cast of his political and philosophic positions, many Brazilian scholars regard him as the precursor of Integralism.

Primary research on Jackson's life activities pointed to some strange contradictions in the man. There seemed to be two Jacksons. The Jackson known through his political writings and public image did not fit the image conveyed by his family, friends, and colleagues. The fiery journalist, the intolerant politician, the glorifier of the strong

[13] Bruce Mazlish, "Clio on the Couch: Prolegomena to Psychohistory," *Encounter* 31 (September 1968): 52.

state stood in stark contrast to the café-loving bohemian who wrote moving and tender letters to his friends, called them his "Second Church," and penned affectionate studies of their modest literary productions. Seemingly, no one could give a lukewarm assessment of either Jackson or his work. His political enemies hated him. His followers spoke only of his "charisma," "compassion," and "humanity." It became increasingly difficult to reconcile his severe religious-political mentality with his personality.

The solution came in the form of a documentary windfall. Alceu Amoroso Lima, Jackson's friend and successor, allowed this investigator to read ten years of personal correspondence from Jackson. Although both men lived in Rio in the 1920s, Jackson corresponded almost daily with Alceu. The utilization of these personal letters, in conjunction with other published and unpublished materials, helped to explicate the connection between his personality, his religion, and his politics.

A word is due here on methodology. The key to a perception of the unconscious lies in the language. Thus, the psychohistorian cultivates the analyst's habit of listening for overtones and undertones. He includes psychoanalysis among his historical tools so as to "hear" disorder, distress, and conflict as a language that, because of repression, cannot be put into words. Finally, he brings his own empathic feelings to bear on the case while, at the same time, remaining aware of the countertransference involved in so doing.

The factor of psychic overdetermination immeasurably assists the verification of the historian's interpretation. "Indeed, it is the latter phenomenon—the fact that the same word or symbol refers to many elements in the unconscious thought process, on the one hand, and that the single unconscious drive or pattern of behavior will manifest itself in innumerable different conscious manifestations, on the other—that warrants the historian in the use of the evidence."[14] Thus, when Jackson speaks of "the Church" he speaks of an unconscious yearning for absolutes, for order, for immutability, for power. And when he strives to conquer disorder, this attempt takes

[14] Ibid.

the form of advocating the death penalty for subversives, the "worst government" over the "best revolution," restricted suffrage, and on the personal level, "the suffocation of the individual."

Sufficient documentation of a psychohistorical nature, that is, documentation that provides answers to the psychohistorical questions put to it, is the *sine qua non* of this type of investigation. Fortunately, not only did Jackson engage in prolonged and constant introspection, but he also wrote about it at great length. Thus, certain recurring personal conflicts can be documented and verified.

Jackson's most basic conflict, his recurring feelings of being "split" into a false and a real self, served as the point of departure for the study. Normal persons experience a good bit of this duality too. With Jackson, however, that part of himself that he saw as "romantic, lunatic, sensual, passionate, musical, sentimental, bohemian, vagabond, physically and morally neurotic,"[15] he sought to attack and destroy as though it were an alien reality, as though it had a separate existence apart from his "real self." He believed his "real self" to be "the intellectual . . . the man of lead or iron or steel."[16]

To some extent Jackson was aware of this split in his personality. He wrote of "the terrible anguish of my interior life which few have penetrated: this unceasing struggle between the man who would like to live like the wind . . . and the other who is all system and partisan."[17]

In examining the development of this conflict through his letters and writings, I came to see Jackson's religio-political thought and activities as part of an unconscious process (in conjunction with conscious aims, to be sure) to assimilate new aspects of identity that might contribute to a resolution of the conflict. From the point of view of Brazilian history, the most significant aspect of the process involved his sense of fusion with and commitment to the Catholic Church.

[15] Jackson de Figueiredo, as quoted in José Fernando Carneiro, *Catolicismo, revolução, reação* (Rio de Janeiro: Agir, 1947), p. 177.

[16] Jackson de Figueiredo to Alceu Amoroso Lima, October 20–21, 1927, p. 3.

[17] Figueiredo to Afrânio Peixoto, August 11–12, 1928. Note the words, "which few have penetrated," one of many oblique references to an inner life imperceptible from the outside.

During his adolescence in high school in Maceió, Jackson became known for his hatred of priests and for his anticlerical activities. On one particularly iconoclastic afternoon, he led a group of fanatical anti-Catholic students on an image-smashing rampage through the churches of the city. In 1909 he moved to Salvador to begin study in the Law Faculty. During these years in Bahia, he flung himself whole-heartedly into the bohemian life, which included wild fights, café brawls, and grimmer battles in cinemas and theatres from which he frequently emerged wounded. He departed from Bahia for a journal-istic career in Rio de Janeiro in 1915. Less than three years later, he made a sudden and personal transition and converted to Catholicism. In 1921, at the age of thirty, he made his first confession.

From then on, Jackson submerged himself in the Church, buried himself in the Church's battles, achieving (or so it seemed) an utter simplicity in his moral being. The Church represented the resolution of earlier struggles toward identity formation manifested in his ex-periments with student radicalism and iconoclasm. After his religious conversion in 1918, an experience that William James has described as that of being "twice-born," the Church became Jackson's source of security. It gave him, moreover, a leader, in the person of Cardinal Sebastião Leme, from whom he received superego sanction to act out his libidinal and aggressive fantasies.

When leaders take upon themselves responsibility for aggression, even implicitly, those who carry out the commands may do so without guilt. A little boy, a servant, a common soldier have no responsibility. (Jackson often referred to himself as Leme's "soldier.") Superego functions are assumed by the leader or by membership in a group that shares the leader's ideals and goals.[18] Many have commented on the perfect complementarity of personality between Leme—the con-trolled, the cautious, the cradle Catholic—and Jackson—the furious, the impassioned, the convert. Jackson's obedience to Leme's directives never swerved. He made the Church a part of himself by introjecting

---

[18] Joseph Sandler, "On the Concept of Superego," in *The Psychoanalytic Study of the Child*, ed. Ruth S. Eissler et al. (New York: International Universities Press, 1960), XV, 156–157.

it. The Church became something of an extension of his own personality. Under these conditions, threats to the group or its members touched the very core of his personality.

In what way did this introjection of the Church assist Jackson in a resolution of his personal conflicts? What messages did Jackson pick up from the Church? What sort of philosophical balm did the Church apply to Jackson's emotional wounds?

The answer to these questions seems to lie in his fear of the "evil forces" inside himself and in his furious struggle to keep those forces quiescent. Catholicism represented for Jackson a means of "permanent revolution against the tyrannical dominance of fallen nature, that is, against the preponderance of instinct and passion."[19] The same man who could speak with understanding and compassion of the weaknesses of his friends, of their scandals, their passions, their adultery, subjected himself to considerable repression in his own instincts and passions—and justified this repression eschatologically. Harmony, Jackson felt, reigned only when one subordinated one's passions to reason and one's reason to God. "I want to do everything so as not to give in to sentiments," he said.[20] Jackson's religion, like his politics, aimed at "suffocating the revolt of the individual."[21] Thus, when he spoke of the Church as "the only force against Force"[22] and of Catholicism as "a characteristically *antirevolutionary* force,"[23] he was unconsciously providing himself with a defense against the feared inner danger of yielding to his own irresistible impulses or "forces."

At least partially, one can comprehend the ideational content of Jackson's thought as a reaction formation, the development of attitudes and interests in conscious life that were the antithesis of his

[19] Jackson de Figueiredo, *A coluna de fogo* (Rio de Janeiro: Edição do Centro Dom Vital, 1925), p. 3.

[20] Figueiredo to Lima, July 24–25, 1928, p. 3.

[21] Jackson de Figueiredo, *Correspondencia*, 3d ed. (Rio de Janeiro: ABC, 1937), p. 29.

[22] Jackson de Figueiredo, *Affirmações* (Rio de Janeiro: Edição do Centro Dom Vital, 1921), p. 1.

[23] Jackson de Figueiredo, *A reação do bom senso* (Rio de Janeiro: Annuario do Brasil, 1922), p. 111.

repressed impulses. Reaction formation directly influenced the development of his political ideology. As he rejected the turmoil and confusion of his affects, so too did he reject the turmoil and confusion of political opposition to the established order. He equated inner disorder with nihilism and external disorder with national chaos. Not surprisingly, he named his polemical journal *Order*.

Jackson matched a violent defense of the authority of the Church with an equally furious defense of established government. Within his set of self-imposed standards, hardness and toughness equalled strength, and softness meant weakness. Accordingly, he strongly advocated throughout his political career such things as states of siege, repression of political dissidents, curtailments of freedom of the press, the breaking of diplomatic relations with anticlerical Mexico, and racist reductions of immigrant entries. Known to his friends as the most tolerant of men, Jackson proved the most intransigent of characters in his public life.

In the process of defending constituted authority, projection served a truly economic function, for it helped canalize his libidinous energy according to the demands of his overstrict superego. Jackson projected onto Protestants, Masons, positivists, indifferent Catholics, Yankee capitalists, and especially Jews and communists his own inadmissible feelings of rage and "low" instincts. These projections provided a defense against the feared inner danger of surrendering to these impulses. He transferred the bogeys of international Judaism and international communism into a receptacle for all kinds of hostile projections—and based his political and religious authoritarianism on these. At the same time, the aggressive action made possible in the service of Church and nation provided him with a cathartic release for his libidinal fantasies. He confessed once to Alceu Almoroso Lima, relating news of a small revolt that had broken out, that "Just this [news] is a sort of balsamic injection for my temperament. I prefer a battle to any type of expectation."[24]

The psychohistorian cannot ignore the historical milieu that influences his subject's vision of options and choices. In the case of Jackson, he must carefully weigh and balance the national and international political context of the 1920s and its effects on the subject.

[24] Figueiredo to Lima, April 24–25, 1928, p. 2.

What Jackson perceived as the increasingly dangerous quality of Brazilian life in the 1920s confirmed his suspicions of impending anarchy. The year 1922 was of particular significance to him. It witnessed the outbreak of the *tenente* uprisings. Jackson believed these uprisings and the reformist rhetoric of *tenentismo* to be a terrible threat to the nation's traditions. Nothing, in his view, warranted the negation of the principle of authority. To contravene the authority principle would lead inevitably to political and moral disintegration.

The growing agitation of the proletariat, foreshadowed by the São Paulo strike of 1917, led in 1922 to the formation of the Brazilian Communist Party (PCB). Since the Russian Revolution, Jackson's fear of communism and of a communist conspiracy to take over Brazil had grown by leaps and bounds. The newly formed PCB now prompted his glorification of Benito Mussolini's fascism, Charles Maurras's Action Française, and Antonio Salazar's Lusitanian Integralism. Partially under the influence of Maurras, Jackson also expressed considerable fear of an international Jewish conspiracy to dominate the world. The anticlerical activities of the "Jew," Plutarco Elías Calles, increased his fears of the "terrible triangle" of Moscow, Mexico, and Madrid. Mexico, he believed, conspired with Brazilian communists and anarchists to transform Brazil into a zone of bolshevism.

Even the 1922 Semana de Arte Moderna received his opprobrium. Modernism offered opposition to, and an alternative to, classical models of art in Brazil. As such, it represented for Jackson a growing tendency toward rebelliousness and antitraditionalism.

When a "Republican Reaction" led by Nilo Peçanha that same year threatened to challenge Artur Bernardes's predetermined (by conventional political accords) ascension to the presidency, Jackson threw the weight of his support to Bernardes. He felt that Peçanha, a Grand Master of the Masonic Order, would unleash the forces of chaos and disorder already at large in Brazil if his bid for the presidency succeeded.

We see through these few examples how political events reinforced Jackson's vision of life as a struggle between good and evil forces, with the necessity of opting for all of one or all of the other. Indeed, Jackson spent the last ten years of his life absorbed professionally and personally in a fight for order. His sense of fusion with the Church undeniably served for a time the function of keeping his self intact in situations that he interpreted as dangerous. Yet the strenuous repression of his instincts involved in this struggle to maintain himself "in the service of a conscience of iron" could not entirely suppress his absorption with primitive desires. These he reinterpreted in terms of fear (communism) and disgust (Jews).

At some point, the psychological devices Jackson employed to avoid inner conflict failed him. Both his public and his private writings in the last year of his life reveal this. He appeared preoccupied by thoughts of suicide. At times he believed himself possessed by the devil. He admitted on occasion to feelings of "panic" and "impotence" that "the constant invasion of the senses in the moral order" provoked in him. He spoke at times of feeling guilty and sinful because of the struggles between his "instinct, so loving of liberty" and his Catholic philosophy.[25]

Throughout the last months of his correspondence, he makes numerous references to feelings of sinking, engulfment, entombment, and drowning. The British psychiatrist R. D. Laing has identified these images as characteristic of the ontologically insecure person, the person who lacks a firm sense of his own identity. The individual experiences himself as a man who saves himself from drowning only by the most constant, strenuous, desperate activity.[26] The sea, waters, sinking, and drowning are constant themes in Jackson's writings from his adolescent journalism to *Aevum*, the autobiography on which he was working at the time of his death.

On November 4, 1928, Jackson slipped from the rocks in Barra de Tijuca while fishing, fell into the waters below, and drowned. Although some contemporary accounts of his death described it as a suicide, most newspapers reported it as an accident.

What is the historical utility of psychobiographical and other psychohistorical studies?

[25] Figueiredo to Lima, December 11–12, 1927, p. 1.
[26] R. D. Laing, *The Divided Self* (Middlesex, Eng.: Penguin Books, 1966), pp. 39–45. Laing uses the word *ontology* in its empirical sense as the adverbial or adjectival derivative of *being*.

One of the aims of psychoanalytic investigation is the deepening of our understanding of the personality of historical personages, always with the underlying hope that some of this understanding will illumine the creative act and the gift of creativity, which are such enigmatic phenomena.

The most obvious historical benefit derived from a psychobiographical study of Jackson de Figueiredo is a heightened sensitivity to the meaning of his political and religious ideas. Such a study does not consider the rightness or the wrongness of these ideas. It does clarify their genesis and the urgency with which Jackson propounded them.

The clue to Jackson's motivations, and the key to all psychohistorical investigation, lies in language. When Jackson lauds the rightist defense of Europe against "disruptive socialism and iconoclastic bolshevism," which "slowly eat away, like leprosy, the body of Europe . . .,"[27] we understand his political concern more fully in the light of his own struggles against internal forces perceived as disruptive. When he proposes the indoctrination of a Catholic vision of the world to defend the "poor carcass" of Brazil from the "onslaught of the [communist] disease,"[28] one perceives that this is partially because Catholicism provided his own "poor carcass" the wherewithal to resist the ravages of psychic disease. Since the Catholic nationalist movement that Jackson fathered centered on the concept of moral regeneration of the nation, the study of his personal struggles to achieve moral regeneration attains a new significance.

Knowledge of Jackson's personal conflicts illuminates even his political imagery. He proudly declared himself a "reactionary" and insisted that ". . . the hour to react, and to react majestically and irresistibly, has finally sounded for Brazil, for the true Brazil: reaction against upstart error, which is like a *schism* within the very social and political *being* of Brazil."[29] He blindly believed that the elimination of dangerous elements from Brazil would unite the nation and remove

[27] Jackson de Figueiredo, as quoted by Virgilio de Mello Franco, *In Memoriam* (Rio de Janeiro: Edição do Centro Dom Vital, 1929).

[28] Figueiredo to Lima, May 8–9, 1928; July 24–25, 1925.

[29] Jackson de Figueiredo, *Literatura reaccionaria* (Rio de Janeiro: Edição do Centro Dom Vital, 1924), p. 40. Italics mine.

its problems. A study of Jackson's methods of dealing with his own personality schism by expunging dangerous instinctual forces would seem peculiarly rewarding in this context.

Finally, one can appreciate best the chronology of Jackson's written production in conjunction with information on his personal development. We see that his most polemical political works, *A reação do bom senso* (1922) and *Literatura reaccionaria* (1924), represent his direct and violent reaction to the *tenente* uprisings of the period, which he viewed as fearful harbingers of chaos and disorder. What was anathema to him on the personal level became anathema to him on the national political level as well.

The above remarks do not imply a simple, causal relationship between personality and ideology, emotional conflict and intellectual development. They do attempt to demonstrate that connections and congruences exist. And because they exist, psychohistory can and does put to its sources a whole new host of provocative questions above and beyond the purely biographical. Does Jackson represent a common political "type"? What conjunction of political and social circumstances render this type of leader appealing to large numbers of people? To what extent do personal psychological variables explain political behavior, leadership, and ideology?

Social scientists frequently rely on psychoanalytic theory to explicate the personality-politics connection. Many have constructed political personality models on the basis of their individual case studies.[30] In a sense this is a natural outcome of perceiving the resemblances between particular research subjects and other political actors.

Jackson, for example, corresponds almost perfectly with most psychological characterizations of the authoritarian personality, which combines "conventionality and authoritarian submissiveness on the ego level, with violence, anarchic impulses and chaotic destructiveness

---

[30] This has been true since Harold Lasswell made his pioneering studies of the relationships between personality and politics in the 1930s. One of the latest psychohistorical examples of this type of work is Victor Wolfenstein's controversial study, *The Revolutionary Personality* (see n. 1). A recent survey article on "personality-politics" research is Fred I. Greenstein's "Systematic Inquiry into Personality and Politics: Introduction and Overview," *Journal of Social Issues* 24 (1968): 1–14.

in the unconscious sphere."[31] The authoritarian subject achieves his own social adjustment by taking pleasure in obedience and subordination. In Jackson's words, "In a society such as ours, I was born a private or a foot soldier, at best a sergeant—and I could not be any other thing but a combatant."[32] The Church's claim to possess the type of immutable power that Jackson greatly admired in medieval institutions satisfied his need for absolutes. In his political life he exhibited tendencies toward unqualified black-white thinking and either-or solutions, oversimplified dichotomizing, stereotyping, and preferences for symmetry, regularity, order, and strong authority. Psychologists have identified these characteristics with the authoritarian personality.[33]

Further analysis reveals that, although Jackson fits neatly into the authoritarian personality model, his authoritarianism was of a particular variety. It came into play only when he entered into supraindividual activities and acted as the representative of a group. In this role, Jackson acquired a sense of respectability and superego satisfaction. He did not act for "selfish" reasons. The individual who acts as a representative of his group sees himself as the embodiment of its purposes and power. He derives feelings of power from the power of his group. He projects upon it all or part of his personality. Membership in the group permits a greatly needed sense of meaningfulness and direction.[34] Jackson frequently spoke of his group (the Church) as his sole reason for being. Accommodation with enemies (for example, Jews), which might be permissible on the "merely"

[31] T. W. Adorno, et al., *The Authoritarian Personality* (New York: Harper and Bros., 1950), p. 675. This now classic work attempts to make the connection between personality and politics through in-depth interviews, psychological questionnaires, and psychological tests. *Studies in the Scope and Methodology of "The Authoritarian Personality,"* ed. Richard Christie and Marie Jahoda (Glencoe, Ill.: The Free Press, 1954), critically examines its concepts and procedures and elaborates on some of the book's moot points.

[32] Figueiredo to Lima, June 19–20, 1928, p. 2.

[33] Else Frenkel-Brunswick, "Environmental Controls and the Impoverishment of Thought," in *Totalitarianism*, ed. Carl Friedrich (Cambridge: Harvard University Press, 1954), p. 183; Adorno, et al., *Authoritarian Personality*, p. 971.

[34] Lewis Coser discusses this in great detail in *The Functions of Social Conflict* (New York: The Free Press, 1966), pp. 112–115.

personal level, became impossible for the representative of the group.

Jackson, then, exhibited personality traits indicative of an authoritarian enlisted in the service of a cause. This typology tells us little in and of itself. But it does force us to raise important and further questions. Would other persons experiencing the same conflicts as Jackson and similar neurotic symptoms hit upon the same or different outlets, channels, or ideologic solutions? Do similar political attitudes serve the same psychological functions for different individuals?

Suppose, for example, that psychohistorical research on Plínio Salgado, leader of the Brazilian Integralist Party, turned up evidence that Salgado exhibited personality conflicts and ego-defensive reactions similar to Jackson's. No serious investigator would make a causal leap of faith from this to political authoritarianism. A considerable range of different motivations may underlie the common act of participation in authoritarian movements. Moreover, Salgado attained national prominence in the 1930s. Jackson acted on the Brazilian political scene in the 1920s. Exhaustive analyses of the political settings and changing options open to political participants between the last years of the Old Republic and the formation of the Estado Novo would be methodologically mandatory before attempting to elucidate personality-politics connections. Alex Inkeles has suggested that personality factors affect mainly the *style* of political action preferred by individuals, with their socioeconomic status being of more importance as a predictor of ideologic choices.[35] The psychohistorian must weigh these factors carefully before attempting to make personality-politics generalizations. To divorce motivation from the social context or to fail to take note of the cultural factors that determine personality factors may provide the historian with psychological explanation, but not with historical explanation.[36]

Psychohistory can deal with the study of groups as well as the

[35] Alex Inkeles, "National Character and Modern Political Systems," in *Psychological Anthropology*, ed. F. L. K. Hsu (Homewood, Ill.: The Dorsey Press, 1961), p. 193.

[36] Bruce Mazlish discusses the issues of causation and determinism in psychohistory. He explains how this type of inquiry offers explanation in terms of correspondences and co-existing processes rather than in causal terms in "Group Psychology and Problems of Contemporary History," pp. 172–173.

study of individuals. For example, the psychobiographical study of Jackson and the psychopolitical congruences we have been discussing lead us to probe the relationships between historical leaders and followers. Why did Jackson achieve so great a popularity among upper-class and professional Catholics in Brazil in the 1920s? Surely they did not all share his psychopathological characteristics. When we speak of his followers, need we distinguish between his close associates, his "lieutenants" of the Centro Dom Vital, and the more numerous but less active sympathizers? What sort of psychological and social congruence existed between Jackson and his followers?

Jackson's lieutenants, the men who joined with him and rose with him in the struggle for Catholic power, possessed neither his color, his charisma, nor his brilliance. In most cases, they were more cultured, polished, and monied. The Brazilian sociologist Alberto Guerreiro Ramos refers to this group as the *jeunesse dorée* because of the high social and economic positions they occupied as well as the intellectual and psychological characteristics they exhibited. These men belonged to "that stratum of well-born intellectuals for whom strictly material difficulties do not exist. . . . By their very existential condition these intellectuals are inclined to a certain asceticism with regard to themselves and life, attempting interior perfection through self-analysis, enlightenment, the exercise of will power, and besides this, through a conception of man and society in preponderantly psychological terms."[37]

Jackson's closest associates came from this group. The most aggressive and militant era of the Centro Dom Vital (1922–1928) corresponds to a key transition period in Brazilian history, one punctuated by military and political turbulence. Bearing these two facts in mind, one can see Jackson's quick and heavy impact on the Church and its elite less as a matter of chance and charisma and more as a matter of psychological and social congruences. He arrived on the ecclesiastical and on the political scene at a moment in which traditional political and religious elites sorely felt the need to take an aggressive position or be left behind in the foreseeable future shuffle.

[37] Alberto Guerreiro Ramos, *A crise do poder no Brasil* (Rio de Janeiro: Zahar, 1961), p. 153.

Jackson displayed publicly an aristocratic distaste for the rabble, which he said should be ruled for its own good by the intelligent. He developed a Catholic intellectual position on all current issues. Both the elitism and the pseudoerudition of Jackson's ideas and his tremendously aggressive tactics in defense of the Church and tradition attracted the *jeunesse dorée* to his organization. Through the Centro Dom Vital, his lieutenants urged the nation to adopt spiritual solutions to societal problems—solutions that excluded neither the Church nor themselves.

Psychohistorical investigations of Jackson's closest associates, the elite of the Church clergy and laity, may bear these speculations out. Almost all of these men freely expressed their ideas in written form, producing among them a remarkably long bibliography of political, philosophical, theological, and literary studies. Several, like Hamilton Nogueira, wrote poetry and novels. Others, for example, Alceu Amoroso Lima (under the pseudonym Tristão de Ataíde), produced volumes of literary criticism and essays. It seems entirely likely, then, that a psychohistorical study of their extant written production, particularly of those works in which the unconscious expresses itself best (novels, poetry, letters, literary essays) would provide us with fascinating insights into the collective or shared psychological motivations for their following Jackson in his religio-political crusades.

Finally, psychohistory furnishes us with a new tool with which to approach the fundamentally historical task of interpreting documents. One detects, for example, a remarkable sameness of tone and imagery in the documents of groups appealing primarily to the traditional Brazilian elites in the 1922–1937 period. Three themes predominate in these writings: the expectation of imminent national catastrophe, the exaggeration beyond reasonable bounds of the power of the nation's and the Church's "enemies," and the call for aggressive action against the forces of chaos.

Representative of the general tenor of these texts is the Collective Pastoral of the Brazilian Episcopacy against the feared "inundation and destruction" of the nation by a communist coup: "The threat is general. Everyone, old and young, rich and poor, educated and ignorant, lay and religious will inexorably and equally share their bitter portion of pain, despair, misery, suffering! Nothing will be respected, either in the moral order or in the material order."[38]

All of these groups (Catholic, Integralist, Neomonarchist, and certain nationalist movements) advocated a similar response to the various enemies of Brazil. The leader of Brazilian Catholicism, Cardinal Leme, spoke of a "conquering crusade" against the powerful non-Catholic minorities of Brazil.[39] The Centro Dom Vital, principal organization of the laity, urged Catholics to gird for combat against liberalism and communism, since "All the great spiritual and idealistic battles in history have been decided on the battlefields. And a Christian, no matter how much of a pacifist he might consider himself, cannot forget this fact."[40] Dr. Alceu, the undisputed lay leader of the Church in the 1930s, called for the articulation of a "united front of Good . . . against the united front of Evil."[41] The Integralists defined themselves as "the Soldiers which the Holy Gospel announced for the definitive fight which is going to separate the decrepit, vice-ridden world from the new, integral, united world vibrating with heroism, without the anarchy which the anti-Christs preach."[42]

It is not possible to argue that the above citations represent the viewpoints of an unbalanced few and that, therefore, they must be discounted in historical attempts to piece together the psychology of an era. In fact, the quotations presented typify the apocalyptic mentality of at least one Brazilian subculture, the members of which joined orthodox Catholic groups and the Integralist Party in droves. Rather more to the point, historians trained in the techniques of psychoanalysis should "listen" to these and similar documents of the period without particular regard to their authorship. From the echoes

38 Episcopado Brasileiro, *Carta pastoral e mandamento do espiscopado brasileiro sobre o comunismo ateu* (Rio de Janeiro: Typ. do Jornal do Commercio, 1937), p. 4.
39 Sebastião Leme, *A carta pastoral de sua eminencia Sr. Cardeal dom Leme, quando arcebispo de Olinda saudando os seus diocesanos*, 3d ed. (Petrópolis: Ed. Vozes, 1938), p. 2.
40 Otto Sachse, "Catolicismo e fascismo," *A Ordem* 1923 (April–June): 189.
41 Alceu Amoroso Lima, "A igreja e o momento politico," *A Ordem* 1935 (July): 13.
42 Custodio de Viveiros, *O sonho do filosofo integralista* (Rio de Janeiro: Livraria H. Antunes, 1935), p. 96.

and resonances that will be heard, the psychohistorian may tell us something of the psychological origins of traditionalism, of conservatism, and of the fear of social change. Such investigation may shed light also on the formation of group self-identity (through the creation or evocation of outside enemies, through its perception of how it is perceived by other groups, etc.) and on the characteristic patterns of defense (denial, projection, aggression) of groups that feel threatened by impending societal changes.

Hopefully this essay has convinced some readers of the potential utility of psychohistory to the Latin American field and of the interpretive possibilities that come open to us with a fusion of the two disciplines. Naturally, not all historians who wish to engage in some psychoanalytic investigation will have an easy task. The kind of evidence needed for a psychobiographical study of Jackson abounded. Jackson was an emotional and a prolific writer. However, as the psychohistorian Cushing Strout warns, ". . . it is wise not to foreclose the possibilities that open up when historians begin to look for evidence that they commonly have not sought. Historical evidence is not a previously known entity, like a continent: when it emerges, it comes in response to questions that need it."[43]

Latin Americanists lag far behind specialists in other historical branches, who have been discussing, debating, and doing psychohistory for many years. As a start to bridging this gap, we might devote several sessions at our formal conferences and less formal seminars to posing and resolving questions of a methodological nature. The proper use of autobiographies and personal memoirs, the reliability of information obtained in interviews, the utility of Latin American literature to psychohistory are but some of the issues that might be raised.

Simultaneously, we should begin to make our graduate students aware, first, of the fact that psychohistory exists and, second, of its viability as an approach to Latin American historical interpretation.

---

[43] Cushing Strout, "Ego Psychology and the Historian," *History and Theory* 7 (1968): 289.

We should encourage these students, especially through the flexible vehicles of seminars and colloquia, to experiment with research projects that require psychoanalytic theory and techniques. Some of the major universities, such as Harvard and UCLA, now offer programs in psychohistory. Berkeley, MIT, Wisconsin, and Princeton offer courses in psychohistory. While extensive development of the field will not be possible or desirable at many of our institutions, it would seem that our students might readily attain at least an introduction to basic psychohistorical readings through historiography and methodology courses.

Finally, some of us must be about the business of doing psychohistory. We would have to wait until the year 2050 for the resolution of all the methodological disputes and problems that inevitably will arise. Initial pathbreaking efforts, however, will help us to clarify the problems and to advance along a rich historical road.

It goes without saying that not every trained Latin American historian will become a psychohistorian by virtue of his interest in the field. In fact, even trained Latin American historians who have undergone a personal analysis do not qualify simply on the basis of that experience, although personal psychoanalysis is a crucial part of psychoanalytic training. Reading Freud and having an intuitive "feel" for psychoanalytic theory will help. But these are not enough. The well-trained psychohistorian might undergo a rigorous and systematic training in one of the more than twenty training institutes in the country approved by the American Psychoanalytic Association. Although most of the training institutes in the past have restricted admission to medical doctors, many have opened their doors to social scientists in more recent years.

Since, however, psychoanalytic training requires years of costly, personal analysis and four to five years of theoretical courses and clinical work, many interested historians will quite rightly hesitate before applying for candidacy. Other alternatives are available. A few of the training institutes offer partial training programs for nonmedical personnel. Partial training generally amounts to four years of seminar work without the clinical exposure. Furthermore, it would seem feasible for the psychoanalytically informed Latin Americanist to undertake psychohistorical projects in collaboration with a trained analyst or psychologist.[44]

This insistence on proper psychoanalytic training reflects the fact that psychohistory, perhaps more than other interdisciplinary approaches to history, is fraught with dangers. For one thing, widespread familiarity with psychosexual interpretation has formed a "whole climate of opinion," as W. H. Auden noted in his memorial poem upon the occasion of Freud's death. People commonly employ psychoanalytic terminology in their daily conversations. This familiarity with certain aspects of the discipline bestirs a curious cultural resonance in those who read psychohistory and, frequently, dilettantism in those who write it. Intuition *cum* jargon replaces the scientific system of concepts, based on clinical data, that is psychoanalysis.

Some writers slap the "psychohistory" label on thinly disguised efforts to grind an ax, political or otherwise.[45] In this regard, Erik Erikson, the man who created (or recreated, after Freud) the subdiscipline of psychohistory, has insisted that those who would write it first openly examine their own prejudices and motives for so doing. Other authors, in their haste to psychoanalyze, reduce historical subjects (including some of the world's most creative artists, politicians, and thinkers) to their psychopathology, neglecting cognitive and other strengths, talents, luck, and the vagaries of social and political events. Yet, properly done, psychohistory is neither a euphemism for exposé nor a medium for heavy-handed interpretations. Rather, it is a thoughtful and imaginative response to a series of facts about people's lives. Reductionism, whether deliberate or unwitting, vitiates the expositor's obligation to the letter and spirit of these lives.

Another danger of psychohistory lies in overextrapolation from the data in the search for the "key" to (for instance) the "Latin

[44] The historian William B. Willcox has done precisely this in his work dealing with the commander-in-chief of the British Army in the War of American Independence. He wrote "Sir Henry Clinton: A Psychological Exploration in History," *William and Mary Quarterly* 16 (1959): 3–26, in collaboration with Frederick Wyatt, a clinical psychologist of Freudian psychoanalytic orientation.

[45] A recent example of this type of work is Nancy Gager Clinch's *The Kennedy Neurosis: A Psychological Portrait of an American Dynasty* (New York: Grosset and Dunlap, 1972).

American mind." In fact, there are no "keys." Psychohistory draws upon several disciplines in the hope of seeing human experience more broadly—that is all. Interest in psychological factors should not blind one to the complexities and the subtleties of history, which does not allow of simplistic, mechanistic approaches. However, when proper and careful research is done, psychohistory can make more intelligible to us events that had a different kind of coherence for others who lived before.

Certainly there is much work to be done. The values and social attitudes that inform the lives (and therefore the history) of Latin Americans urgently need investigation of a psychohistorical nature. Such supposedly "traditional" Latin characteristics as fatalism, religiosity, and familism tremendously influence the developmental process in Latin America. Yet historians to date offer interpretation of these phenomena most hesitantly, and then in preponderantly "rational" terms. It is time to lay at rest the notion that history rests only on conscious, rational foundations.

Since the Latin American field is still devoid of basic psychohistorical studies of attitudinal development and value formation, one logical place to start work would be the history of the family and of child-rearing practices. Individuals learn values and attitudes in the context of family. Parents themselves reflect in their prohibitions the pressures of the society.[46] Investigations of this nature will illuminate such fundamental issues as the *patrón-sirvienta* mentality, the role of women in society, and aggression. Moreover, since so many Latin American institutions reflect family social values, as partially exemplified by nepotism, *parentelas*, paternalism, lack of cooperation in com-

[46] A graduate student at the University of Minnesota, Margarita Gangotena of Ecuador, has written a most interesting psychohistorical study on child-rearing in Ecuadorean upper- and middle-class families. Among other things, Gangotena demonstrates how the self-esteem of children is threatened when the individuals with whom they have identified (servants who raise them) receive little respect from other, more powerful, adult figures (parents, uncles, aunts). Paternalism (a reaction-formation defense) and hostility (a displacement defense) towards *cholo* servants in particular and peasants in general, results from the psychological conflicts generated in the home. I would like to thank Professor Stuart Schwartz for sending me a copy of this paper, "The Denial of the Peasant Heritage" (unpublished, 1971).

munity projects, and even reliance on foreign institutional models, such studies provide an optimum jumping-off point for larger macrocosmic interpretation. Psychohistory gives us the tool to negotiate the transition from individual to societal (collective) issues.

The doing of psychohistory requires an awareness of its pitfalls. We can avoid reductionism, that is, the reducing of subjects to their pathological characteristics, by conscientious attention to the concrete social and political environments in which these people operated. We can guard against overextrapolation or false extrapolation from the data by strict adherence to the evidence of the documents. Finally, the psychohistorian must make it clear that he does not seek the "causes" of history or *the* explanation of history. Rather, he seeks nothing more, or less, than another level of historical illumination.

Political Legitimacy in Spanish America

PETER H. SMITH

Events of the last ten years have sharply challenged the view that Latin America is moving along the road to "democratic" political development. In late 1973, the overthrow of Salvador Allende's constitutional regime in Chile was only the latest, and perhaps most shocking, sign of a pervasive pattern. Military regimes were flourishing in Bolivia, Brazil, Ecuador, Paraguay, Peru, and most of Central America (including Panama!). Mexico, sometimes regarded as a one-party democracy, had revealed a brutal capacity for denying civil liberties. Uruguay, the erstwhile "utopia" of the Americas, had fallen under siege. Argentina had returned to electoral politics, but there the atmosphere was tentative; to many observers, it was only a matter of time before the next coup. And even where multiparty competition had fairly solid roots—Colombia, Costa Rica, Venezuela—the prospects for democracy remained uncertain.[1]

NOTE. I wish to acknowledge the indirect assistance of undergraduate and graduate students in Latin American history at the University of Wisconsin; over the years, their insistent curiosity and criticism have helped me delineate and sharpen many of the key concepts in this essay. Several of the other contributors to this book also offered specific comments on an early draft, but errors of fact or interpretation are mine alone. Time to write the paper was obtained with financial support from the Graduate School of the University of Wisconsin and the Institute for Advanced Study at Princeton, New Jersey, where I did much of my work on the coediting of the volume as a whole.

[1] As of 1969 only Costa Rica and Uruguay (now a dubious case) qualified as

This situation may seem perplexing, especially for North Americans, because it climaxes a widely heralded "decade of development." Spurred by expansion in trade, credit, and investment, Latin America's economies enjoyed a period of substantial and sustained growth. In varying degrees, countries of the hemisphere came closer to fulfilling the alleged socioeconomic "requisites" of political democracy.[2] Then why the resurgence of dictatorships?

One line of argument would deny the importance of current events. According to this view, recent years have produced a temporary aberration in the general trend of Latin American politics away from dictatorship and towards democracy. Until the transition is complete, the continent remains in a state of "permanent instability." As one proponent of this viewpoint writes: "stability on the basis of a non-democratic official ideology is not possible. Attempts to achieve such stability are made from time to time but today they are bound to fail. Short of a totally democratic stability, there can only be either a state of permanent instability or an unstable state modified in the direction of greater fidelity to democratic norms. It has been repeatedly made evident that politically conscious Latin Americans accept without question the norms of the complex of democratic public ideas, at least *as* norms."[3]

I disagree with this opinion. In the first place, I see authoritarian politics, in the broadest sense of the term, as the prevalent mode

---

fully inclusive "polyarchies"; Chile was (and is no longer) a "limited polyarchy"; Colombia, the Dominican Republic, and Venezuela were "near-polyarchies." See Robert A. Dahl, *Polyarchy: Participation and Opposition* (New Haven: Yale University Press, 1971), Appendix B, pp. 246–249. On p. 8, Dahl defines polyarchies as "relatively (but incompletely) democratized regimes, . . . regimes that have been substantially popularized and liberalized, that is, highly inclusive and extensively open to public contestation."

[2] See Seymour Martin Lipset, *Political Man: The Social Bases of Politics* (Garden City, N.Y.: Doubleday and Company, 1963), Ch. 2, "Economic Development and Democracy," pp. 27–63; also Dahl, *Polyarchy*, Ch. 5 and citations therein (pp. 62–80).

[3] Martin C. Needler, *Political Development in Latin America: Instability, Violence, and Evolutionary Change* (New York: Random House, 1968), pp. 3–42; the quote is from p. 27.

throughout Latin American history.[4] I also believe that political practice in Latin America has generally complied with cultural norms, rather than defied them. This does not mean that political systems of the area have not been undergoing significant change, because they undoubtedly have, but it raises doubt about the inherently "democratic" tendencies of such transition.

My evidence is mainly circumstantial. The undeniable fact is that, ever since the wars of independence, most regimes in Latin America have been unequivocally nondemocratic. This denouement cannot have been an accident. There can be many explanations for this situation, which undoubtedly has complex roots. Here I would like to emphasize merely one facet of the problem: the cultural determinants of politics.

This is pretty unfashionable stuff. In the past, cultural interpretations of Latin American politics have often degenerated into racism or deprecatory "national-character" arguments. Reliance on the "Ibero-Mediterranean ethos" can be unsatisfactory, since it does not (by itself) account for the evident variability in political behavior throughout the continent. Besides, culture is not easily quantifiable, and it thus defies the recent trends toward statistical measurement.[5] Finally, I suspect that North Americans, believing democracy to be the most desirable form of political life, have felt that the ascription of nondemocratic values to Latin America would be a mark of condescension and disdain; thus ethnocentrism, in the guise of good-

---

[4] For the sake of convenience I shall employ the adjective *authoritarian* interchangeably with *nondemocratic*. But I regard an authoritarian regime as one particular and specific type of nondemocratic polity. See Juan J. Linz, "An Authoritarian Regime: Spain," most easily consulted in *Mass Politics: Studies in Political Sociology*, ed. Erik Allardt and Stein Rokkan (New York: The Free Press, 1970), pp. 251–283 and 374–381.

[5] One recent study seeks a proxy measure for the "Ibero-Mediterranean ethos" in such (unspecified) variables as "the institutional role of the Church, the relative size of the *mestizo* population and the prevailing system of land tenure." The author openly acknowledges "the remoteness of such aggregate data as indicators of psychocultural dispositions," but I see the distance between concept and measure as more than remote. See Philippe C. Schmitter, "Paths to Political Development in Latin America," in *Changing Latin America: New Interpretations of Its Politics and Society*, ed. Douglas A. Chalmers, *Proceedings of the Academy of Political Science* 30, no. 4 (August 1972): 83–105, with the quotations on p. 102.

neighborliness, has discouraged attention to the cultural underpinning of dictatorship.

In this paper I confront three aspects of the problem. First, I examine the content of political culture in Spanish America, with specific regard to the concept of political legitimacy, and I attempt to modify and expand conventional Weberian approaches to this phenomenon. Second, I try to outline some of the analytical challenges presented by the concept, especially insofar as legitimacy relates to (but differs from) the durability and power of political regimes. Third, I seek to demonstrate the usability of quantitative content analysis as a methodological tool for detecting operative codes or claims for political authority. There is little, if anything, that is genuinely "new" in the pages that follow. I shall merely try to outline salient aspects of the problem in a clear and systematic way.

At bottom, my argument contains a fundamental plea. I believe we should cease to employ a simple democratic-nondemocratic dichotomy in classifying and describing Latin America's political systems.[6] Since most of the continent's political experience has been patently nondemocratic, insistence on this dichotomy had led us to comprehend Latin American politics for what they are *not* instead of for what they *are*.[7] This tendency has slackened in recent years, but it still pervades an inordinate amount of literature on the subject. In addition to asking why democracy has failed, we should also be asking why dictatorship has succeeded.[8]

----

[6] The "we" includes Latin American scholars as well as North Americans. Overuse of the democratic-nondemocratic dichotomy seems to be more prevalent in this country than below the Río Grande—but, for better or for worse, North Americans produce a disproportionate share of the literature on Latin American politics.

[7] For a classic expression of this tendency see W. W. Pierson, ed., "The Pathology of Democracy in Latin America: A Symposium," *American Political Science Review* 44, no. 1 (March 1950): 100–149.

[8] I make this statement as the author of "The Breakdown of Democracy in Argentina, 1916–1930" (Paper presented at the Seventh World Congress of Sociology, Varna, Bulgaria, September 1970). In fact my own research has not, in general, followed the specific prescriptions set forth in this essay; but my efforts to deal with political conflict, elite recruitment, and other prima facie "uncultural" matters have led to a firm belief in the importance and desirability of approaching the relationship between culture and politics in a rigorous way.

In this connection I would urge the adoption of a flexible, dispassionate, systematic approach toward the concept of dictatorship. Several years ago Juan Linz presented a pathbreaking definition of *authoritarianism* as a kind of "limited pluralism" that is analytically and empirically distinct from the antipluralistic domination characteristic of truly "totalitarian" states. More recently he has broken the concept of authoritarianism down into a series of component subtypes. Philippe C. Schmitter has also offered speculation about the dynamics of transition from one type of regime to another.[9] My point is that, in order to understand the pattern of historical change in Latin American politics, we must be willing to recognize significance in the transition from one kind of nondemocratic policy to another. Calling a regime "dictatorial" is not, in the final analysis, saying much at all.

This is not to argue that we must favor or tolerate dictatorship, authoritarian or otherwise, merely because it exists. Nor am I suggesting that historians need suspend all moral and political judgments about the past, probably an impossible feat anyway. What I am saying is that we must improve our intellectual awareness of political phenomena in Spanish America before we can make serious evaluations. Historical judgments, like any other ethical decision, acquire much of their ultimate significance from the soundness of their cognitive basis.

POLITICAL CULTURE AND CODES OF LEGITIMACY

By *political culture*, in this essay, I mean "the system of empirical beliefs, expressive symbols, and values which defines the situation in which political action takes place. It provides the subjective orientation to politics."[10] Political culture defines the cultural medium or

---

9 Linz, "An Authoritarian Regime"; idem, "Notes toward a Typology of Authoritarian Regimes" (Paper presented at the annual meeting of the American Political Science Association, Washington, D.C., September 1972); Schmitter, "Paths to Political Development"; and Howard J. Wiarda, "Toward a Framework for the Study of Political Change in the Iberic-Latin Tradition: The Corporative Model," *World Politics* 25, no. 2 (January 1973): 206–235.

10 Sidney Verba, "Comparative Political Culture," in *Political Culture and Political Development*, ed. Lucian W. Pye and Sidney Verba (Princeton: Princeton University Press, 1965), p. 513.

idiom through which political behavior is seen, interpreted, and understood. By imposing conceptual (and often moral) order on patterns of action, it finds significance and "meaning" in politics; it can also furnish prescriptions for behavior.[11]

One of the most critical dimensions in any political culture involves the notion of *political legitimacy*, that is, the set of beliefs that lead people to regard the distribution of political power as just and appropriate for their own society. Legitimacy provides the rationale for voluntary submission to political authority. Obviously, concepts of legitimacy can vary greatly from culture to culture: a political order that is morally acceptable for members of one society might be totally abhorrent for members of another.

My basic proposition is that authoritarian polities have dominated Spanish American history because they have been to some degree "legitimate." No doubt some people have accepted dictatorship as a matter of self-serving convenience; other people, possibly large sectors of the population, have been too frightened to resist; others have been indifferent. Still others have resisted authoritarian rule because of democratic convictions, though this does not mean that all opponents of dictatorship have acted for the same reason. But I maintain that, over time, politically relevant segments of Latin American society have considered authoritarian structures as legitimate and therefore worthy of acceptance or support.

The immediate task is to identify strains in the political culture that have given rise to this situation. For this purpose, and as a heuristic device, I shall in this section examine the content of claims to legitimacy that have been made by political leaders in Spanish America. This practice involves some intrinsic distortion, since claims made by leaders may well differ from the beliefs and attitudes of the community at large; and, as emphasized below, not all rulers are legitimate.

To begin, all modern analysis of political legitimacy must come to terms with Max Weber. In his famous treatment of "imperative co-

---

[11] Note the different conception of political culture in Richard R. Fagen's *The Transformation of Political Culture in Cuba* (Stanford: Stanford University Press, 1969), pp. 5–6.

ordination," Weber posited three modal categories or "ideal types" of political legitimacy: traditional, legal, and charismatic.[12]

Traditional authority, in Weber's usage, rests on "an established belief in the sanctity of immemorial traditions and the legitimacy of the status of those exercising authority under them."[13] A political order is here viewed as proper simply because of its immutability over time: since the rules for allocating authority "have always been this way," they should therefore continue to exist. Under these conditions obedience is typically owed to the person of the traditionally anointed leader, who has considerable discretion in authority but who must also stay within the bounds of tradition itself. Thus precedent, as both custom and law, assumes paramount importance.

Traditional claims to authority have occupied a prominent place in Spanish American history, particularly during the colonial period. Obedience had *always* been due to the crown, which demanded—and for centuries received—recognition on precisely these grounds. Noting the extensive networks of personal loyalty, some writers have emphasized the "patrimonial" qualities of traditional authority under the empire, while John Leddy Phelan has stressed the complexity of imperial claims to rule.[14]

Almost by definition, separation from Spain nullified the possibility of relying explicitly on traditional authority. With new polities to govern, leaders in the postindependence period would have to present new, or at least different, claims to authority.

Some of these demands fit Weber's category of *legal* authority,

[12] See Max Weber, *The Theory of Social and Economic Organization*, ed. Talcott Parsons (New York: The Free Press, 1964), pt. 3, "The Types of Authority and Imperative Co-ordination," pp. 324–423.

[13] Ibid., p. 328.

[14] Richard R. Morse, "The Heritage of Latin America," in *The Founding of New Societies*, ed. Lewis Hartz (New York: Harcourt, Brace, and World, 1964), pp. 123–177, esp. pp. 157–159; Magali Sarfatti, *Spanish Bureaucratic-Patrimonialism in America* (Berkeley: Institute of International Studies, University of California, 1966); John Leddy Phelan, *The Kingdom of Quito in the Seventeenth Century: Bureaucratic Politics in the Spanish Empire* (Madison: University of Wisconsin Press, 1967), esp. pp. 320–337, where he also deals with the concept of "historical bureaucratic empires" as presented by S. N. Eisenstadt in *The Political Systems of Empires* (New York: The Free Press, 1963).

which rests upon "a belief in the 'legality' of patterns of normative rules and the right of those elevated to authority under such rules to issue commands."[15] In contrast to the traditional case, obedience is here owed to the legally established order itself, instead of to the persons who occupy the special offices. Typically, legal legitimacy derives from the generalized acceptance of rational rules for distributing power. The rules are consistent, unambiguous, and universally applied.

The most obvious evidence of legal claims to legitimacy in Spanish American history lies, of course, in the many constitutions that have proliferated since independence. Such documents represent a clear effort to codify and promulgate rules for the allocation and acceptance of authority. Standard interpretations have long asserted that constitutional rule, inspired by French and North American models, evinced persistent attempts to implant democracy in Spanish America. By this same logic, illegal seizures of power thrust the continent into a "legitimacy vacuum," and defiance of the constitutions signaled the weakness of democracy.

While this view may be partially true, at least in some specific instances, there is no inherent reason for legal legitimacy to be necessarily democratic. (Weber's own example of the archetypal legal system was a corporate bureaucracy, in many ways an antidemocratic structure.)[16] As Glen Dealy has argued, Spanish American constitutions have contained a large number of authoritarian features. Rejecting the notion that constitutional ideals were imported from the United States and France, Dealy asserts: "Eighteenth-century political liberalism was almost uniformly and overwhelmingly rejected by Spanish America's first statesmen. Though there is wide variety in the form and content of the early charters, not one could be construed as embodying constitutional liberalism, however loosely that term may be defined."[17]

[15] Weber, *Theory*, p. 328.

[16] H. H. Gerth and C. Wright Mills, eds., *From Max Weber: Essays in Socoiology* (New York: Oxford University Press, 1958), pp. 224–226.

[17] Glen Dealy, "Prolegomena on the Spanish American Political Tradition," *Hispanic American Historical Review* 48, no. 1 (Febraury 1968): 37–58; the quote is from p. 43.

According to Dealy's analysis, most constitutions placed power in the state and not in the people. In explicitly elitist fashion, they defined the major requirement for holding political office as moral superiority rather than popular support. And they put virtually no restrictions on governmental authority. Civil rights existed at the tolerance of the state and could readily be set aside, usually by the chief executive. At all times the collective interest reigned supreme. "Politics is the achievement of the public good, which is in constant opposition to private interest."[18]

Without presenting traditional grounds for authority in Weber's sense of the term, Spanish American constitutions have thus drawn upon time-honored canons of medieval and Hispanic political philosophy. There persist, in constitutional form, the Thomist notions of divine, natural, and human law. The purpose of political organization is to rise above the innate fallibility of its mortal constituency and, through moral purification and leadership, attain a social order that complies with natural (and ultimately divine) prescription. Since human judgment is erroneous, so are election results. The true political leader must respond not to his constituency but to the imperatives of higher morality. Insofar as he follows that precept, he commands, and deserves, absolute power.[19]

Thus legal claims to legitimacy have often been made, but not necessarily in democratic fashion. In fact one might well construe these constitutions as efforts to legalize dictatorship rather than to implant democracy. Moreover, the acceptability of the resulting political order has depended entirely upon the moral quality of its leaders. An inferior leader betrays an inferior constitution, which, being the product of fallible men, should therefore be overthrown. In this sense Spanish American constitutions have contained implicit provision for their own abandonment. Coups thus become part of a cultural pattern, rather than a deviation from it.

18 Ibid., p. 57.
19 See Morse, "Heritage," pp. 151–159, esp. the statement on p. 154 that according to Spanish political philosophy "the people do not *delegate* but *alienate* sovereignty to their prince." For excellent general background see Otto Gierke, *Political Theories of the Middle Age*, trans. Frederic William Maitland (Cambridge: Cambridge University Press, 1951).

A third kind of legitimacy consists of *charisma*, which Weber defines as "devotion to the specific and exceptional sanctity, heroism or exemplary character of an individual person, and of the normative patterns or order revealed or ordained by him."[20] Literally, charisma means "the gift of grace." The exceptional powers of the charismatic leaders are not available to the ordinary person, and they are held to be either exemplary or of divine origin. The charismatic leader typically represents a movement, a cause, or some higher truth. His followers, out of their commitment to the ultimate mission, obey the leader from a sense of moral duty.

Charismatic leaders have played prominent parts in Spanish American history, and political missionaries have pursued a wide range of varied goals: collective redemption, national salvation, social justice, and so on. Fidel Castro and Juan Perón offer classic instances of charismatic types, and there have been many others too. As Dealy has shown, constitutions were often designed to bring men with a kind of "gift of grace" to power—and to this extent, Spanish American constitutions can be understood as efforts to "routinize" charisma.[21] For reasons spelled out below, however, I think the concept of charisma has often been misused.

Most writers who have dealt with the problem of political legitimacy have stayed within the Weberian framework. According to the standard logic, if a leader cannot make effective claims to a traditional, legal, or charismatic authority or a proper combination of the three, his rule is ipso facto illegitimate. The absence of legitimacy means there is a legitimacy vacuum. A legitimacy vacuum begets instability. Ergo, the absence of traditional or legal or charismatic authority means there must be instability.

What this reasoning fails to consider is the possibility that, at least in Spanish America, there might be additional types of legitimacy. This oversight is particularly unfortunate in view of the thoroughly relativistic quality of the concept of legitimacy. Weber himself recognized the limits of his ideal construct and introduced his own typology

---

[20] Weber, *Theory*, p. 328.
[21] On the routinization of charisma see Weber, *Theory*, pp. 363–373.

with a clear disclaimer: "the idea that the whole of concrete historical reality can be exhausted in the conceptual scheme about to be developed," he wrote, "is as far from the author's thoughts as anything could be."[22]

It is my intention to propose two additional categories of political legitimacy that, in my judgment, have appeared in Spanish American history. Whether or not they have existed elsewhere is a question that far transcends the narrow limits of my own expertise. But even if my analysis of Spanish American political culture is wrong, the methodological lesson remains: we should try to explore political legitimacy in terms that derive from the immediate culture.

The first of my categories, which could be called *dominance*, rests on a somewhat tautological assertion that those in power ought to rule because they are in power. By gaining power, people demonstrate their suitability for it. In a sense, this precept simply inverts a traditional canon of Hispanic philosophy, which holds that the law of the prince loses force "if the majority has already ceased to obey it."[23] The principle of dominance maintains that the law of the prince acquires force if the majority (or at least a major segment of the population) starts to obey it. Power, in short, should go to the strong.

According to this code, the central means of asserting dominance is through physical coercion. A sexual component of this theme, *machismo*, concerns domination of women. The more explicitly political component involves demonstration of the capacity for wielding violence. In this way violence has occupied a central place in Spanish American political culture. Its appearance does not necessarily indicate a disregard for social norms; on the contrary, it can bespeak compliance with accepted norms. Strikes, riots, coups, and assassinations do not always mean the system is breaking down; they can be part of the system itself.[24] (Here I would offer a distinction between *gov-*

22 Ibid., p. 329.
23 Morse, "Heritage," p. 154.
24 See Eric R. Wolf and Edward C. Hansen, "*Caudillo* Politics: A Structural Analysis," *Comparative Studies in Society and History* 9 (1966–1967): 168–179; Francisco José Moreno and Barbara Mitrani, eds., *Conflict and Violence in Latin American Politics: A Book of Readings* (New York: Crowell, 1971).

236   *New Approaches to Latin American History*

ernmental stability and *systemic* stability; individual governments may tumble while the system as a whole remains intact.)[25]

An implicit claim in the concept is that dominance, once recognized and obeyed, will bring about political order. In the well-known *Cesarismo democrático*, for instance, Laureano Vallenilla Lanz conceived of the caudillo as "the necessary policeman" to establish social control. "The authority of [José Antonio] Páez" after the wars of independence, he wrote, "like that of all the caudillos of Spanish America, was based on the *unconscious suggestion* of our majority. Our people, who can be regarded as an *unstable* social group . . . instinctively followed the strongest, the bravest and the smartest, whose personality had become a legend in the popular imagination and from whom the people expected absolute protection."[26]

In this connection Vallenilla Lanz traced out the routinization, not of charisma, but of dominance: "leaders do not get elected," said the Venezuelan, "they impose themselves. Election and inheritance to office . . . constitute a subsequent process."[27] Thus Vallenilla Lanz regarded dominance as a transitory (but conceptually distinct) type of legitimacy that creates the conditions for legal or traditional rule. Of course one's interpretation of the length and kind of transition would depend upon one's position. But, most importantly, Vallenilla Lanz did not condemn violence. He linked it to social order, to dominance, and by implication to charisma.

One practical consequence of legitimation through dominance is uncertainty. It is possible to proclaim dominance only so long as one is dominant (or becoming dominant). By definition, the loss of power entails a loss of legitimacy. Since people obey authority only

[25] As Kalman H. Silvert has said: "If the normal way of rotating the executive in a given country is by revolution, then it is not being facetious to remark that revolutions are a sign of stability—that things are marching along as they always have" (*The Conflict Society: Reaction and Revolution in Latin America*, rev. ed. [New York: American Universities Field Staff, 1966], p. 19). I would prefer a term like *coup* or *violent overthrow* to *revolution* in this context.

[26] Laureano Vallenilla Lanz, *Cesarismo democrático: Estudios sobre las bases sociológicas de la constitución efectiva de Venezuela* (Caracas: Empresa El Cojo, 1919), p. 188, 276, and passim.

[27] Ibid., p. 189.

because it is supreme, the fallen leader quickly finds his following in disarray. Partly for this reason there are very few instances of once-dominant leaders who have made successful political comebacks.

Dominance is a relatively primitive claim to political legitimacy, and on the national level it has generally (but not exclusively) been associated with the rule of nineteenth-century caudillos. It runs throughout the pages of Domingo Sarmiento's classic book, *Facundo: Civilization and Barbarity*, a transparent attack on Juan Manuel de Rosas.[28] And it finds exemplary expression in the career of Mariano Melgarejo, who ruled Bolivia from 1864 to 1871. According to one account: "Melgarejo got into power by killing the country's dictator, [Manuel Isidoro] Belzú, in the presidential palace. The shooting took place before a great crowd which had gathered in the plaza to see the meeting of the two rivals. When Belzú fell dead into the arms of one of his escorts, Melgarejo strode to the window and proclaimed: 'Belzú is dead. Now who are you shouting for?' The mob, thus prompted, threw off its fear and gave a bestial cry: 'Viva Melgarejo!' "[29]

It is extremely important to distinguish dominance from charisma. In the first place, the dominant leader does not represent a revealed truth or moral purpose; he represents strength and, in a way, order, but not a spiritual cause.[30] Second, the followers of a dominant person do not obey out of a sense of duty; they do so on the basis of a rational calculation, a kind of bet—that leader X will stay in power for some time—and when his time is up they commonly desert. Third, the leader pays constant attention to the size and strength of his following; without substantial recognition of his dominant qualities, he

---

[28] Domingo Sarmiento, *Facundo: Civilización y barbarie*, trans. Mrs. Horace Mann as *Life in the Argentina Republic in the Days of the Tyrants; or, Civilization and Barbarism* (New York: Hurd and Houghton, 1868).

[29] Quoted in Wolf and Hansen, "*Caudillo* Politics," p. 174.

[30] One could conceivably argue that dominance reveals "exemplary qualities" and therefore qualifies as a kind of charisma rather than as a separate type of legitimacy; but as I understand Weber's description of charisma, personal qualities of the leader become "exemplary" only because they symbolize or provide a metaphor for some concept of ethics or morality. Most decidedly, the qualities called forth by dominance per se do not meet this condition, though it is possible for a dominant leader to be charismatic too.

would have no credible claim to authority at all. The truly charismatic leader, by contrast, is wholly concerned with his mission; as Weber writes, in what I take to be an overstatement, "no prophet has ever regarded his quality as dependent on the attitudes of the masses toward him."[31]

The distinction between dominance and charisma offers at least one means of classifying and analyzing the phenomenon of *personalism*. There has been a widespread tendency in literature on Spanish American politics to identify personalistic leadership with charismatic leadership. I consider this semantic equation to be theoretically untenable and empirically incorrect. It has created confusion, and, lamentably, it has also devalued the concept of charisma in the analytical marketplace. Some personalistic leaders have undoubtedly been charismatic; but others have not, and their claims to authority have really rested upon dominance. The difference is essential.[32]

Just as legitimation through dominance prevailed in early nineteenth-century Spanish America, more recent developments have given rise to yet another assertion of political legitimacy, which I shall refer to as *achievement-expertise*. This notion rests on the claim that authority should reside in the hands of people who have the knowledge, expertise, or general ability to bring about specific achievements—usually, but not always, economic achievements. In this case authority derives essentially from the desirability of the achievement itself; the commitment is to the goal, not the means.

Political obedience is thus demanded, and presumably accorded, for nonpolitical reasons. The political structure per se loses importance. Leaders are free to adopt any method, no matter how repressive, as long as they can demonstrate progress toward the sought-after goal.

---

[31] Weber, *Theory*, pp. 359–360. To borrow a phrase from Richard M. Morse, the dominant ruler takes a fundamentally "Machiavellian" view of political life; the genuinely charismatic figure would not. See Morse, "Toward a Theory of Spanish American Government," *Journal of the History of Ideas* 15, no. 1 (January 1954): 71–93, esp. pp. 80–83; an excerpted version of this article appears in *Dictatorship in Spanish America*, ed. Hugh M. Hamill, Jr. (New York: Alfred A. Knopf, 1966), pp. 52–68.

[32] Note the apparent discomfort with which Morse categorized all personalistic caudillos as charismatic leaders ("Toward a Theory," p. 85).

This claim first gained currency in the late nineteenth century, as the positivistic slogan of "order and progress" offered a respectable rationale for dictatorial rule. The outstanding example was the Mexican regime of Porfirio Díaz, whose *científico* advisers expressed open scorn for democratic pretensions.[33] "Rights!" exclaimed Francisco G. Cosmes:

People are fed up with them; what they want is bread. To constitutions teeming with sublime ideas which no one has ever seen functioning in practice . . . they prefer an opportunity to work in peace, security in their personal pursuits, and the assurance that the authorities, instead of launching forth on wild goose chases after ideals, will hang the cheats, the thieves, and the revolutionaries. . . . Fewer rights and fewer liberties in exchange for more order and more peace. . . . Enough of utopias. . . . I want order and peace, albeit for the price of all the rights which have cost me so dear. . . . I daresay the day is at hand when the nation will declare: We want order and peace even at the cost of our independence.[34]

By this argument, political authoritarianism—Díaz's "honest tyranny," as it was called—would provide the key to socioeconomic development. Material achievement, in turn, could justify a political system. As another *científico* said, "The day we find that our charter has produced a million settlers, we may say that we have found the right constitution, a constitution no longer amounting to merely a phrase on our lips, but to ploughs in our hands, locomotives on our rails, and money everywhere."[35] When Porfiristas spoke of "freedom," as they often did, they meant economic freedom—not political freedom. And, not surprisingly, when Francisco Madero started attacking Díaz, he did so on the exclusively political questions of reelection and the presidential succession.

[33] Needler takes notes of the "order and progress" justification for dictatorship but regards it as a historical phenomenon that lost relevance by 1930 (*Political Development*, pp. 33–40). On the contrary, I see achievement-expertise as gaining currency in recent years.

[34] Quoted in Leopoldo Zea, "Positivism and Porfirism in Latin America," in *Ideological Differences and World Order*, ed. F. S. C. Northrop (New Haven: Yale University Press, 1949), p. 174.

[35] Ibid., p. 182.

In our own century, achievement-expertise has become a common claim of military dictatorships. Even Rafael Leonidas Trujillo Molina, who tyrannized the Dominican Republic for thirty straight years, made fervent claims to political legitimacy. He called his regime a democracy but ignored the problem of personal rights. Instead, he said, "Democracy is action: economic, religious, political, social, human action—in a word, action which evolves and operates in accordance with the traditions, the history, the ethnology, and the geography of each group provided of course it is primarily directed towards the improvement of the community." Looking back on his first days in office and the devastation then caused by a hurricane, Trujillo modestly acknowledged: "I had the patience and the faith to undertake and carry out a program of government which was embodied in a single word: *build!*"[36]

More recent military governments have made extensive use of the achievement-expertise claim. During the 1950s Marcos Pérez Jiménez proudly proclaimed *la reforma del medio físico* in Venezuela. Since 1964 the Brazilian regime has stressed its modernizing capabilities and organizational efficiency. The "Argentine Revolution" of 1966 took place in the name of order and economic development. Examples abound, echoing the well-known refrain from Mussolini's Italy: The trains now run on time.[37]

In summary, I perceive five distinct, nondemocratic types of political legitimacy in Spanish American history: tradition (mainly in the colonial period), legality, charisma, dominance, and achievement-expertise. Naturally, this does not exhaust the entire range of possibilities. It would be going too far to assert that there is *no* democratic tradition in Spanish American legalism; my point is that legality qua legality can be *either* democratic or authoritarian. Cuba's current ef-

[36] Rafael Leonidas Trujillo Molina, *The Evolution of Democracy in Santo Domingo* (Ciudad Trujillo, 1950), pp. 4, 13.

[37] Seymour Martin Lipset's concept of *effectiveness* is analogous to my notion of achievement-expertise, though he specifically distinguishes it from legitimacy—partly because he adheres to the standard Weberian typology (*Political Man*, pp. 64–70). It remains my observation that achievement-expertise constitutes a distinct kind of legitimacy, probably claimed by authoritarian regimes more often than by democratic governments.

forts to create a "new socialist" man may offer yet another alternative.[38] In any case, the prevalence of nondemocratic, authoritarian ideals in Spanish America strongly suggests that dictatorship is not an aberration. It would seem to be a logical expression of the political culture.

Of course there is all the difference in the world between a *claim* to political legitimacy and a *state* of political legitimacy. All leaders seek voluntary submission from their citizenry, to one extent or another, and all make some sort of claim to legitimacy. It is not particularly surprising to find nondemocratic leaders making nondemocratic claims.

The question is whether the constituent population accepts the claim as appropriate—in other words, whether there is congruence between claims of the leaders and the values of the people.[39] Where there is congruence, there is a state of legitimacy. Where there is no congruence, there is a state of illegitimacy. The implication here is obvious: if dictatorial claims to legitimacy comply with basic societal values, then dictatorship (in one form or another) may well have been legitimate throughout much of Spanish American history. If not, then why did leaders make such claims?

Of course this begs another question: why should Spanish American political culture possess a propensity to perceive dictatorial rule as legitimate? A historian might instinctively respond that this was so because such tendencies rested in the cultural tradition, but this reply seems tautological to me. The question then becomes, why do people follow and accept tradition? And if some ideas about legitimacy (such as democratic legality, perhaps also achievement-expertise) are essentially imported, rather than derived from local tradition, how is it that some of these cultural transplants are successful and others are not? The issue is extraordinarily complex, and, partly for this reason, I shall take the liberty of ruling that it lies outside the scope of this essay. At the same time I must also acknowledge its importance.

38 See Fagen, *Transformation*.
39 See Harry Eckstein, *Division and Cohesion in Democracy: A Study of Norway* (Princeton: Princeton University Press, 1966), Appendix B and passim.

POSSIBILITIES AND PROBLEMS FOR RESEARCH

Whether or not my suppositions are correct, there should be little doubt that the concepts of political culture and political legitimacy in Spanish America deserve serious attention from historians. But this is more easily said than done. At the very least, comprehensive analysis of legitimacy must take account of leaders, followers, and the situational context of leader-follower relationships.

One elementary step is to concentrate on the claims to legitimacy made by rulers (or aspirants to rule). This kind of research demands considerable imagination. For all the imperfections of my own analysis, I hope to have demonstrated the general need for suspending ethnocentric assumptions and for extending the Weberian typology. In practice, this work can focus on the standard written sources: speeches, reports, memoirs, letters, and so on. Pompous, apparently empty titles—"Well-Deserving of the Fatherland," "The Great Democrat," "The Illustrious American"—can furnish additional clues to the content of claims.

The scrutiny of leadership should concentrate upon the search for underlying patterns or configurations of claims to legitimacy. The differing types of legitimacy are not mutually exclusive; they are strongly interdependent, and virtually all leaders make more than one sort of claim. The problem is one of determining the relative emphasis and the relative meaning of the various claims. An oversimplified, but useful, illustration of the point could take the form of an equation:[40]

Claims to
Political   = Claims to (Tradition + Legality + Charisma
Legitimacy   + Dominance + Achievement-Expertise).

Eventually, it may prove possible to demonstrate that certain types of leaders tend to make certain types (or clusters of types) of claims

[40] Instead of simple additive equations, one could employ multiplicative models, replacing $x = y + z$ by some such conceptualization as $x = yz$. The idea of using an equation first struck me in reading Lucian W. Pye's "The Legitimacy Crisis," in *Crises and Sequences in Political Development*, by Leonard Binder et al. (Princeton: Princeton University Press, 1971), p. 149n.; Pye, in turn, got the idea from Dankwart A. Rustow.

to legitimacy. As an example, one might correlate legitimacy claims with the kinds of political resources possessed by elites or leadership types.[41] The early caudillos, who relied essentially upon physical coercion, tended to emphasize dominance. "Integrating dictators," usually men of military background who built their power upon centralized national authority, often stressed a mixture of dominance, achievement-expertise, and legality (nondemocratic). Professional military men, in accord with their training—plus the absence of a civilian political base—have shown a tendency to appeal to achievement-expertise, either to purge the body politic before relinquishing power to civilians or to push the country on the road to economic development. Technocrats, whose access to power presumably depends upon their knowledge, have also stressed achievement-expertise. Career politicians, whose main resource is control over votes, commonly claim that legality (often democratic) is on their side. Almost by definition, populists are charismatic: mass leaders like Perón because they articulate a social order in traditional terms, social revolutionaries because of their vision of the promised land. Solely for heuristic purposes, Table 1 sets forth these speculations.[42]

In addition to examining the claims of leaders, we need to explore the popular values and "civic culture" of political constituencies in Latin America. In this regard we have much to learn from both literary sources and survey research.[43] Some time ago I utilized

[41] Regarding typologies of Latin American leaders see Kalman H. Silvert, "Leadership Formation and Modernization in Latin America," *Journal of International Affairs* 20, no. 2 (1966): 318–331; William A. Welsh, "Methodological Problems in the Study of Political Leadership in Latin America," *Latin American Research Review* 5, no. 3 (Fall 1970): 3–33; and the essay by Richard Graham in this volume.

[42] To avoid confusion I have restricted my focus to national leaders. For a subtle analysis of local bossism in rural Mexico see Paul Friedrich, "The Legitimacy of a Cacique," in *Local-Level Politics: Social and Cultural Perspectives*, ed. Marc J. Swartz (Chicago: Aldine, 1968), pp. 243–269; though Friedrich's terminology differs from mine, he clearly reveals the importance of dominance and achievement-expertise in the local context. For further reference on this type of leader see *The Caciques: Oligarchical Politics and the System of Caciquismo in the Luso-Hispanic World*, ed. Robert Kern, with the assistance of Ronald Dolkart (Albuquerque: University of New Mexico Press, 1973).

[43] But *not* surveys loaded with ethnocentric bias, such as Gabriel Almond and

Table 1.

*Some Hypothetical Relationships between Leadership
Types and Claims to Political Legitimacy*

Leadership Type	Predominant Claims to Legitimacy*
Caudillos	Dominance
Integrating dictators	Dominance, achievement-expertise, legality (nondemocratic)
Military professionals	Achievement-expertise (political or economic)
Technocrats	Achievement-expertise (economic)
Career politicians	Legality (democratic), possibly charisma
Mass populists	Charisma (in traditional terms)
Social revolutionaries	Charisma (for a new society)

* It should be understood that predominant claims were almost always supported and reinforced by secondary claims, which are not listed in this table.

historiographical polemics over a nineteenth-century dictator in order to trace changing conceptions of political legitimacy in Ecuador.[44] Aside from sources of this sort, we could investigate the political content of popular media—songs, cartoons, cheap novels, schoolbooks, and so on. One particularly intriguing research strategy would be to trace dictionary definitions of such politically relevant terms as *poder, elección, dictador, compromiso.* It would be especially important to examine not only the substance of operative values, but also their cohesiveness. A reasonably consistent, widely held notion of legitimacy has one implication for the political order; an inconsistent or divided set of strictures means something else again.

We can also benefit from careful analysis of the institutions that form, perpetuate, and pass on political values. This raises the whole question of what has come to be known as "political socialization," a field that has developed a substantial literature of its own.[45] At least two institutions come readily to mind: the Church and the schools, sometimes closely related if not synonymous. Richard Fagen's excel-

Sidney Verba's *The Civic Culture: Political Attitudes and Democracy in Five Nations* (Boston: Little, Brown, 1965).

[44] Peter H. Smith, "The Image of a Dictator: Gabriel García Moreno," *Hispanic American Historical Review* 45, no. 4 (February 1965): 1–24.

[45] See Richard E. Dawson and Kenneth Prewitt, *Political Socialization* (Boston: Little, Brown, 1969).

lent study on Cuba has shown how the Castro regime has consciously utilized the educational process in order to inculcate new and revolutionary values; but schools have performed political functions throughout history, not just under Castro, and Fagen's approach to the problem offers a promising paradigm for research in this area.[46]

In this connection, we must take care to relate political values (however plumbed) to the sociopolitical structure of the society under study. The basic question is beguilingly straightforward: *Whose* political values? As one approach to the problem, students of political culture have come to recognize three distinct strata or subcultures: (*a*) the *participant* population, which takes active and effective interest in political affairs; (*b*) the *subject* population, passive but aware of politics; and (*c*) the *parochial* population, unconcerned and ignorant of politics.[47]

It is virtually impossible to determine the size or composition of these subcultures with much precision, but rough estimates are feasible. Literacy rates and newspaper circulation figures, for instance, might circumscribe the participant-plus-subject group. In his stimulating study of political culture in twentieth-century Mexico, Robert E. Scott uses data on class structure for this same general purpose.[48] Distinguishing between the participant and subject strata is much more difficult. Scott leans on survey results; historians would have to employ other sources (electoral participation might be useful but misleading).

Although these distinctions defy clear translation into empirical terms, they provide an analytical criterion for focusing upon salient political constituencies. At this juncture the study of legitimacy becomes inextricably linked to the study of power. To maintain functional authority, a government needs recognition and support from the active power centers in society—not necessarily from a statistical ma-

---

[46] Fagen, *Transformation*.

[47] See Almond and Verba, *Civic Culture*, passim. These broad distinctions strike me as valid concepts—although, as noted above, I believe that Almond and Verba applied the concepts in a very biased way.

[48] Robert E. Scott, "Mexico: The Established Revolution," in *Political Culture*, ed. Pye and Verba, esp. pp. 342–345.

jority of people. It is possible for a regime to be widely viewed as illegitimate but stay in power if a small but predominant sector of the participant stratum sees it as legitimate.

So there is a critical distinction between the *durability* and the *legitimacy* of regimes. A totally illegitimate government can keep office under either of two conditions: (*a*) if domestic power groups support it for the sake of convenience, rather than out of conviction; or (*b*) if it is imposed or maintained by a foreign power. Trujillo's thirty-year rule in the Dominican Republic, for example, may have met both these conditions. Quite rightly, Juan Linz has classified it as a "sultanistic" regime devoid of internal legitimacy,[49] propped up partly by the United States government.

In defining the relevant constituency or political "audience," one must take special note of foreigners. For most (if not all) of the period since independence, participant strata have included foreign investors, organizations, and governments. In deference to the ideological (or terminological) predilection for "democracy" in the United States, many dictators—even Trujillo—have trumpeted the democratic virtues of their governments. Recent concerns with economic performance have lent international respectability to legitimation by achievement-expertise. Ironically enough, the now-defunct Alliance for Progress may have encouraged dictatorship because of its emphasis on economic development; in many quarters, a growing GNP and a stable currency can justify repression.

The distribution of power within subject and participant subcultures offers one means for comprehending the dynamic *processes* of legitimation and delegitimation.[50] Change can take place in one of two ways: a leader can gain or lose legitimacy among specific constituent groups; or, more fundamentally, the over-all constituency may undergo alteration. In twentieth-century Argentina, for instance, transition of the urban working class from subject to participant status (among

---

[49] Linz, "Notes toward a Typology."

[50] It is essential to stress this aspect of change. As Paul Friedrich has observed, "Much essentially scholastic debate could be obviated if legitimacy were thought of as a matter of process and flux rather than a static thing with fixed and proper attributes" ("The Legitimacy of a Cacique," p. 244).

other things) has not only altered the power equation but also created a profound split in political values among the country's actively contending groups. And the result, since the 1930s, has been a pervasive crisis of legitimacy.[51]

Finally, we must place the leaders, the audience, and their values in their historical and socioeconomic context. Experience—the passage of events—doubtless affects the type and effectiveness of legitimacy claims. It would appear that the wars of independence exerted a double impact on codes of legitimacy in Spanish America: first, by eliminating direct recourse to traditional claims; second, by lending prestige to feats of military prowess, thus strengthening the notion of dominance. Brazil had no such wars and retained a traditionalistic empire throughout most of the nineteenth century. Perhaps this difference helps account for the alleged de-emphasis on violence in Brazilian political culture, with a corresponding scarcity of legitimacy through dominance.[52] In this paper I have limited my discussion to Spanish America precisely in order to hold this historical factor constant, but Brazil offers a fascinating prospect for comparative analysis. Needless to say, variations in historical experience (i.e., the incidence of wars, the level of technological development) might also contribute to an understanding of variability in political cultures among the countries of Spanish America.

Ultimately, we should strive for a holistic view of political legitimacy that would integrate actors, values, and social relationships in a coherent and systematic way. Specifically, we need to ask which kinds of political *leaders* make which kinds of *claims* to legitimacy to which kind of *audience* with what kind of *success* under what kind of contextual or historical *conditions*. This paradigm not only offers a means of dealing with legitimacy at a single point in time. It also suggests an approach to the sequential processes of legitimation and delegitimation. Which variables seem to bring about changes in which others? What are the causal relationships? By what means does a leader (or regime) most commonly gain or lose legitimacy?

[51] See Lucian W. Pye, "The Legitimacy Crisis," in *Crises*, by Binder et al.
[52] James L. Busey, "Brazil's Reputation for Political Stability," *Western Political Quarterly* 18, no. 4 (December 1965): 866–880.

Obviously it would be impossible for any single researcher to deal with all these issues in a solid empirical way. It is not my purpose, however, to lay down a grand design for decades of research. My intention is to emphasize these linkages in order to encourage scholars to maintain a sense of the whole, even while working on only a part.

IN SEARCH OF VALUE CONFIGURATIONS

The practical analysis of political legitimacy can be as difficult as it is fruitful. "Operationalization of the conceptual framework," in the awesome jargon of contemporary social science, presents a formidable challenge. Here I shall take up only one piece in the puzzle—the problem of identifying a configuration of claims to legitimacy that a political leader might make. How can we best comprehend the priorities and relationships among various available types of legitimacy?

Obviously one approach—and an essential one—is to read the available documents with thoroughness, sensitivity, and care. One simply has to get a "feel" for the material, to discern its logical structure, to sense its underlying emphasis, to perceive its unwritten assumptions, and to understand its hidden messages. As Clifford Geertz has said of ideology:

... it is ... the attempt of ideologies to render otherwise incomprehensible social situations meaningful, to so construe them as to make it possible to act purposefully within them, that accounts both for the ideologies' highly figurative nature and for the intensity with which, once accepted, they are held. As metaphor extends language by broadening its semantic range, enabling it to express meanings it cannot or at least cannot yet express literally, so the head-on clash of literal meanings in ideology—the irony, the hyperbole, the overdrawn antithesis—provides novel symbolic frames against which to match the myriad "unfamiliar somethings" that, like a journey to a strange country, are produced by a transformation in political life. Whatever else ideologies may be—projections of unacknowledged fears, disguises for ulterior motives, phatic expressions of group solidarity— they are, most distinctively, maps of problematic social reality and matrices for the creation of collective conscience. Whether, in any particular case, the map is accurate or the conscience creditable is a separate question . . .[53]

[53] Clifford Geertz, "Ideology as a Cultural System," in *Ideology and Discontent,*

Particular claims to political legitimacy may or may not amount to an ideology, depending on one's definition, but the methodological strictures still apply. We must deal with language, even political language, as an integral cultural form.[54] We cannot expect it to be "rational" in terms that are congruent with our own values.

Getting a "feel" for the data has to be the first analytical step, and it may prove to be the only necessary one. Yet it can also be subject to erroneous interpretation. As a means of checking this tendency, I would suggest the use of quantitive content analysis.

Content analysis has gained considerable notoriety as a historiographical tool. Critics charge that it demands oversimplification for the purpose of misleading codification, that it invariably culminates in the fallacy of misplaced concreteness. In truth, however, content analysis is just like any other form of historical analysis. *All* historians sort, codify, and classify themes in documents as "more" or "less" important—usually according to some implicitly quantitative criterion, such as frequency of mention. Content analysis simply attempts to make this process rigorous; as Ole Holsti has defined it, content analysis is "any technique for making inferences by objectively and systematically identifying specified characteristics of messages."[55] If quantification is to be used, it is obviously necessary to know what to count (i.e., the "specified characteristics"), and this is why I have devoted so much attention to the concept of political legitimacy. Once this issue is settled (I do not pretend that it is), statistical devices can be of great help.

As a simple example of content analysis, Table 2 presents some

---

ed. David E. Apter (New York: The Free Press, 1964), pp. 47–76; the quotation is from p. 64. See also *Daedalus* 101, no. 1 (Winter 1972), an issue dedicated to "the systematic study of meaningful forms."

[54] The same point applies to the study of "ideas" as distinct from "ideology." See Charles A. Hale, "The Reconstruction of Nineteenth-Century Politics in Spanish America: A Case for the History of Ideas," *Latin American Research Review* 8, no. 2 (Summer 1973): 53–73; and Dahl, *Polyarchy*, pp. 124–188.

[55] Ole R. Holsti, *Content Analysis for the Social Sciences and Humanities* (Reading, Mass.: Addison-Wesley, 1969), p. 14; see also Robert C. North et al., *Content Analysis: A Handbook with Applications for the Study of International Crisis* (Evanston, Ill.: Northwestern University Press, 1963).

Table 2

*Frequency of Self-References by Gabriel García Moreno**

	Period 1 1845–1859 No. %		Period 2 1859–1865 No. %		Period 3 1865–1869 No. %		Period 4 1869–1875 No. %		Net % (Average) 1859–1875
Tradition	—	—	—	—	—	—	—	—	—
Legality									
Opponent of tyranny	5		—		—		—		
Disinterested servant	—		20		7		2		
Total	5	25	20	15.6	7	8.8	2	1.4	8.6
Charisma									
Patriot, national savior	7		17		13		4		
Champion of morality	5		8		8		17		
Protected by God	3		4		29		13		
Protector of Church	—		4		9		35		
Total	15	75	33	25.8	59	73.8	69	47.6	49.1
Dominance									
Necessarily strong leader	—		5		—		—		
Guardian of peace	—		32		13		5		
Total	—	—	37	28.9	13	16.3	5	3.4	16.2
Achievement-Expertise									
Fiscal reformer and "master builder"	—		25		—		60		
Total	—	—	25	19.5	—	—	60	41.4	20.3
Other									
Commander-in-chief	—		13		1		9		
Total	—	—	13	10.2	1	1.3	9	6.2	5.9
General Total	20	100	128	100	80	100	145	100	100

* Based on 100-page samples for each of four separate periods from García Moreno's private papers: *Cartas de Gabriel García Moreno*, ed. Wilfrido Loor, 4 vols. (Quito: La Prensa Católica, 1953–1956). Percentage details may not add up to 100 because of rounding.

findings on claims to legitimacy made by Gabriel García Moreno, ruler of Ecuador in 1859–1865 and 1869–1875. Standard views of his career imply that García Moreno, a religious fanatic, claimed legitimacy through his devotion to the mission of the Roman Catholic Church. Charisma, of allegedly divine inspiration, would constitute his major demand for authority.

In compiling these data I have taken one-hundred-page samples of his writings from four main periods of his life: born in 1821, he became increasingly active in national politics from 1845 to 1859; from 1859 to 1865 he was the country's dominant figure, first as the leader of a ruling triumvirate; then, from 1861, as constitutional president; he was out of power between mid-1865 and 1869; and then he ruled again from 1869 to 1875. For each sample I simply counted the number of times that García Moreno referred to himself in ways that could be related to political or quasi-political images: "Protector of the Church," "Champion of Morality," "Guardian of Public Peace," and so on. Then, letting knowledge of the context guide my intuition, I collated all these themes under headings of legitimacy (with all due respect to subtle ambiguities). The point of it all is to see which themes he emphasized and whether the configuration of claims underwent change over time. The findings are hardly definitive, but I believe they are suggestive.

First, it is clear that García Moreno's political self-consciousness intensified a great deal, as the total number of references for the one-hundred-page samples climbed from only 20 in the years before power to 145 during his second presidential term. He seems to have acquired a sense of charismatic self-importance; he did not have it all the time. One might even construe the intensification of his ideology (or self-image) as a response to, or part of, the exigencies of political events.

Second, in his search for legitimacy, García Moreno made no overt or direct references to traditional authority, in keeping with the general trend of nineteenth-century Spanish America. But as I shall indicate below, he did make indirect appeals to this theme.

Third, he made very few references to legal authority, less than 10 percent during the period of his most active political participation (1859–1875). It is possible that the infrequency of this claim is partly due to my use of private papers for the sample, rather than public statements, but it is still notable that he did not portray himself as "Protector of the Laws" or "Father of the Constitution" during either administration—even though he supervised the adoption of a new national charter in 1869. In fact, having upheld the "necessity of a strong Government" during a constitutional convention in 1861, he was sorely disappointed with the resulting document and as president even vowed to break it: "we must execute whoever helps invaders," he once said, "despite the Constitution."[56] The basic point is this: García Moreno was not apologizing for the authoritarian quality of his regime; he was trying to justify it.

Fourth, García Moreno made clear references to both dominance and achievement-expertise, with a clear pattern emerging over time. During his first term in office, while establishing his personal authority and leading his country in war, his most frequent claim to power was through dominance (28.9 percent). By 1869–1875, however, he turned his attention to material achievement (41.4 percent).

Fifth, García Moreno changed emphasis at different times. Before taking power in 1859, he viewed his political purpose as in some vague way serving the Ecuadorean nation and liberating it from tyranny. During his first presidency, he combined this belief with an insistence upon dominance and the need for achievement-expertise. After stepping down in 1865, he began to stress a hitherto latent theme: a claim to charismatic authority (73.8 percent in Period 3) because of his devotion to Christian morals and the Catholic Church. "Special providential care," he wrote at the time, "convinces me that God wants me to keep discharging the difficult mission of consolidating liberty on morality, with Religion as the guarantee. . . . Let us have faith, and God will protect us."[57] Thus García Moreno claimed authority by a kind of "divine right," though not a hereditary one. His reliance on the Church added a traditional dimension to his claims: the Church had embodied God's will from time immemorial, and García Moreno's close association with it sanctified him as the spokesman for sacred tradition.

When he came to power for the second time, García Moreno demanded that the people accept him "unanimously," wrote a theocratic sort of constitution, and struck an eclectic combination. He tried to assert *charismatic* authority as God's chosen instrument and through

[56] Gabriel García Moreno, *Cartas de Gabriel García Moreno*, ed. Wilfrido Loor, 4 vols. (Quito: La Prensa Católica, 1953–1956), II, 225, 316.

[57] García Moreno, *Cartas*, III, 364. There is some ambiguity in the Spanish text of this passage—as to whether God or García Moreno is to discharge the mission—but it is clear from the context (and from another quote on this same page) that García Moreno viewed himself as God's chosen agent on earth.

identification with the *traditional* role of the Church, the outward manifestation of his anointment being his *achievement-expertise.* The constitution furnished *legal* recognition of the situation and, presumably, a means for the routinization of charisma. In possible testimony to the effectiveness of these claims, and also to the prevailing behavioral codes, García Moreno's opponents had to shoot him out of power in 1875.

Thus content analysis can bring about considerable refinement in our historical perception of political legitimacy. I should stress that this example demonstrates only the crudest sort of content analysis, based on simple frequency counts. Advanced techniques exist for determining the intensity, context, and latent characteristics of messages too. Sophisticated computer programs, such as the series of programs known as the General Inquirer, offer major resources for this kind of work.[58]

While my demonstration has referred only to claims made by a political leader, I am confident these techniques would be equally applicable to the study of popular values. Content analysis can be performed on any sort of document, including school textbooks or popular songs. The most difficult problem is finding salient and workable categories of analysis. It is for this reason, again, that I have used so much space to elaborate and define basic types of political legitimacy.

SUMMARY

This paper has set forth a number of related propositions about the historical study of Spanish American politics. In retrospect they seem exceedingly simple, if not simplistic, but a brief summary can schematize the structure of my argument.

1. Dictatorial government has so dominated Spanish American history that it seems illusory to consider this fact as an accident.

2. Socioeconomic development, however construed, does not appear to create political democracy, though there may be a loose positive correlation between the two phenomena.[59]

---

[58] Holsti, *Content Analysis*, pp. 150-194.

[59] Evidence on this point is far from complete, and one recent study has argued that authoritarianism in Latin America may be a *consequence* of socioeconomic de-

3. There is no convincing reason to believe that Spanish American politics is moving, even gradually, towards democracy.[60] A democratic-nondemocratic dichotomy is therefore not a useful conceptual tool.

4. In the absence of other clear explanations, one reason for the prevalence of authoritarianism might be cultural.

5. A central dimension in any political culture involves the concept of political legitimacy.

6. Studies of political legitimacy have been hampered by over-reliance on Max Weber's classification of legitimacy as traditional, legal, and charismatic (despite Weber's own warnings). My interpretation of Spanish American political culture suggests the existence of two other distinct types, which I have called *dominance* and *achievement-expertise*.

7. In order to make sufficient allowance for the (very real) possibility that dictatorships can be legitimate, we must place legitimacy claims in their full historical and cultural context.

8. Claims to legitimacy may or may not be recognized by relevant political constituencies. It is therefore necessary to study the political values of constituent groups as well as the content of leadership claims.

9. It is conceivable for a government to be largely or even totally illegitimate and yet remain in power. There is a crucial difference between governmental durability and governmental legitimacy.

10. Quantitative content analysis can be of great help in exploring the configuration of legitimacy claims by leaders, and it also has potential for the study of popular values.

My most elementary message, however, stands apart from these specific propositions and questions about their validity. Fundamentally, I want to extend the reconceptualization of political phenomena in

velopment. See Guillermo A. O'Donnell, *Modernization and Bureaucratic-Authoritarianism: Studies in South American Politics* (Berkeley: Institute of International Studies, University of California, 1973), esp. pp. 1–114.

[60] Needler has constructed a graph that shows a secular decline in the over-all "incidence of dictatorship" in Latin America between 1935 and 1964 (*Political Development*, pp. 41–42, 171 n.). His definition of *dictatorship* seems very limited, however, and he does not report his country-by-country classifications over time.

Spanish America that other scholars have already started and to focus attention on the concept of political culture. In particular, I would urge North American historians to (*a*) suspend blatantly ethnocentric and naively normative criteria, (*b*) present assumptions and relevant preferences in explicit fashion, and (*c*) analyze political culture in its own terms. My own views of Spanish American politics might well be entirely wrong; but by following these rules, someone else might turn out to be right.

GLOSSARY

agregado: a free man attached by ties of blood, godparentage, or some other form of obligation to the head of an urban household or rural establishment.

alcalde del crimen: a judge of a lower court, the *sala de crimen*, attached to the *audiencias* of Mexico and Lima to exercise criminal jurisdiction.

alcalde mayor: in colonial Spanish America, an official in charge of a province or district (often equivalent to a *corregidor*).

amparo: a judicial writ similar to habeas corpus.

antioqueño: native or resident of the former province and state (now department) of Antioquia, in western Colombia.

audiencia: the highest court of justice in a Spanish-American kingdom, with some administrative and political functions.

bandeirante: originally, a term applied to sixteenth- and seventeenth-century pathfinders and slavecatchers based in São Paulo, Brazil; currently synonymous with *paulista*.

barbarie: barbarity, backwardness.

bárbaro. See *caudillo bárbaro*.

bogotano: native or resident of Bogotá, Colombia.

bolas: weapon used by Argentine gauchos, adapted from the Araucanian Indians; also known as *boleadoras*.

bozal: an African-born slave.

cabildo: in Spain and Spanish America, the town council.

cacique: originally, an Indian chieftain; currently used in Spanish America to indicate a local or regional political boss.

caciquismo: the political system characterized by caciques.

carne y hueso: flesh and blood.

Casa de Contratación: Sevillian-based institution, analogous to a Board of Trade, that dealt with all matters of trade and emigration to the Indies.

caucano. See *negro caucano*.

caudillismo: in Spanish America, the political system characterized by the overwhelming control and influence of a single individual.

caudillo: in Spanish America, a dominant political leader on the national or regional level.

caudillo bárbaro: term applied to Bolivia's more violent mid-nineteenth-century dictators by the Bolivian author, Alcides Arguedas.

censos: quit-rents or annuities, usually paid at the rate of 5 percent upon a certain value of property, often to a Church organization, hospital, or some other pious institution and in consideration for a loan.

científico: literally, scientist or scientific; applied with particular reference to university-trained Positivists in late nineteenth- and early twentieth-century Mexico.

cimarrones: runaway slaves.

civilización: civilization.

clientela: group of dependents or persons owing favors.

colegio: institution of higher education, now exclusively secondary; in the colonial era and on occasion in the nineteenth century, however, a university-level institution might be called a *colegio mayor*.

colegio mayor. **See** *colegio.*

compadrazgo: ritual godparentage.

compromiso: engagement, commitment, or pledge; occasionally, compromise.

Comunero rebellion: popular rebellion of 1780–1781 against tax increases in the Viceroyalty of New Granada.

consulado: Spanish merchants' guild.

consulta: record of a discussion in council; by extension, a council's decision.

coronelismo: political bossism of large landowners in twentieth-century Brazil.

corregidor: in the Spanish colonial system, an official with administrative, political, and judiciary authority over a province; subordinate to viceroy and *audiencia.*

corregimiento: provincial administrative unit governed by a *corregidor.*

cortes: Spanish parliament composed of delegates selected by major town councils (*cabildos*) ; lasted from medieval era into the nineteenth century.

costumbrismo: literary description of local manners and folk customs.

criollo: a person of European descent born in the New World.

cuartelazo: barracks revolt.

desamortización: the liberation for legal sale and the selling of property, usually that of the Church, that according to the original bequest could not be legally alienated by its recipient.

dictador: dictator.

diezmo: 10 percent tax on most agricultural and livestock products, collected by the Spanish crown and, for a time, by the successor republican governments for the support of the Church and pious works.

elección: election.

enchufe: political influence or "pull." **See also** *pistolão*.

encomendero: individual who received, from the Spanish crown, the right to Indian tribute in payment of services rendered to the crown.

estanquero: in colonial or early republican Spanish America, a person associated with one of the government monopolies, especially the tobacco monopoly; in Chile, *estanqueros* were political followers of Diego Portales, who held the country's tobacco monopoly from 1824 to 1826.

fiscal: a crown attorney serving as one of the superior magistrates of an *audiencia* and overseeing the royal treasury.

ganho. **See** *negro de ganho*.

hacendado: owner of a large landed estate.

hidalguismo: in Spain, pride in and glorification of one's descendance from noble blood.

ladino: an African or Indian who has acquired most of the external cultural attributes of the Spaniard.

letrado: a university graduate; term often synonymous with lawyer or judge.

limeño: native or resident of Lima, Peru.

limpieza de sangre: literally, purity of blood; also, Spanish pride in ancestry untainted by genetic mixture with Jews, Moors, or heretics.

los que mandan: those in control; phrase refers to title of book by the Argentine sociologist, José Luis de Imaz.

machismo: literally, maleness or masculinity; more frequently used to denote unpredictable aggressiveness and violence on the part of men and the exaltation of this type of behavior.

medio físico: physical environment. See *reforma del medio físico*.

memoria: summary report of viceroy's administration prepared by him at the end of his term, partly to assist the new viceroy.

mercedes: royal grants of office, title, Indian tribute, or other benefits in return for services rendered to the crown.

mocambo: Portuguese term for small community of escaped slaves; today, used to refer to a slum. **See also** *quilombo*.

moderado: "moderate," self-designation used by New Granadan politicians of the 1830s who supported the resumption of parliamentary republican government after Simon Bolívar's dictatorship of 1828-1830 but also favored a policy of conciliation toward Bolívar's adherents, in opposition to a more doctrinaire group of liberals whom they called the *exaltados*.

morador: free peasant in Northeast Brazil.

município: subdivision of a Brazilian state, in most respects equivalent to a county.

negro caucano: term used by citizens of Bogotá to describe the lower classes of the Cauca Valley, a term which particularly came into play in 1861 when an army from Cauca was about to invade Bogotá.

negro de carne y hueso: a flesh-and-blood black man.

negro de ganho: a black slave who seeks employment on his own, turning over the earnings to his master.

oidor: judge who served on an *audiencia*.

palanca: literally, a lever or simple instrument to move or lift weights; in colloquial Brazilian, the word refers to the use of one's acquaintances for "leverage" in attaining perquisites or benefits.

panelinha: intimate but informal mutual-aid society in Brazil, often based on friendships made early in life.

parentela: kinship group or ancestor-oriented family; also used in Brazil to denote a system of interlocking social, political, and business obligations binding members of such a group.

paternalismo: paternalism, a relation involving care and control on the part of the government for the governed, on the part of the employer for the employed, etc.

patrón: in Spanish America, the owner or boss or, more generally, the person in a superior position.

paulista: native or resident of the state of São Paulo, Brazil; as adjective, referring to the state of São Paulo.

pelucones: literally, "big wigs" or people wearing them; term applied to conservative element in Chile in the 1820s and 1830s, usually associated with large landowners.

pensador: person involved in philosophical or speculative pursuits, usually oriented toward questions of public policy.

personalismo: personalism, the control and influence of a single leader on a government, a business, or some other organization; also, the attachment of followers to dominant individuals rather than to ideals, principles, or some other form of loyalty.

pistolão: literally, pistol, in Brazil, but meaning "pull"; the use of political influence to obtain jobs, contracts, favors. **See also** *enchufe*.

pocho: slang term, often used pejoratively, to denote a person of Mexican descent living across the border in the United States; the term originated in northern Mexico and antedates the word *chicano*.

poder: power.

política dos governadores: political system characteristic of early twentieth-century Brazil in which the federal president allowed each governor to rule virtually undisputed as long as he sent pliable delegations to the national congress.

populacho: the populace, usually used with derogatory implication (as in the English "rabble").

Porfiriato: period in Mexican history when Porfírio Díaz was in control, 1876–1911.

pronunciamento: proclamation or decree, often of a Spanish American military chief or dictator.

quilombo: Portuguese-Brazilian term for a runaway slave community. **See also** *mocambo*.

Reforma: period of pronounced liberal-conservative struggle in Mexico (1855–1867), during which liberals adopted a new federalist constitution and assaulted the power of the Church.

reforma del medio físico: reform or transformation of the physical environment.

residencia: judicial review of an official's conduct at the end of his term in office.

sede: seat of a Brazilian *município*.

sindicato: officially recognized interest-group association in Brazil.

sirvienta: female servant.

tenente: in Brazil, an army lieutenant; the word is often used to denote those junior army officers during the 1920s and 1930s who favored social, economic, and political reforms.

tenentismo: in Brazil, the reform movement led by young military officers in the 1920s and 1930s; the term also refers to the military revolts of these young officers, particularly in 1922 and 1924.

valido: royal favorite.

visita: inspection of an administration carried out by a special commissioner called a *visitador*.

visita general: an occasional investigation of the conduct of an *audiencia*.

voodún: animistic religious beliefs and practices, possibly originating in Dahomeh, with magic and witchcraft as prominent features; in Latin America, particularly associated with the black population of Haiti.

NOTES ON CONTRIBUTORS

MARGARET E. CRAHAN, born in Catskill, New York, in 1939, received her B.A. from the College of New Rochelle, her M.A. from Georgetown University, and her Ph.D. from Columbia University. She has published articles on the role of the Church in Latin America and is an assistant professor of history at Herbert H. Lehman College of the City University of New York.

RICHARD GRAHAM was born in Anápolis, Brazil, in 1934. He earned his B.A. from the College of Wooster and his M.A. and Ph.D. from the University of Texas. He has taught at Cornell University and the University of Utah and is now a professor of history at the University of Texas at Austin. His books include *Britain and the Onset of Modernization in Brazil, 1850–1918*, winner of the Bolton Prize; *A Century of Brazilian History since 1865*; and *Independence in Latin America*.

MICHAEL M. HALL, born in Houston in 1941, is assistant professor of history at Newcomb College of Tulane University. An undergraduate at Stanford University, he did his graduate work at Columbia University and has taught at the University of North Carolina and the Universidade Estadual de Campinas, São Paulo, Brazil.

JOHN V. LOMBARDI, born in Los Angeles in 1942, is associate professor of history and director of the Latin American Studies Program at Indiana University. He earned his degrees at Pomona College and Columbia Univerity and has done extensive research on eighteenth- and nineteenth-century Spanish America. He is the author of *The Decline and Abolition of Negro Slavery in Venezuela, 1820–1854*.

JOSEPH L. LOVE was born in Austin, Texas, in 1938, obtained his B.A. degree from Harvard University, his M.A. from Stanford University, and his Ph.D. from Columbia University. He has published *Rio Grande do Sul and Brazilian Regionalism, 1882–1930,* and coedited a volume entitled *Quantitative Social Science Research on Latin America.* He is associate professor of history at the University of Illinois (Urbana-Champaign).

FRANK SAFFORD, born in El Paso in 1935, graduated from Harvard in 1957 and received his Ph.D. from Columbia University in 1965. Associate professor of history at Northwestern University, he has conducted extensive research on economic history in Latin America and is the author of a forthcoming study, *Colombia's Struggle to Form a Technical Elite.*

STUART B. SCHWARTZ, born in 1940, earned his B.A. from Middlebury College and his Ph.D. from Columbia University. He has published numerous articles on colonial Latin America and is the author of *Sovereignty and Society in Colonial Brazil: The High Court of Bahia and Its Judges, 1609–1751.* He is associate professor of history at the University of Minnesota and has also taught at the University of California at Berkeley.

PETER H. SMITH was born in Brooklyn, New York, in 1940 and received degrees from Harvard and Columbia universities. His research has focused on political behavior in twentieth-century Latin America, and he has published *Politics and Beef in Argentina.* He is professor of history at the University of Wisconsin at Madison.

MARGARET TODARO WILLIAMS, born in Brooklyn, New York, in 1942, did her undergraduate work at Trinity College in Washington, D.C., studied at the University of Madrid, and obtained a Ph.D. from Columbia University in 1971. She is a clinical associate at the Los Angeles Psychoanalytic Institute and an assistant professor of history at the University of Southern California.

INDEX

abolitionism, 162–163
achievement-expertise: in career of García Moreno, 252; explanation of, 238; manifestations of, in Spanish America, 239–240
Action Française, 211
administrative-institutional history: achievements of, 5–6; relationship of, to social history, 9; shortcomings of, 6–7
administrators: relationship of, with landholders, 83
Aevum, 212
Africans, enslavement of, 62
agregado, 169
Alamán, Lucas, 82, 86, 90
Aldermanic Landowner: description of, 132; nature of dominance of, 134; on spectrum of political participation, 133
Alexandrine bulls, 39
Alford, Robert, 154
Alienation of Church Wealth in Mexico, 88
Allende, Salvador, 225
American Historical Association, 194
American Psychoanalytic Association, 221
American Revolution: and the commercial elite, 66
American South: position of slaves in, 157
Andalusia: alliance of, with Castilian interests, 40, 41
Antioquia (Colombia): conservatism of,

105–106, 108; regional analyses of, 143
Antuñano, Esteban de, 90
Anuário Estatístico, 147
A Ordem, 205
Aragon: subordination of, to Castile, 38
Aramoni, Ancieto, 195
A reação do bom senso, 214
Areche, Antonio de, 34
Arévalo, Juan José, 196
Argentina: achievement-expertise leadership in, 240; Aldermanic Landowners in, 132; Armed Landowners in, 130; challenges to landed power in, 127; changing status of working class in, 246–247; immigrant entrepreneurship in, 186–187; immigrants as modernizers of, 181; importance of immigration to, 177; landholder power in, 135; landowner lobby in, 123–124; political alignments in, 72; political atmosphere in, 225; position of caudillos in, 82; power of Aldermanic Landowners in, 134; regional interests in, 94, 95; size of migration to, 176; socioeconomic setting of, 72
Armed Landowners: basis for dominance of, 134; description of, 130–131; on spectrum of political participation, 133
artisans: as topic for study, 170
assimilation of Italian immigrants in São Paulo, 188–192
Ataíde, Tristão de. See Lima, Alceu Amoroso
Auden, W. H., 222